Interactive C#

Fundamentals, Core Concepts and Patterns

Vaskaran Sarcar

Foreword by A. Rajendram and S. Ghosh

Apress®

Interactive C#

Vaskaran Sarcar
560066, Karnataka, India

ISBN-13 (pbk): 978-1-4842-3338-2   ISBN-13 (electronic): 978-1-4842-3339-9
https://doi.org/10.1007/978-1-4842-3339-9

Library of Congress Control Number: 2017962428

Cover image designed by Freepik (www.freepik.com)

Managing Director: Welmoed Spahr
Editorial Director: Todd Green
Acquisitions Editor: Celestin Suresh John
Development Editor: Matthew Moodie
Technical Reviewer: Shekhar Kumar Maravi
Coordinating Editor: Sanchita Mandal
Copy Editor: Kim Burton-Weisman
Compositor: SPi Global
Indexer: SPi Global
Artist: SPi Global

Distributed to the book trade worldwide by Springer Science+Business Media New York, 233 Spring Street, 6th Floor, New York, NY 10013. Phone 1-800-SPRINGER, fax (201) 348-4505, e-mail orders-ny@springer-sbm.com, or visit www.springeronline.com. Apress Media, LLC is a California LLC and the sole member (owner) is Springer Science + Business Media Finance Inc (SSBM Finance Inc). SSBM Finance Inc is a **Delaware** corporation.

For information on translations, please e-mail rights@apress.com, or visit http://www.apress.com/rights-permissions.

Apress titles may be purchased in bulk for academic, corporate, or promotional use. eBook versions and licenses are also available for most titles. For more information, reference our Print and eBook Bulk Sales web page at http://www.apress.com/bulk-sales.

Any source code or other supplementary material referenced by the author in this book is available to readers on GitHub via the book's product page, located at www.apress.com/978-1-4842-3338-2. For more detailed information, please visit http://www.apress.com/source-code.

Printed on acid-free paper

Table of Contents

Foreword by Ambrose Rajendram

I have spent most of my career working in R&D and related activities. During this time, I have come in contact with many engineers across many disciplines and of differing caliber and attitudes. As a rule, engineers spend most of their life acquiring knowledge, which is even truer in today's fast-changing technological landscape. Vaskaran is one such engineer who is on an eternal quest to try new boundaries. What makes Vaskaran different, though, is that he has an unbridled passion to share his knowledge and make it available to the world. It is an honor and a privilege to write this foreword.

In the connected world we live in, there is an abundance of knowledge. It sometimes seems that textbooks are superfluous, as this information is available free on the Internet. However, what this book does is take the reader through a set of logical steps from the basics to advanced concepts. This flow is very important to understand the fundamental building blocks. Once the reader has a grasp of this, it will be relatively easy to advance further.

This book concentrates on what is required to understand the subject and leaves out unnecessary things. Each chapter introduces a new concept and the author has anticipated questions that the reader may have and preempts this through simple Q&A analogies as would happen in a classroom. This provides insights that lead to a deeper understanding of the concepts.

Object-oriented programming is the most essential concept in software engineering today and understanding this is crucial to good programming. The author has done a phenomenal job of presenting this in a simple way that is easy to understand. Use this book as a companion guide on your journey through the complex world of object-oriented programming. I hope that this book will be as useful to you as it was to me.

—Ambrose Rajendram

About Ambrose Rajendram

Ambrose is a Master Technologist at Hewlett-Packard's R&D Centre in India. He is an electronics engineer by education but his passion for technology has led him to different areas, from mechanical engineering to robotics and machine learning. He is presently working on applying machine learning to robotics to solve everyday problems.

Foreword by Siddhartha Ghosh

 There is no dearth of books on any programming language, particularly on a programming language as popular as C#. There are definitive textbooks by authors who are active contributors to the development of the language. Most of the time, however, these books prove too challenging for a normal reader to understand. On the other hand, there are books that are very easy to read, but they compromise the accuracy of the concepts covered. Vaskaran, having been a teacher himself in the initial phase of his career, understands the challenges faced by the students in developing a solid foundation in programming. His unique student-teacher dialog approach provides the reader a strong foundation on fundamental concepts without making matters overly complex. In addition to the strong fundamentals, Vaskaran has also included some crucial pieces of information from his professional life. The chapter on memory cleanup is an example of this. I am very sure that this book is going to provide the readers a good understanding of the topics in a clear and interesting way.

—Siddhartha Ghosh

About Siddhartha Ghosh

Siddhartha is postgraduate in statistics and information technology. He is working as a Solutions Architect in enterprise print domain at Hewlett-Packard's R&D division in Bangalore. He has more than 18 years of experience in the IT industry in various roles and capacities. He obtained his MBA in quality management and he always tries to discover ways in which he can apply his acquired skills set at work.

About the Author

Vaskaran Sarcar, ME (software engineering), MCA, is a Senior Software Engineer and Team Lead in Hewlett-Packard's R&D Centre in India. He has more than 12 years of experience in education and the IT industry. He is an alumnus of prestigious institutions in India, such as Jadavpur University, Vidyasagar University, and Presidency University (formerly Presidency College). He started his teaching career in 2005; later he entered the software industry. Reading and learning new things are his passion. You can connect with him at vaskaran@rediffmail.com or find him on LinkedIn at https://www.linkedin.com/in/vaskaransarcar

Other books by the author include *Java Design Patterns* (Apress, 2016), *Interactive Object-Oriented Programming in Java* (Apress, 2016), *Design Patterns in C#* (CreateSpace, 2015), C# *Basics: Test Your Skill* (CreateSpace, 2015), and *Operating System: Computer Science Interview Series* (CreateSpace, 2014).

About the Technical Reviewers

Shekhar Kumar Maravi is a System Software Engineer, whose main interest and expertise are programming languages, algorithms, and data structures. He obtained his M.Tech degree from Indian Institute of Technology, Bombay in computer science and engineering.

After his graduation, he joined Hewlett-Packard's R&D hub in India to work on printer firmware. Currently, he is working as a technical lead in Siemens Healthcare India, Strategy and Innovation Division, on automated lab diagnostic device firmware and software.

He can be reached by email at shekhar.maravi@gmail.com or find him on LinkedIn at https://www.linkedin.com/in/shekharmaravi

Ravindra T. Bharamoji is a Tech Lead whose main interests and expertise are programming languages and testing. He obtained his BE degree in electronics and communication engineering from Karnataka University. After graduation, he joined Wipro Technologies. Currently, he is working as a technical lead at HP. He can be reached by email at aarushsowmya@gmail.com or find him on LinkedIn at https://www.linkedin.com/in/ravindrabharamoji

Acknowledgements

First, I thank the Almighty. I sincerely believe that with His blessings only, I could complete this book.

I extend my deepest gratitude and thanks to

Ratanlal Sarkar and Manikuntala Sarkar, my parents. With your blessings only, could I complete the work.

Indrani, my wife, and Ambika, my daughter. Sweethearts, without your love, I could not proceed at all. I know that we needed to limit many social gatherings and invitations to complete this work on time.

Sambaran, my brother. Thank you for your constant encouragement.

Shekhar, Anupam, Ravindra, Idris, and Naveen, my best friends and technical advisors. I know that whenever I was in need, your support was there. Thank you one more time.

Ambrose Rajendram and Siddhartha Ghosh, my colleagues cum seniors. A special thanks to you for investing your time to write a foreword for my book. When experts like you agreed to write for me, I get additional motivation to enhance the quality of my work.

Lastly, I extend my deepest gratitude to my publisher, the editorial board members, and everyone who directly or indirectly supported this book.

Preface

The successful completion of a work brings relief. But if you are working to fulfill your heart's desire, that feeling of relief is transformed into a feeling of satisfaction. And if your desire is to help others, the completion of that task gives you tremendous satisfaction. The same kind of feeling is applicable here.

In 2015, I wrote C# *Basics: Test your Skill*, which covered some fundamental concepts in C#. In 2017, the book was enhanced and *Interactive Object-Oriented Programming in C#* was born. Immediately after its release, it became the "No.1 New Release" in C# and object-oriented programming categories on Amazon.com. Based on readers' feedback, the work was further fine-tuned and this book was born. Since the book covers more than pure object-oriented programming, the words *object-oriented* and *programming* were removed from the title.

As an author, my initial goal was to complete this book successfully. But during the process, my aim became higher. I wanted to make this book *interactive*. I did not want to explain only in an informative way. I also wanted you to take this journey with me. You must agree that you can complete a journey along an unknown path if you have a partner who is not only knowledgeable but also loving and caring. Learning a new programming language through a book is a journey, which was always on my mind. So, in this book, I present a loving teacher to assist you throughout your journey. You can ask him questions. He will try to answer them in a simple way. He may ask you some questions also, so that you can think about and analyze them yourself. In most of the cases, he will write full programs and then display the corresponding output as screenshots, so that you get maximum benefits through the visualization process.

If you are curious to know about the most important and unique characteristics of this book, I would say that it is interactive and very simple. The goal was not to demonstrate how good a programmer I am by including typical and tough programs using all the latest features of C#. On the contrary, the true goal is to fuel your creativity by illustrating the core programming concepts of C#. The word *core* is more important than *the latest* when you are learning a new technology. Whatever is the latest today, will be outdated tomorrow. But "core concepts" are evergreen.

So, welcome to the journey. It is my privilege to present *Interactive C#*. Before we jump into the topics, I want to highlight a few points about the goal of the book and the organization of the topics.

- The goal of this book is to help you to learn from a classroom environment. I have been involved in teaching since 2005. I have taken classes at both engineering and non-engineering colleges. Fortunately, most of my teaching was based on object-oriented programming. That was the true motivation to introduce a book like this.

- This book does not invest time in topics that are easily available, such as how to install Visual Studio on your system, or how to write a "Hello World" program, and so forth. Your teacher expects that before you enter the classroom, you must have done your basic homework and your coding environment must be ready. Your teacher starts from the basic object-oriented concepts that we can implement in C#. He focuses on the key features of C#. And he explains how these concepts can be learned and used effectively.

- But do not worry! To assist you with asking better questions in the classroom, an entire section is dedicated at the end of the book (Appendix A). This appendix talks about some key concepts in C# and it helps you evaluate your skills in the language basics. You may need to come back to this section many times, because it acts as a reference. Gradually, upon repeated practice, you will become familiar with it. So, even if you are new to programming or if you have some idea about other programming languages, those information will assist you a lot. It will also help you prepare for a job interview or an examination by answering some tricky questions that may seem very easy at the beginning.

- This book uniquely presents a two-way communication between the teacher and students. So, with this book, you have a feel that you are learning C# in a classroom environment (or you are talking to your private tutor), where your teacher discusses problems/topics and asks you questions. At the same time, you can clear your doubts by asking the teacher questions. This kind of approach was intended because many students do not feel comfortable asking questions in an open forum. If you are dedicated to this subject and think about these Q&A sessions, you will surely develop confidence in this language, which benefits you in the programming world.

- Many of us are afraid of large books because they do not promise that we can learn the subject in one day or 7 days, but learning is a continuous process. I believe that no real mastery can be achieved in 24 hours or in 7 days. So, the motto of the book is "to learn the core topics of C#, whatever effort I need to put, I am OK with that." Still, simple arithmetic says that if you can complete two topics per week, you can complete the book within two months (your learning speed depends only on your capabilities and dedication). The book is designed in such a way that upon completion of the book, you will know the core OOP concepts in C# in detail, and most importantly, you will know how to go further.

- The programs are tested with Visual Studio IDE. (The project started with Visual Studio 2012 and finished with Visual Studio 2017.) I have taken care that the code is compatible with all the latest versions. Also, it is not mandatory for you to learn Visual studio 2017 (or any upcoming version) in detail. You can simply run these programs in your preferred IDE. I chose Visual Studio because it is the most common IDE for exploring C#, and this book presents screenshots from that IDE.

Lastly, I have tried my best to help you in these pages. I believe that you will benefit from this work and find the book very useful.

Guidelines for Using the Book

Welcome. Here are some suggestions for using this book.

- If you have just learned the basics of C#, or if you have some coding experience with other languages, such as C++, Java, and so forth, I recommend that you quickly go through Appendix A. The Preface section will help you become familiar with the basic syntax and fundamental concepts of C#.

- If you are confident with what's covered in the appendix A, you can enter Part I of the book.

- All the book parts are connected. I suggest that you only start Part II when you are confident about Part I.

- In Part III, an overview of design patterns are presented. Around 1995, four authors—Erich Gamma, Richard Helm, Ralph Johnson, and John Vlissides—presented their book, *Design Patterns: Elements of Reusable Object-Oriented Software* (Addison-Wesley, 1995), in which they initiated the concept of design pattern in software development. These authors became known as the Gang of Four (GoF). They introduced the concepts and categorized 23 identified patterns into three categories. I discuss one pattern in each of these categories. Part III of the book introduces real-world challenges and shows how to handle them programmatically. The topics covered in Part I, Part II, and Appendix A are sufficient for understanding the patterns described in this book.

- You can download and install the Visual Studio IDE from `https://www.visualstudio.com/downloads/`.

You can use the Visual Studio Community Edition because it is free.

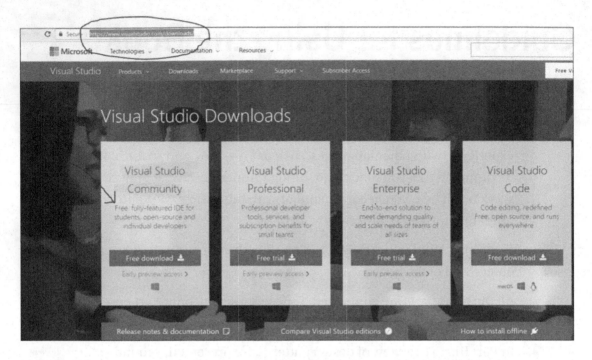

Note At the time of this writing, this link works fine and the information is correct, but the link and policies may change in the future.

An Important Note Before You Begin

In this book, you will often see the phrases like *Teacher says:*, *Teacher clarifies:*, *Students ask:*, and so forth (this type of conversation starts in Chapter 2). In my teaching career, my students used to call me "Sir." But you may call your teacher by his first/last name or something like "Mr. X"—all are fine. The author is open-minded. He knows that it depends on the particular culture. So, by using the word "Sir" he does not represent himself as a superior person. Instead, you can imagine him as a loving guide in this journey.

Similarly, with "Students ask," the author refers various students. No single student asks all of these questions. The author has encountered several questions from his students, peers, and other experts in these topics. Sometimes, he himself acts like a student—curious to learn more details; he got support from peers, teachers, and experts. Therefore, *Students* simply refer to this whole domain (including himself) of the curious who want to learn more. The author loves his students and respects all. Therefore, the meaning of *Students* should not be misinterpreted.

PART I

Enter into the World of OOP

This section's highlights:

- What is object-oriented programming (OOP)?

- Why do we need this type of programming?

- How can we cover the fundamental concepts of OOP with the core building blocks of C#?

- How can we make our C# applications attractive and efficient?

CHAPTER 1

Object-Oriented Programming Concepts

Welcome to object-oriented programming (OOP). You may already be familiar with the proverb "Necessity is the mother of invention." The same concept applies here. If we have a basic idea about why we introduced this type of programming, or how these concepts will make real-world programming easy, our learning paths will be enjoyable and we will be able to extend our learnings in various directions. Therefore, I'll try to address some common questions then I'll provide an overview of object-oriented programming.

I have just two warning messages for you.

- Do not get discouraged if you do not understand everything after your first pass. Sometimes it may seem complicated, but gradually it will seem easier to you.

- There are many criticisms against OOP. Do not forget, each human mind has a tendency to criticize a new thing. So, even if you want to criticize these concepts, I suggest that you first try to understand and use the concepts, and then make your own decision whether to appreciate or criticize.

Now let us begin the journey...

We started computer programming with binary codes, and mechanical switches were needed to load those programs. You can guess that a programmer's job was very challenging in those days. Later, some high-level programming languages were developed to make their lives easier. They started writing simple English-like instructions to serve our purpose. In turn, the compilers used to translate those instructions into binaries because a computer can understand instructions in a binary language only. So, we became happy to develop those high-level languages.

© Vaskaran Sarcar 2018
V. Sarcar, *Interactive C#*, https://doi.org/10.1007/978-1-4842-3339-9_1

But over a period of time, the computer capacity and capabilities increased a lot. As an obvious result, we needed to expand our vision and we started trying to implement more complex concepts in computer programming. Unfortunately, none of the programming languages that were available at that time was mature enough to implement those concepts.These were our primary concerns:

- How can we reuse the existing codes to avoid duplicate efforts?

- How can we control the use of global variables in a shared environment?

- How do we debug the code when too much jumping is occurring (with keywords like goto) in an application?

- Suppose a new programmer has joined a team. He found it extremely difficult to understand the overall structure of the program. How can we make his/her life easier?

- How can we maintain a large code base in an effective way?

To overcome these problems, expert programmers came up with the idea of breaking big problems into smaller chunks. The idea behind this was very simple: *If we can solve each of the small problems/chunks, eventually we will solve that big problem.* So, they started breaking large problems into small parts and the concept of functions (or procedure or subroutines) came into the picture. Each of these functions was dedicated to solve one small problem area. At a high level, managing the functions and their interaction became the key areas of focus. *In this context, the concept of structured programming came into picture.* Structured programming started gaining its popularity because small functions are easy to manage and easy to debug. In addition to this, we started limiting the use of global variables, which were replaced with local variables in the functions (in most of the cases).

Structured programming maintained popularity for almost two decades. During this time, the capacity of hardware increased significantly and as an obvious effect, people wanted to achieve more complex tasks. Gradually, the drawbacks and limitations of structured programming drew our attention; for example

- Suppose, we have used a particular data type across multiple functions in an application. Now if we need to change the data type, we have to implement the changes across all functions across the products.

- It is difficult to model all real-world scenarios with the key components of structured programming (i.e., data + functions). In the real world, whenever we create a product, there are two areas we need to focus on.

  - *Purpose.* Why do we need this product?

  - *Behavior.* How does the product make our lives easier?

Then the idea of objects came into existence.

POINTS TO REMEMBER

The fundamental difference between structured programming and object-oriented programming can be summarized as : Rather than the operations on data, we focus on the data itself.

There are few principles at the heart of object-oriented programming. You can easily guess that we will cover them in detail in rest of the book. First, I'll introduce each of them.

Class and Objects

These are the core of OOP. A *class* is the blueprint or the template for its objects. *Objects* are instances of a class. In simple language, we can say that in structured programming, we segregate or divide our problems into functions, and in OOP, we divide our problems into objects. In computer programming, we are already familiar with data types like *int, double, float,* and so forth. These are called *built-in data types* or *primitive data types* because they are already defined in the corresponding computer languages. But when we need to create our own datatype (e.g., Student), we need to create a Student class. Just as when we need to create an integer variable, we need to refer the int first, similarly, when we need to create a student object (e.g., John), we need to refer our Student class first. Similarly, we can say Ronaldo is an object from a Footballer class, Hari is an object from an Employee class, your favorite car is an object from a Vehicle class, and so on.

Encapsulation

The purpose of encapsulation is at least one of the following:

- Putting restrictions so that the components of an object cannot be accessed directly

- Binding the data with methods that will act on that data (i.e., forming a capsule)

In some OOP languages, the hiding of the information is not implemented by default. So, they come up with an additional term called *information hiding*.

Later we will see that data encapsulation is one of the key features in a class. In ideal cases, this data is not visible to the outside world.Only through the methods defined inside the class, we can access these data. Therefore, we can think of these methods as the interface between the objects' data and the outside world (i.e., our program).

In C#, we can implement encapsulation through the proper use of access-specifiers (or modifiers) and properties.

Abstraction

The key purpose of abstraction is to show only essential details, and hiding the background details of implementation. Abstraction is also very much related to encapsulation, but the difference may be easily understood with a simple day-to-day scenario.

When we press a button on our remote control to switch on the TV, we do not care about the internal circuits of the TV or how the remote control is enabling the TV. We simply know that different buttons on the remote control have different functionalities, and as long as they work properly, we are happy. So, the user is isolated from the complex implementation details, which is *encapsulated* within the remote control (or TV). At the same time, the common operations that can be performed through the remote control can be thought of as an *abstraction* in a remote control.

Inheritance

Whenever we talk about reusability, we generally refer to inheritance, which is a process in which one class object acquires the properties of another class object. Consider this example. Bus is one type of Vehicle because it fulfills the basic criteria of a Vehicle that is used for transportation purposes. Similarly, Train is another type of Vehicle. In the same way though Goods Trains and Passenger Trains are different, we can say that both of them inherit from Train category (or class) because ultimately both of them fulfill the basic criteria of a Train, which in turn is a Vehicle. So, we can simply say that hierarchical classifications are supported with the concept of inheritance.

In the programming world, inheritance creates a new child class from an existing class (known as a *base class* or a *parent class* in C#), which is placed one level up in that hierarchical chain. Then we can add new functionalities (methods) or modify the base class functionalities (override) into the child class. We must remember that due to these modifications, the core architecture should not be affected. In other words, if you derive Bus class from Vehicle class, and add/modify the functionalities in Bus class, those modifications should not hit the original functionalities that were described for the Vehicle class.

So, the key advantage is that we can avoid lots of duplicate codes with this mechanism.

Polymorphism

Polymorphism is generally associated with *one name with many forms*. Consider the behavior of your pet dog. When it sees an unknown person, it is angry and starts barking a lot. But when it sees you, it makes different noises and behaves differently. In the coding world, you can think of a very popular method, Addition. With addition in the context of two integers, we expect to get a sum of the integers. But for two strings, we expect to get a concatenated string.

Polymorphism can be of two types.

- *Compile-time polymorphism*: The compiler can decide very early as to which method to invoke in which situation once the program is compiled. It is also known as *static binding* or *early binding*.

- *Runtime polymorphism*: The actual method calls are resolved at runtime. In compile time, we cannot predict which method will be invoked when the program runs (e.g., the program may behave differently with different inputs). Take a very simple use case: suppose, we want to generate a random number at the very first line when we execute a program. And if the generated number is an even number, we will call a method, Method1( ), which prints "Hello"; otherwise, we'll call a method whose name is same but it prints "Hi". Now, you'll agree that if we execute the program, then only we can see which method is invoked (i.e., the compiler cannot resolve the call in compile time). We do not have any clue as to whether we will see "Hello" or "Hi" prior to the program's execution. This is why sometimes it is also termed as *dynamic binding* or *late binding*.

Summary

This chapter discussed the following topics.

- ✓   An introduction of object-oriented programming
- ✓   Why did it evolve?
- ✓   How is it different from structured programming?
- ✓   What are the core characteristics of object-oriented programming?

CHAPTER 2

The Building Blocks: Class and Objects

Class

A class is a blueprint or a template. It can describe the behaviors of its objects. It is the foundation for how the object is built or instantiated.

Object

An object is an instance of a class.

Object-oriented programming (OOP) techniques primarily depend on these two concepts—class and objects. With a class, we are creating a new data type, and objects are used to hold the data (fields) and methods. Object behavior can be exposed through these methods.

If you are familiar with the game of football (or *soccer*, as it's known in the United States), we know the players who are participating in a game are selected for their skills in various positions. In addition to these skills, they need to have a minimum level of match fitness and general athletic capabilities. So, if we say that Ronaldo is a footballer (a.k.a. soccer player), we can predict that Ronaldo has these basic abilities as well as some skills specific to football (even though Ronaldo is unknown to us). So, we can simply say that Ronaldo is an object of a Footballer class.

Note   Still, you may feel that it is a chicken-or-the-egg type of dilemma. You can argue that if we say, "Mr. X is playing like Ronaldo," then in that case, Ronaldo is acting like a class. However, in object-oriented design, we make things simple by deciding who comes first and we mark that guy as the class in the application.

© Vaskaran Sarcar 2018
V. Sarcar, *Interactive C#*, https://doi.org/10.1007/978-1-4842-3339-9_2

Now consider another footballer, Beckham. We can predict again that if Beckham is a footballer, then Beckham must be excellent in many aspects of football. Also, he must possess a minimum fitness level to participate in a match.

Now say both Ronaldo and Beckham are participating in the same match. It is not difficult to predict that although both Ronaldo and Beckham are footballers, their playing style and performance will be different from each other in that match. In the same way, in the world of object-oriented programming, the performance of objects can be different from each other, even though they belong to the same class.

We can consider any different domain. Now you can predict that your pet dogs or cats can be considered as objects of the Animal class. Your favorite car can be considered an object of a Vehicle class. Your favorite novel can be considered as an object of a Book class, and so on.

In short, *in the real-world scenario, each of the objects must have two basic characteristics: state and behavior.* If we consider the objects—Ronaldo or Beckham from the Footballer class, we notice that they have states like "playing state" or "non-playing state." In the playing state, they can show different behaviors—they can run, they can kick, and so forth.

In a non-playing state, their behaviors will also change. In this state, they can take a much needed nap, or they can eat their meals, or they can simply relax by doing activities like reading a book, watching a movie, and so forth.

Similarly, we can say that the televisions in our home, at any particular moment, can be in either an "on" state or an "off" state. It can display different channels if, and only if, it is in *switched on* mode. It will not show anything if it is in *switched off* mode.

So, to begin with object-oriented programming, it is always suggested that you ask yourself questions like these:

- What are the possible states of my objects?

- What are the different functions (behaviors) that they can perform in those states?

Once you get the answers for these questions, you are simply ready to proceed. It is because the same pattern is followed by software objects in any object-oriented program: their states are stored in fields/variables and their capabilities/behaviors are described through different methods/functions.

Let's get to the programming now. To create objects, we need to decide first in which class they will belong to; that is, in general, if we want to create objects, we need to create a class first.

Note   There are some exceptional cases (e.g., the ExpandoObject class in the System.Dynamic namespace). It can represent an object whose members can be added or removed at runtime. But you have just started the journey of class and objects. Let's make the things very much simple. We can ignore those corner cases at this moment.

POINTS TO REMEMBER

In general, if we want to use objects, we need to have a class first.

Suppose we have created a class and we have given the name of this class as A. Now we can create an object obA of class A with the following statement:

```
A obA=new A();
```

The preceding line can be decomposed of the following two lines:

```
A obA;//Line-1
obA=new A();//Line-2
```

At the end of the line 1, obA is a reference. Until this point, there is no memory allocated. But once the new one comes into the picture, the memory is allocated.

If you notice carefully, you will observe that in the second line, the class name is followed by a parenthesis. We have used this to construct the object. These are *constructors* that are used to run initialization codes. Constructors can have different arguments (i.e., they can vary with different number of parameters or different type of parameters).

In the following example, class A has four different constructors.

```
class A
{
    A()
    {
        //some code
    }
    A(int a)
    {
        //some code
    }
    A(int a, int b)
    {
        //some code
    }
    A(double a)
    {
        //some code
    }
}
```

But if we do not supply any constructor for our class, C# will supply a default one.

POINTS TO REMEMBER

If we do not supply any constructor for our class, C# will supply a default parameterless public constructor for you. But if you supply any constructor, then the compiler will not generate the default constructor for you.

So, when we see something like the following, we are sure that a parameterless constructor is used.

```
A obA=new A();
```

But to know whether it is a user-defined constructor or it was provided by C# (in other words, a default constructor), we need to examine the class body; for example, if in a class definition, we have written codes like those in the following.

```
class A
{
    A()
    {
        //some code
    }
    //remaining body -if any

}
```

We can conclude that here we have used the user-defined parameterless constructor. So, in this scenario, the C# compiler will not generate any default constructors for us.

Class Demonstrations

If you have reached this point, it means that you can guess that classes are simply the building blocks of our programs. We encapsulate the variables (known as *fields*) and methods inside a class to make a single unit. These variables are called as instance variables (static variables will be discussed in later part of the book) because each object of this class (i.e., each instance of the class) contain their own copies of these variables. (Later, you'll learn that fields can be any implicit data type, different class objects, enumerations, structures, delegates, etc.). *Methods*, on the other hand, contain a block of codes. These are nothing but a series of statements that perform specific actions. Instance variables are generally accessed through methods. Collectively, these variables and methods are called *class members*.

POINTS TO REMEMBER

- As per the C# language specification, apart from fields and methods, a class can contain many other things—constants, events, operators, constructors, destructors, indexers, properties, and nested types. But for simplicity, we have started with methods and fields, which are the most common. I will cover other topics in their respective chapters in later parts of this book.

- Fields and methods can be associated with different kind of modifiers.

  - Field modifiers can be any of them—static, public, private, protected, internal, new, unsafe, read-only, and volatile.

  - Method modifiers can be either of these—static, public, private, protected, internal, new, virtual abstract override, or async.

Most of these are covered in upcoming chapters.

Consider a simple example. Now we have created a class called ClassEx1 and we have encapsulated only one integer field, MyInt, into it. We have also initialized the value 25 into that field. So, we can predict that whenever we create an object of this class, that object will have an integer named myInt in it and the corresponding value will be 25.

For your ready reference, we have created two objects—obA and obB from our ClassEx1 class. We have tested the values of the variable MyInt inside the objects. You can see that in both cases, we are getting the value 25.

Demonstration 1

```
using System;

namespace ClassEx1
{
    class ClassEx1
    {
        //Field initialization is optional.
        public int MyInt = 25;
        //public int MyInt;
    }
    class Program
    {
        static void Main(string[] args)
        {
            Console.WriteLine("*** A class demo with 2 objects ***");
            ClassEx1 obA = new ClassEx1();
            ClassEx1 obB = new ClassEx1();
```

```
        Console.WriteLine("obA.i ={0}", obA.MyInt);
        Console.WriteLine("obB.i ={0}", obB.MyInt);
        Console.ReadKey();
    }
  }
}
```

Output

```
*** A class demo with 2 objects ***
obA.i =25
obB.i =25
```

Additional Comments

- It is not necessary to initialize the MyInt in this way. We are just
  starting up. So, we are starting with a very simple example. In other
  words, *field initialization is optional.*

- If you do not supply any initialization for your field, it will take some
  default value. We will cover those default values shortly.

- Suppose that in the preceding example, you did not initialize the
  field. Then your class will look like this:

```
class ClassEx1
{
    //Field initialization is optional.
    //public int MyInt = 25;
    public int MyInt;
}
```

Still, you can instantiate your object and then supply your intended value like this:

```
ClassEx1 obA = new ClassEx1();
obA.MyInt = 25;//setting 25 into MyInt of obA
```

If you are familiar with Java, to print in console, you may like this kind of format. C# also allows this.

```
Console.WriteLine("obA.i =" + obA.MyInt);
Console.WriteLine("obB.i =" + obB.MyInt);
```

Students ask:

Sir, please tell us something more about constructors.

Teacher says: We must remember these key points:

- Constructors are used to initialize objects.

- The class name and the corresponding constructor's name(s) must be the same.

- They do not have any return types.

- We can say that there are two types of constructors: *parameterless constructors* (sometimes referred as constructors with no argument or *default constructor*) and constructors with parameter(s) (known as *parameterized constructors*). In C# parlance, it does not matter whether we are creating our own parameterless constructor or if it is created by the C# compiler. In both cases, we generally call it a *default constructor*.

  OR

  We can also distinguish constructors based on whether it is a static constructor or a non-static constructor (or an *instance constructor*). You are becoming familiar with instance constructors in this chapter. Instance constructors are used to initialize instances (objects) of the class, whereas static constructors are used to initialize the class itself when it appears for the first time. I discussed "static" in another chapter.

- In general, the common tasks, like initialization of all the variables inside a class, are achieved through constructors.

Students ask:

Sir, constructors do not have any return type. With this statement, did you mean that their return type is void?

Teacher says: No. Implicitly, a constructor's return type is same as its class type. We should not forget that even void is also considered a return type.

Students ask:

Sir, we are little bit confused about the use of a user-defined parameterless constructor and a C# provided default constructor. Both appear to be the same. Is there any key difference between them?

Teacher says: I already mentioned that in C# parlance, it does not matter whether we created our own parameterless constructor or if it was created by the C# compiler. In both cases, we generally call it a default constructor. Sometimes both may appear to be same. *But always remember that with a user-defined constructor, we can have some flexibility. We can put our own logic and have some additional control on object creation.*

Consider the following example and analyze the output.

Demonstration 2

```
using System;

namespace DefaultConstructorCaseStudy
{
    class DefConsDemo
    {
        public int myInt;
        public float myFloat;
        public double myDouble;
        public DefConsDemo()
        {
            Console.WriteLine("I am initializing with my own choice");
            myInt = 10;
            myFloat = 0.123456F;
            myDouble = 9.8765432;
```

```
        }
    }
    class Program
    {
        static void Main(string[] args)
        {
            Console.WriteLine("***Comparison between user-defined and  C#
            provided default constructors***\n");
            DefConsDemo ObDef = new DefConsDemo();
            Console.WriteLine("myInt={0}", ObDef.myInt);
            Console.WriteLine("myFloat={0}", ObDef.myFloat.
            ToString("0.0####"));
            Console.WriteLine("myDouble={0}", ObDef.myDouble);
            Console.Read();
        }
    }
}
```

Output

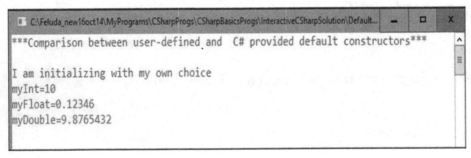

Analysis

You can see that before we set the values to our variables, we have printed one additional line saying, "I am initializing with my own choice."

But if you simply do not supply this parameterless constructor and you want to use the C# provided default constructor, you will get the output shown in the next section.

Additional Comments

To see the following output, you need to comment out or remove the constructor definition in the preceding example. Now you can see that each of these values are initialized with the corresponding default values of that type.

```
***Comparison between user-defined and  C# provided default constructors***
myInt=0
myFloat=0.0
myDouble=0
```

You must remember another key point. *We can use our own access modifiers for user-defined constructors.* So, if you provide your own parameterless constructor, you can make it other than public.

Let's see what the C# language specification tells us about this case.

If a class contains no instance constructor declarations, a default instance constructor is automatically provided. That default constructor simply invokes the parameterless constructor of the direct base class. If the class is abstract, then the declared accessibility for the default constructor is protected; otherwise, the declared accessibility for the default constructor is public. Thus, the default constructor is always of the following form:

protected C(): base() {}

or

public C(): base() {}

C is the name of the class. If an overload resolution is unable to determine a unique best candidate for the base class constructor initializer, then a compile-time error occurs.

Soon, you will be familiar with these new terms: access modifiers, overload, and base. So, do not panic. You can learn these concepts and then come back to this part of answer.

So, in simple terms, the following declaration

```
class A
    {
        int myInt;
    }
```

is equivalent to this:

```
class A
    {
        int myInt;
        public A():base()
        { }
    }
```

Students ask:

Sir, we are seeing that the C# provided default constructor is initializing the instance variables with some default values. What are the default values for other types?

Teacher says: You can refer to the following table for your reference.

Type	Default Values
sbyte, byte, short, ushort, int, uint, long,ulong	0
char	'\x0000'
float	0.0f
double	0.0d
decimal	0.0m
bool	false
struct	All value types to their default values and all reference types to null*
enum E	0(converted to type E)

*We will discuss value types and reference types in detail later in the book.

Students ask:

Sir, it appears to us that we can call some methods to initialize those variables. Then why do we choose constructors?

Teacher says: If you think from that point of view, then you must agree that to do that job, you need to call the method explicitly; that is, in simple language, that call is not automatic. But with constructors, we are performing automatic initialization each time we create objects.

Students ask:

Sir, which occurs first—field initializations or initialization through a constructor?

Teacher says: Field initializations occur first. And this initialization process follows the declaration order.

Quiz

Can you predict the output?

```
using System;
namespace ConsEx2
{
    class ConsEx2
    {
        int i;
        public ConsEx2(int i)
        {
            this.i = i;
        }
    }
    class Program
    {
        static void Main(string[] args)
        {
            Console.WriteLine("***Experiment with constructor***");
            ConsEx2 ob2 = new ConsEx2();
        }
    }
}
```

Output

Compilation error: *'ConsEx2' does not contain a constructor that takes 0 arguments.*

Error List						
Entire Solution ▾	⊗ 1 Error	⚠ 0 Warnings	① 0 Messages		Build + IntelliSense ▾	
Code	Description			Project	File	Line
⊗ CS1729	'ConsEx2' does not contain a constructor that takes 0 arguments			ConsEx2	Program.cs	17

Explanation

See the following Q&A. We will also discuss the keyword "this" shortly.

Students ask:
Sir, we should have a default constructor from C# in this case. Then why is the compiler complaining about a 0 argument constructor?

Teacher says: I already mentioned that in C#, we can get a default 0 argument constructor if, and only if, we do not provide any constructor. But, in this example, we already have a parameterized constructor. So, in this case, the compiler will not provide a default 0 argument constructor for us.

So, if you want to remove this compilation error, you have following choices:

- You can define one more custom constructor like this:

```
public ConsEx2() { }
```

- You can remove the custom constructor declaration (that you already defined but not used) from this program.

- You can supply the necessary integer argument inside your `Main()` method like this:

```
ConsEx2 ob2 = new ConsEx2(25);
```

Students ask:
Sir, can we say that class is a custom type?

Teacher says: Yes.

Students ask:

Sir, can you please elaborate the concept of reference?

Teacher says: Yes. When we write `ClassA obA=new ClassA();` an instance of ClassA will be born in memory, and it creates a reference to that instance and stores the result inside the obA variable. So, we can say objects in memory are referenced by an identifier called "reference".

Later, when you learn more about memory management, you will see that in C#, we mainly use two types of data—value types and reference types. The value types are stored on a stack and reference types are stored on a heap. Since objects are reference types, they are stored on a heap. But the important catch is that the reference itself is stored on a stack. So, when we write

```
ClassA obA=new Class A();
```

you can imagine something like the following:

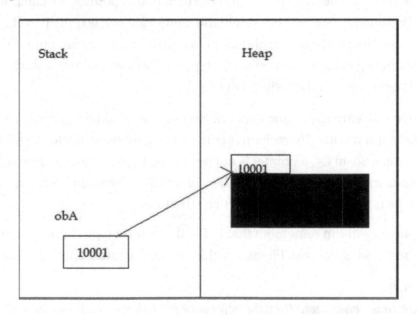

We are assuming the object is stored in the heap address 10001 and obA is holding this clue in stack.

Students ask:
Sir, why do we use both a stack and a heap?

Teacher says: The simplest answer at this level is that when a reference variable goes out of scope, it is removed from the stack, but actual data still exists on the heap until the program terminates or the garbage collector clears that memory. So, we can have control over the lifetime of a particular data.

Students ask:
Sir, then reference is basically used to point to an address. Is this correct?

Teacher says: Yes.

Students ask:
Sir, then references are similar to pointers in C/C++. Is this correct?

Teacher says: It may appear that references are a special kind of pointer. But we must note the key difference between these two. With a pointer, we can point to any address (basically, it is a number slot in the memory).So, it is quite possible that with a pointer, we can point to an invalid address and then we may encounter unwanted outcomes during runtime. But reference types will always point to valid addresses (in a managed heap) or they will point to null.

Shortly, we will learn about one key concept in C#. It is called a *garbage collection mechanism* and it is used to reclaim memory. The garbage collector is unaware of these pointers. So, in C#, a pointer is not permitted to point to a reference. Later, you'll also learn that if a structure (in C#, called a *struct*) contains a reference, a pointer type is not allowed to point to that structure.

For simplicity, you can remember that in C#, the pointer type comes into the picture only in the "unsafe" context. I'll discuss this "unsafe" context later in the book.

Students ask:
Sir, how can we check whether the reference variable is pointing to null or not?

Teacher says: The following simple check can serve your purpose. For your ready reference, I could have added these few lines in the preceding programs.

```
    ......
ConsEx2 ob2 = new ConsEx2(25);
if (ob2 == null)
```

```
  {
   Console.WriteLine("ob2 is  null");
  }
 else
 {
  Console.WriteLine("ob2 is  NOT null");
 }
     .....
```

Students ask:

Sir, can multiple variables reference the same object in memory?

Teacher says: Yes. The following type of declaration is perfectly fine:

```
ConsEx2 ob2 = new ConsEx2(25);
ConsEx2 ob1=ob2;
```

Demonstration 3

In the following example, we have created two objects of the same class but the instance variable (i) is initialized with different values. To do this job, we have used a parameterized constructor that can accept one integer argument.

```
using System;

namespace ClassEx2
{
    class ClassA
    {
        public int i;
        public ClassA(int i)
        {
            this.i = i;
        }
    }

    class Program
    {
```

```
        static void Main(string[] args)
        {
            Console.WriteLine("*** A class demo with 2 objects ***");
            ClassA obA = new ClassA(10);
            ClassA obB = new ClassA(20);
            Console.WriteLine("obA.i =" + obA.i);
            Console.WriteLine("obB.i =" + obB.i);
            Console.ReadKey();
        }
    }
}
```

Output

```
*** A class demo with 2 objects ***
obA.i =10
obB.i =20
```

Explanation

Students ask:

Sir, what is the purpose of this?

Teacher says: Good question. Sometimes we need to refer the current object, and to do that, we use the "this" keyword. In the preceding example, instead of using the "this" keyword, we could also write something like the following to achieve the same result.

```
class ClassA
{
        int i;//instance variable
        ClassA(int myInteger)//myInteger is a local variable here
        {
          i=myInteger;
        }
}
```

You are familiar with code like a=25; here we are assigning 25 to a. But are you familiar with code like 25=a;? No. The compiler will raise an issue.

In the preceding example, myInteger was our *local variable* (seen inside methods, blocks, or constructors) and i was our *instance variable* (declared inside a class but outside a method, block, or constructor).

So, instead of myInteger, if we use i, we need to tell the compiler about our direction of assignment. It should not be confused about "which value is assigned where." Here we are assigning the value of the local variable to the instance variable, and the compiler should clearly understand our intention. With this.i=i;, the compiler will clearly understand that the instance variable i should be initialized with the value of the local variable i.

I can also explain the scenario from another point of view. Suppose, by mistake, you have written something like i=i in the preceding scenario. Then there will be confusion from compiler's point of view. Because in that case, it is seeing that you are dealing with two local variables that are the same. (Although your intention was different, you meant that the i on the left side is the field and the other one is the method parameter).Now if you create an object, obA for ClassA, try to see the value of obA.i, with codes like this:

```
ClassA obA = new ClassA(20);
Console.WriteLine("obA.i =" + obA.i);
```

You will get 0 (the default value of an integer). So, your instance variable cannot get your intended value, 20. Our Visual Studio Community Edition IDE also raises a warning in this case: "Assignment made to same variable, did you mean to assign something else?"

> ⚠ CS0649   Field 'ClassA.i' is never assigned to, and will always have its default value 0
>
> ⚠ CS1717   Assignment made to same variable; did you mean to assign something else?

POINTS TO REMEMBER

A method parameter with the same name as a field hides the entire field in the method body. In this type of scenario, the keyword "this" helps us to identify which one is a parameter and which one is a field.

Demonstration 4

In the following demonstration, we are using two different constructors. The user-defined parameterless constructor is always initializing the instance variable i with the value 5, but the parameterized constructor can initialize the instance variable with any integer value that we supply.

```
using System;
class ClassA
{
    public int i;
    public ClassA()
    {
        this.i = 5;
    }
    public ClassA(int i)
    {
        this.i = i;
    }

}
class ClassEx4
{
    static void Main(string[] args)
    {
        Console.WriteLine("*** A Simple class with 2  different constructor
        ***");
        ClassA obA = new ClassA();
        ClassA obB = new ClassA(75);
        Console.WriteLine("obA.i =" + obA.i);
        Console.WriteLine("obB.i =" + obB.i);
        Console.ReadKey();
    }
}
```

Output

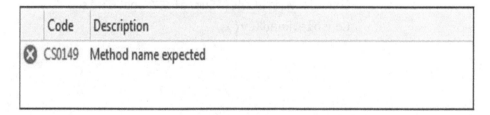

```
*** A Simple class with 2  different constructor ***
obA.i =5
obB.i =75
```

Additional Comments

- Earlier, we used the same constructor to create different objects that were initialized with different values. In this example, we used a different constructor to create different objects that are initialized with different values.

- In Java, we could use this (5) instead of this.i=5. But in C#, that kind of coding is not allowed. For that kind of coding, we will encounter a compilation error like the following:

Code	Description
⊗ CS0149	Method name expected

Demonstration 5

I mentioned that a class can have both variables and methods. So, now we are going to create a class with a method that will return an integer. This method is used to accept two integer inputs, and in turn, it will return the sum of those integers.

```csharp
using System;

namespace InstanceMethodDemo
{
    class Ex5
    {
        public int Sum(int x, int y)
        {
            return x + y;
        }
    }

    class Program
    {
        static void Main(string[] args)
        {
            Console.WriteLine("*** A Simple class with a method
            returning an integer ***\n\n");
            Ex5 ob = new Ex5();
            int result = ob.Sum(57,63);
            Console.WriteLine("Sum of 57 and 63 is : " + result);
            Console.ReadKey();

        }
    }
}
```

Output

```
*** A Simple class with a method returning an integer ***

Sum of 57 and 63 is : 120
```

Object Initializers

Teacher continues: Now we are going to learn two different techniques in object creation. We can use them as per our need. Consider the following program, which followed by the output and analysis.

Demonstration 6

```csharp
using System;

namespace ObjectInitializerEx1
{
    class Employee
    {
        public string Name;
        public int Id;
        public double Salary;
        //Parameterless constructor
        public Employee() { }
        //Constructor with one parameter
        public Employee(string name) { this.Name = name; }
    }
    class Program
    {
        static void Main(string[] args)
        {
            Console.WriteLine("***Object initializers Example-1***");

            //Part-1:Instantiating without Object Initializers

            //Using parameterless constructor
            Employee emp1 = new Employee();
            emp1.Name = "Amit";
            emp1.Id = 1;
            emp1.Salary = 10000.23;
            //Using the constructor with one parameter
            Employee emp2 = new Employee("Sumit");
```

```
        emp2.Id = 2;
        emp2.Salary = 20000.32;

        //Part-2:Instantiating with Object Initializers

        //Using parameterless constructor
        Employee emp3 = new Employee { Name = "Bob", Id = 3, Salary =
        15000.53 };
        //Using the constructor with one parameter
        Employee emp4 = new Employee("Robin") { Id=4,Salary = 25000.35 };

        Console.WriteLine("Employee Details:");
        Console.WriteLine("Name ={0} Id={1} Salary={2}", emp1.Name,
        emp1.Id,emp1.Salary);
        Console.WriteLine("Name ={0} Id={1} Salary={2}", emp2.Name,
        emp2.Id,emp2.Salary);
        Console.WriteLine("Name ={0} Id={1} Salary={2}", emp3.Name,
        emp3.Id, emp3.Salary);
        Console.WriteLine("Name ={0} Id={1} Salary={2}", emp4.Name,
        emp4.Id, emp4.Salary);
        Console.ReadKey();
    }
  }
}
```

Output

```
***Object initializers Example-1***
Employee Details:
Name =Amit Id=1 Salary=10000.23
Name =Sumit Id=2 Salary=20000.32
Name =Bob Id=3 Salary=15000.53
Name =Robin Id=4 Salary=25000.35
```

Analysis

Notice the following section carefully.

```
//Part-1:Instantiating without Object Initializers

//Using no argument constructor
Employee emp1 = new Employee();
emp1.Name = "Amit";
emp1.Id = 1;
emp1.Salary = 10000.23;
//Using the constructor with one argument
Employee emp2 = new Employee("Sumit");
emp2.Id = 2;
emp2.Salary = 20000.32;

//Part-2:Instantiating with Object Initializers

//Using no argument constructor
Employee emp3 = new Employee { Name = "Bob", Id = 3, Salary = 15000.53 };
//Using the constructor with one argument
Employee emp4 = new Employee("Robin") { Id=4,Salary = 25000.35 };
```

In Part-2 of this example, we have introduced the concept of *object initializers*. We can see that in the top portion (Part-1), we needed to code more lines to complete the objects (emp1 and emp2) compared to the bottom portion (part 2). In Part-2, a single line of code was sufficient to instantiate each of the objects(emp3 and emp4).We also experimented with the different types of constructors. But it is evident that in all cases, object initializers simplify the instantiation process. This concept was introduced in C# 3.0.

Optional Parameters

Teacher continues: Now consider the following program and output.

Demonstration 7

```csharp
using System;

namespace OptionalParameterEx1
{
    class Employee
    {
        public string Name;
        public int Id;
        public double Salary;
        public Employee(string name = "Anonymous", int id = 0, double
        salary = 0.01)
        {
            this.Name = name;
            this.Id = id;
            this.Salary = salary;
        }
    }
    class Program
    {
        static void Main(string[] args)
        {
            Console.WriteLine("***Optional Parameter Example-1***");

            Employee emp1 = new Employee("Amit", 1, 10000.23);
            Employee emp2 = new Employee("Sumit", 2);
            Employee emp3 = new Employee("Bob");
            Employee emp4 = new Employee();

            Console.WriteLine("Employee Details:");
            Console.WriteLine("Name ={0} Id={1} Salary={2}", emp1.Name,
            emp1.Id, emp1.Salary);
            Console.WriteLine("Name ={0} Id={1} Salary={2}", emp2.Name,
            emp2.Id, emp2.Salary);
            Console.WriteLine("Name ={0} Id={1} Salary={2}", emp3.Name,
            emp3.Id, emp3.Salary);
```

```
            Console.WriteLine("Name ={0} Id={1} Salary={2}", emp4.Name,
            emp4.Id, emp4.Salary);
            Console.ReadKey();
        }
    }
}
```

Output

```
***Optional Parameter Example-1***
Employee Details:
Name =Amit Id=1 Salary=10000.23
Name =Sumit Id=2 Salary=0.01
Name =Bob Id=0 Salary=0.01
Name =Anonymous Id=0 Salary=0.01
```

Analysis

Here we have used the concepts of optional parameters in a constructor. This constructor needs three arguments: one for the employee's name, one for the employee's ID, and one for the employee's salary. But if we pass fewer arguments, the compiler will not complain at all. On the other hand, our application is picking the default values that we already set in the optional parameter's list. From the last line of output, you can see that the default values of an employee object were *Anonymous,0 and 0.01* (corresponding to the employee's name, ID, and salary).

Students ask:

Sir, in OOP we see that codes are always bundled inside objects. What are the benefits of this type of design in real-world scenarios?

Teacher says: Actually, there are many advantages. Think from a real-world scenario; for example, consider your laptop or your printer. If any of the parts in your laptop malfunctions, or if your print cartridge runs out of ink, you can simply replace those parts. You do not need to replace the entire laptop or the entire printer. The same concept applies to other real-world objects.

And, you can reuse the same parts in similar model of a laptop or a printer.

Apart from this, you must agree that we do not care how these functionalities are actually implemented in those parts. If those parts are working fine and serve our needs, we are happy.

In object-oriented programming, objects play the same role: they can be reused and they can be plugged in. At the same time, they are hiding the implementation details. For example, in Demonstration 5, we can see when we invoke the Sum()method with two integer arguments (57 and 63), we know that we'll get the sum of those integers. An outside user is totally unaware of the inner mechanisms of the method. So, we can provide a level of security by hiding this information from the outside world.

Lastly, from another coding point of view, assume the following scenario. Suppose that you need to store employee information in your program.If you start coding like this:

```
string empName= "emp1Name";
string deptName= "Comp.Sc.";
int empSalary= "10000";
```

Then for a second employee, we have to write something like this:

```
string empName2= "emp2Name";
string deptName2= "Electrical";
int empSalary2= "20000";
```

And so on.

Can we really continue like this? The answer is no. To make it simple, it is always a better idea to make an Employee class and process like this:

```
Employee emp1, emp2;
```

It is much cleaner and readable, and obviously, a better approach.

Students ask:
Sir, so far, we have talked about constructors but not destructors. Why?

Teacher says: I will discuss destructors with garbage collections in Chapter 14 (Memory Cleanups).

Summary

This chapter discussed the following topics.

- ✓ The concepts of class, object and reference

- ✓ The differences between an object and a reference

- ✓ The differences between a pointer and a reference

- ✓ The differences between a local variable and an instance variable

- ✓ The different types of constructors and their usage

- ✓ The differences between a user-defined parameter less constructor and a C# provided default constructor

- ✓ The this keyword

- ✓ The concept of object initializers

- ✓ The concept of optional parameters

- ✓ The benefits of object-oriented approach in real-world programming

CHAPTER 3

The Concept of Inheritance

Teacher starts the discussion: The main objective of inheritance is to promote reusability and eliminate redundancy (of code). The basic idea is that a child class can obtain the features/characteristics of its parent class. In programming terms, we say that a child class is derived from its parent/base class. Therefore, the parent class is placed at a higher level in the class hierarchy.

Types

In general, we deal with four types of inheritance.

- *Single inheritance*: A child class is derived from one base class

- *Hierarchical inheritance*: Multiple child classes can be derived from one base class

- *Multilevel inheritance*: The parent class has a grandchild

- *Multiple inheritance*: A child can derive from multiple parents

---

POINTS TO REMEMBER

- C# does not support multiple inheritance (through class); that is, a child class cannot derive from more than one parent class. To deal with this type of situation, we need to understand interfaces.

- There is another type of inheritance known as *hybrid inheritance*. It is a combination of two or more types of inheritances.

© Vaskaran Sarcar 2018
V. Sarcar, *Interactive C#*, https://doi.org/10.1007/978-1-4842-3339-9_3

Diagram	Type with Code Format

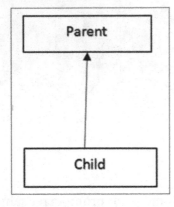
 	
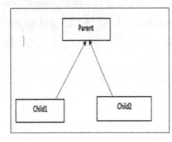
	Single inheritance:
	`#region Single Inheritance`
	`    class Parent`
	`    {`
	`        //Some code`
	`    }`
	`    class Child : Parent`
	`    {`
	`        //Some code`
	`    }`
	`#endregion`
	
	Hierarchical inheritance:
	`#region Hierarchical Inheritance`
	`    class Parent`
	`    {`
	`        //Some code`
	`    }`
	`    class Child1 : Parent`
	`    {`
	`        //Some code`
	`    }`
	`    class Child2 : Parent`
	`    {`
	`        //Some code`
	`    }`
	`#endregion`

(continued)

Diagram	Type with Code Format

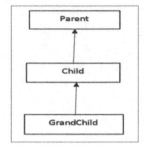	Multilevel inheritance:
	
	`#region Multilevel Inheritance`
	`    class Parent`
	`    {`
	`        //Some code`
	`    }`
	`    class Child : Parent`
	`    {`
	`        //Some code`
	`    }`
	`    class GrandChild : Child`
	`    {`
	`        //Some code`
	`    }`
	`#endregion`

Multilevel inheritance:

```
#region Multilevel Inheritance
    class Parent
    {
        //Some code
    }
    class Child : Parent
    {
        //Some code
    }
    class GrandChild : Child
    {
        //Some code
    }
#endregion
```

Multiple inheritance:

Not supported in C# through classes. We need to learn about interfaces. Here is an example:

```
#region Multiple Inheritance
    interface IInter1
    {
        //Some Code
    }
    interface IInter2
    {
        //Some code
    }
    class MyClass : IInter1, IInter2
    {
        //Some code
    }
#endregion
```

Let's start with a simple program on inheritance.

Demonstration 1

```csharp
using System;
namespace InheritanceEx1
{
    class ParentClass
    {
        public void ShowParent()
        {
            Console.WriteLine("In Parent");
        }
    }
    class ChildClass :ParentClass
    {
    }
    class Program
    {
        static void Main(string[] args)
        {
            Console.WriteLine("***Testing Inheritance***\n\n");
            ChildClass child1 = new ChildClass();
            //Invoking ShowParent()through ChildClass object
            child1.ShowParent();
            Console.ReadKey();
        }
    }
}
```

Output

```
C:\Feluda_June12,2017Onwards\MyPrograms\CSharpProgs\CSharpBasicsProgs\InteractiveCSh
***Testing Inheritance***


In Parent
```

Additional Comments

We have invoked the ShowParent()method through a child class object.

POINTS TO REMEMBER

- Remember that in C#, Object is the root for all classes in the .NET framework. In other words, System.Object is the ultimate base class in the type hierarchy.

- Apart from constructors (instance and static) and destructors, all members are inherited (i.e., it does not matter on the access-specifiers).But due to their accessibility restrictions, all the inherited members may not be accessible in the child/derived class.

- The child class can add new members but it cannot remove the definition of the parent member. (Just as you can choose a new name for yourself but you cannot change the surname of your parents).

- The inheritance hierarchy is transitive; that is, if class C inherits class B, which in turn is derived from class A, then class C contains all the members from class B and class A.

Students ask:

Then this means that private members also inherited. Is this understanding correct?

Teacher says: Yes.

Students ask:

How can we examine the fact that private members are also inherited?

Teacher says: You can refer to the program and output shown in Demonstration 2.

Demonstration 2

```
using System;

namespace InheritanceWithPrivateMemberTest
{
    class A
    {
        private int a;
    }
    class B : A { }

    class Program
    {
        static void Main(string[] args)
        {
            B obB = new B();
            A obA = new A();
            //This is a proof that a is also inherited. See the error
            message.
            Console.WriteLine(obB.a);//A.a is inaccessible due to its
            //protection level
            Console.WriteLine(obB.b);//'B' does not contain a definition
            //for 'b' and no extension ......
            Console.WriteLine(obA.b);//'A' does not contain a definition
            //for 'b' and no extension ......
        }
    }
}
```

Output

❌	CS0122	'A.a' is inaccessible due to its protection level
❌	CS1061	'B' does not contain a definition for 'b' and no extension method 'b' accepting a first argument of type 'B' could be found (are you missing a using directive or an assembly reference?)
❌	CS1061	'A' does not contain a definition for 'b' and no extension method 'b' accepting a first argument of type 'A' could be found (are you missing a using directive or an assembly reference?)

Analysis

We have encountered two different types of errors: CS0122 and CS1061.

- CS0122: A.a is inaccessible due to its protection level. It indicates that the private member a from class A is inherited in the child class B.

- CS1061: We tested the output with another field, which is not present in this class hierarchy (i.e., the field is not present—neither in A nor in B). When we tried to access the member with a class A or class B object, we encountered a different error. Therefore, if a is absent in class B, then you should get a similar error.

Students ask:
Why doesn't C# support multiple inheritance through class?

Teacher says: The main reason is to avoid ambiguity. It can cause confusion in typical scenarios; for example, let's suppose that we have a method named Show() in our parent class. The parent class has multiple children—say Child1 and Child2, who are redefining (in programming terms, *overriding*) the method for their own purposes. The code may look like what's shown in Demonstration 3.

Demonstration 3

```
class Parent
    {
        public void Show()
        {
        Console.WriteLine("I am in Parent");
        }
    }
    class Child1: Parent
    {
        public void Show()
        {
        Console.WriteLine("I am in Child-1");
        }
    }
```

```
class Child2:Parent
{
    public void Show()
    {
    Console.WriteLine("I am in Child-2");
    }
}
```

Now, let's say another class called Grandchild derives from both Child1 and Child2, but it has not overridden the Show() method.

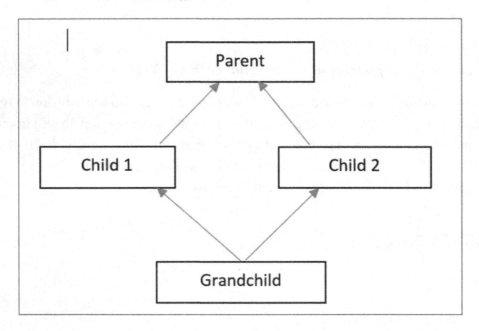

So, now we have ambiguity: from which class will the grandchild inherit/call Show()—Child1 or Child 2? To avoid this type of ambiguity, C# does not support multiple inheritance through class. This is known as the *diamond problem*.

So, if you code like this:

```
class GrandChild : Child1, Child2//Error: Diamond Effect
{
    public void Show()
    {
        Console.WriteLine("I am in Child-2");
    }
}
```

The C# compiler will complain with this error:

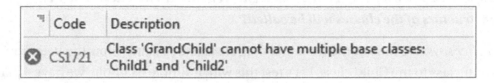

	Code	Description
❌	CS1721	Class 'GrandChild' cannot have multiple base classes: 'Child1' and 'Child2'

Students ask:

So, programming languages do not support multiple inheritance. Is this understanding correct?

Teacher says: No. The decision is made by the designers of the programming language (e.g., C++ supports the concept of multiple inheritance).

Students ask:

Why do C++ designers support multiple inheritance? It seems that the diamond problem can impact them too.

Teacher says: I am trying to explain from my point of view. They probably did not want to discard multiple inheritance (i.e., they wanted the feature to be included to make the language rich). They supplied you with the support but left the control of proper usage to you.

On the other hand, C# designers wanted to avoid any unwanted outcomes due to this kind of support. They simply wanted to make the language simple and less error-prone.

Teacher asks:

Is there hybrid inheritance in C#?

Teacher explains: Think carefully. Hybrid inheritance is a combination of two or more types of inheritance. *So, the answer to this question is yes if you are not trying to combine any type of multiple inheritance through class.* But if you try to make a hybrid inheritance with any type of multiple inheritance (through class), the C# compiler will raise its concern immediately.

Teacher asks:

Suppose we have a parent class and a child class. Can we guess in which order constructors of the classes will be called?

Teacher says: We must remember that the constructor's calls follow the path from the Parent class to the Child class. Let's test this with a simple example: we have a parent class-Parent, a child class-Child, and a grandchild class-GrandChild. As the names suggest, the Child class derives from the Parent class and the Grandchild derives from the Child class. We have created an object of the grandchild class. Notice that constructors are called in the order of their derivation.

Demonstration 4

```
using System;

namespace ConstructorCallSequenceTest
{
    class Parent
    {
        public Parent()
        {
            Console.WriteLine("At present: I am in Parent Constructor");
        }
    }
    class Child : Parent
    {
        public Child()

        {
            Console.WriteLine("At present: I am in Child Constructor");
        }
    }
    class GrandChild : Child
    {
        public GrandChild()
        {
```

```
            Console.WriteLine("At present: I am in GrandChild
            Constructor");
        }
    }

    class Program
    {
        static void Main(string[] args)
        {
            Console.WriteLine("***Testing the call sequence of
            constructors***\n\n");
            GrandChild grandChild = new GrandChild();
            Console.ReadKey();
        }
    }
}
```

Output

```
***Testing the call sequence of constructors***


At present: I am in Parent Constructor
At present: I am in Child Constructor
At present: I am in GrandChild Constructor
```

Explanation

Students ask:

Sir, sometimes we are uncertain. Who should be the parent class and who should be the child class in an inheritance hierarchy? How can we tackle this kind of situations?

Teacher says: You can try to remember a simple statement: a footballer is an athlete but the reverse is not necessarily true. Or, a bus is a vehicle but the reverse is not necessarily true. This type of "is-a" test can help you to decide who should be the parent; for example, "athlete" is the parent class and "footballer" is the child class.

We also take this "is-a" test to determine in advance whether we can place a class in the same inheritance hierarchy or not.

A Special Keyword: base

In C#, there is a special keyword called *base*. It is used to access the members of the parent class (also called the base class) in an efficient way. Whenever a child class wants to refer to its immediate parent, it can use the *base* keyword.

Let's examine the different uses of the base keyword in two simple examples.

Demonstration 5

```
using System;

namespace UseOfbaseKeywordEx1
{
    class Parent
    {
        private int a;
        private int b;
        public Parent(int a, int b)
        {
            Console.WriteLine("I am in Parent constructor");
            Console.WriteLine("Setting the value for instance variable
            a and b");
            this.a = a;
            this.b = b;
            Console.WriteLine("a={0}", this.a);
            Console.WriteLine("b={0}", this.b);
        }
}
```

```csharp
class Child : Parent
{
    private int c;
    public Child(int a, int b,int c):base(a,b)

    {
        Console.WriteLine("I am in Child constructor");
        Console.WriteLine("Setting the value for instance variable c");
        this.c = c;
        Console.WriteLine("c={0}", this.c);
    }

}


class Program
{
    static void Main(string[] args)
    {
        Console.WriteLine("***Testing the use of base keyword.
        Example-1***\n\n");
        Child obChild = new Child(1, 2, 3);
        //Console.WriteLine("a in ObB2={0}", obChild.a);// a is private,
//so Child.a is inaccessible
        Console.ReadKey();
    }
}
}
```

Output

```
***Testing the use of base keyword. Example-1***

I am in Parent constructor
Setting the value for instance variable  a and b
a=1
b=2
I am in Child constructor
Setting the value for instance variable c
c=3
```

Analysis

We need to understand why it is necessary to use the keyword base. If we did not use it in the preceding example, we would need to write code similar to this:

```
public Child(int a, int b, int c)
     {
          this.a = a;
          this.b = b;
          this.c = c;
     }
```

There are two major issues with this kind of approach. You are trying to write repeated code to initialize the instance variables a and b. In this particular case, you will receive a compilation error because both a and b are inaccessible due to their protection level (note that they are private). With the use of the "base" keyword, we handled both scenarios efficiently. Although we have written the word "base" after the subclass constructor declaration, the parent class constructor invoked before the child class constructor. Ideally, this was our true intention.

POINTS TO REMEMBER

Earlier you saw that when we initialize an object, the constructor bodies executed in the direction of the parent class to its child class. But the reverse direction of initialization (i.e., child to parent) occurs with the initialization of fields (and also with arguments to parent class constructor calls).*

In C#, you cannot use one instance field to initialize another instance field outside a method body.

---

* I believe that it's worth reading the following MSDN resources:

- https://blogs.msdn.microsoft.com/ericlippert/2008/02/15/
  why-do-initializers-run-in-the-opposite-order-as-
  constructors-part-one/

- https://blogs.msdn.microsoft.com/ericlippert/2008/02/18/
  why-do-initializers-run-in-the-opposite-order-as-
  constructors-part-two/

Quiz

What is the output?

```
using System;

namespace FieldInitializationOrderEx1
{
    class A
    {
        int x = 10;
        int y = x + 2;//Error
    }
    class Program
    {
        static void Main(string[] args)
        {
            Console.WriteLine("*** Analyzing C#'s field initialization
            order ***");
            int x = 10;
            int y = x + 2;//ok
            Console.WriteLine("x={0}", x);
            Console.WriteLine("y={0}", y);
            Console.ReadKey();
        }
    }
}
```

Output

❌ CS0236   A field initializer cannot reference the non-static field, method, or property 'A.x'

Analysis

This restriction was implemented by the designers of C#.

Students ask:

Why have C# designers placed this restriction (related to error CS0236)?

Teacher says: There are many discussions on this topic. The statement y=x+2; in the preceding example is equivalent to y=this.x+2; "this" means the current object So, if we want to make a call like this.x, the current object needs to be completed first. But the current object may not be completed at this point in some situations (e.g., if x is a property (instead of a field) that is not created yet or it is a part of another instance, etc.) We will learn more about properties shortly. We should also remember that the constructors are created to handle this kind of initialization. So, if these types of constructs are allowed, they can also question the purpose of constructors.

Teacher continues: Now let's examine another use of base keyword in the following example. Note that in this example, we are calling a parent class method (ParentMethod()) through the base keyword from a derived class method.

Demonstration 6

```csharp
using System;

namespace UseOfbaseKeywordEx2
{
    class Parent
    {
        public void ParentMethod()
        {
            Console.WriteLine("I am inside the Parent method");
        }
    }
    class Child : Parent
    {
        public void childMethod()
        {
                Console.WriteLine("I am inside the Child method");
```

```
            Console.WriteLine("I am calling the Parent method now");
            base.ParentMethod();
        }
}

    class Program
    {
        static void Main(string[] args)
        {
            Console.WriteLine("***Testing the use of base keyword.
            Example-2***\n\n");
            Child obChild = new Child();
            obChild.childMethod();
            Console.ReadKey();
        }
    }
}
```

Output

```
***Testing the use of base keyword. Example-2***

I am inside the Child method
I am calling the Parent method now
I am inside the Parent method
```

POINTS TO REMEMBER

- As per the language specification, base class access is permitted only in a constructor, an instance method, or an instance property access.

- The keyword "base" should not be used in a static method context.

- It is similar to the "super" keyword in Java and the "base" keyword in C++. It is almost identical to C++'s base keyword, from which it was adopted. However, in Java, a restriction says that "super" should be the first statement. Oracle Java documents say that the invocation of a superclass constructor must be the first line in the subclass constructor.

Students ask:

Sir, suppose there are methods that have a common name in both the parent class and its child class. If we create a child class object and try to invoke the same named method, which one will be called?

Teacher says: You are trying to introduce the concept of method overriding here. We will discuss it further in the chapter on polymorphism. But to answer your question, consider the following program and output.

Demonstration 7

```
using System;

namespace UseOfbaseKeywordEx3
{
    class Parent
    {
        public void ShowMe()
        {
            Console.WriteLine("I am inside the Parent method");
        }
    }
    class Child : Parent
    {
        public void ShowMe()
        {
            Console.WriteLine("I am inside the Child method");
            //base.ParentMethod();
        }
    }

    class Program
    {
        static void Main(string[] args)
        {
```

```
        Console.WriteLine("***Testing the use of base keyword. Example--
        3***\n\n");
        Child obChild = new Child();
        obChild.ShowMe();
        Console.ReadKey();
    }
  }
}
```

Output

```
***Testing the use of base keyword. Example-3***

I am inside the Child method
```

Analysis

In this case, your program was compiled and run, but you should note that you are receiving a warning message saying that your derived class method hides the inherited parent class method, like this:

```
▷  ⚠ CS0108   'Child.ShowMe()' hides inherited member 'Parent.ShowMe()'. Use the new
              keyword if hiding was intended.
```

So, if you want to invoke the Parent class method, you can simply use the code inside the Child class method, like this:

```
class Child : Parent
{

    public void ShowMe()
    {
        Console.WriteLine("I am inside the Child method");
        base.ShowMe();
    }
}
```

59

The base keyword can be used in either of the following scenarios:

- To call a hidden/overridden method defined in a parent class.

- We can specify the particular base-class constructor version when we create instances of the derived class (see Demonstration 5).

Students ask:

It appears to me that a subclass can use its superclass methods. But is there any way by which a superclass can use its child class methods?

Teacher says: No. You must remember that a superclass is completed before its subclass, so it has no idea about its subclass methods. It only announces something (think about some contract/methods) that can be used by its children. It is only giving without any expectation to get return from its children.

If you notice carefully, you will find that the "is-a" test is one-way (e.g., a footballer is always an athlete, but the reverse is not necessarily true; so there is no concept of backward inheritance).

Students ask:

Sir, so whenever we want to use a parent class method and put additional stuff in it, we can use the keyword base. Is this understanding correct?

Teacher says: Yes.

Students ask:

Sir, in OOP, inheritance is helping us reuse the behavior. Is there any other way to achieve the same?

Teacher says: Yes. Although the concept of inheritance is used in many places, it does not always provide the best solution. To understand it better, you need to understand the concept of design patterns. A very common alternative is to use the concept of composition, which is covered later.

Students ask:

Sir, it appears that if a user already made a method for his application, we should always reuse the same method through the concept of inheritance to avoid duplicate efforts. Is this understanding correct?

Teacher says: Not at all. We should not generalize inheritance in this manner. It depends on the particular application. Suppose that someone has already made a Show( ) method to describe the details of a Car class. Now let's say that you have also created a class called Animal and you also need to describe the characteristics of an animal with a method. Suppose that you also believe that the name "Show()" best suits your method. In this case, since we already have a Show( ) method in a class called Car and if you think that you need to reuse the method for your Animal class, You would write something like this:

Class Animal: Car{...} .

Now think for a moment. "Is this a good design?" You must agree that there is no relationship between a car and an animal. So, we should not relate them in the same inheritance hierarchy.

Students ask:

How can we inherit a constructor or a destructor?

At the beginning of the chapter, I mentioned that constructors (both static and non-static) and destructors are not inherited.

Summary

This chapter covered the following topics.

- ✓ The concept of inheritance

- ✓ The different types of inheritance

- ✓ Why C# does not support multiple inheritance through class

- ✓ The kind of hybrid inheritance allowed in C#

- ✓ The different uses of the "base" keyword

- ✓ A brief comparison between C#'s base keyword and Java's super keyword

- ✓ The constructor calling sequence in an inheritance hierarchy

- ✓ How to call a parent class method if its child class also contains a method with the same name

- ✓ How to put classes in an inheritance hierarchy

- ✓ The proper use of the concept of inheritance

And more.

CHAPTER 4

Get Familiar with Polymorphism

Teacher starts the discussion: Let's recollect what we discussed about polymorphism in the beginning of this book. Polymorphism is generally associated with *one name with many forms;* for example, if we have two integer operands with the *addition* operation, we expect to get a sum of the integers, but if the operands are two strings, we expect to get a concatenated string. I also mentioned that polymorphism can be of two types: compile-time polymorphism and runtime polymorphism.

Here we will start our discussion with compile-time polymorphism.

In compile-time polymorphism, the compiler can bind the appropriate methods to the respective objects during the compile time because it has all the necessary information (e.g., method arguments). So, it can decide which method to call much earlier once the program is compiled. This is why it is also known as *static binding* or *early binding.*

In C#, compile-time polymorphism can be achieved with method overloading and operator overloading.

POINTS TO REMEMBER

In C#, method overloading and operator overloading can help us to achieve compile-time polymorphism.

Method Overloading

Teacher continues: Let's start with a program. Consider the following program and the corresponding output. Do you notice any specific pattern?

© Vaskaran Sarcar 2018
V. Sarcar, *Interactive C#*, https://doi.org/10.1007/978-1-4842-3339-9_4

Demonstration 1

```
using System;

namespace OverloadingEx1
{
    class OverloadEx1
    {
        public int Add(int x, int y)
        {
            return x + y;
        }
        public double Add(double x, double y)
        {
            return x + y;
        }
        public string Add(String s1, String s2)
        {
            return string.Concat(s1, s2);
        }
    }
    class Program
    {
        static void Main(string[] args)
        {
            Console.WriteLine("***Concept of method Overloading***\n\n");
            OverloadEx1 ob = new OverloadEx1();
            Console.WriteLine("2+3={0}", ob.Add(2, 3));
            Console.WriteLine("20.5+30.7={0}", ob.Add(20.5, 30.7));
            Console.WriteLine("Amit + Bose ={0}", ob.Add("Amit","Bose"));
            Console.ReadKey();
        }
    }
}
```

Output

```
***Concept of method Overloading***


2+3=5
20.5+30.7=51.2
Amit + Bose =AmitBose
```

Analysis

Students respond: Yes. We are seeing that all the methods have the same name "Add" but from their method bodies, it appears that each method is doing different things.

Teacher says: Correct observation. When we do this kind of coding, we call it method overloading. But you should also notice that in this case, method names are the same but the method signatures are different.

Students ask:
What is a method signature?

Teacher says: Ideally, a method name with the number and types of parameters consist of its signature. A C# compiler can distinguish among methods with same name but different parameter lists; for example, for a C# compiler, double Add(double x, double y) is different from int Add(int x, int y).

Quiz

The following code segment is an example of method overloading. Is this right?

```
class OverloadEx1
  {
      public int Add(int x, int y)
      {
          return x + y;
      }
      public double Add(int x, int y, int z)
      {
```

```
        return x + y+ z;
    }
}
```

Answer

Yes.

Quiz

Is the following code segment an example of method overloading?

```
class OverloadEx1
{
    public int Add(int x, int y)
    {
        return x + y;
    }
    public double Add(int x, int y)
    {
        return x + y;
    }
}
```

Answer

No. The compiler will not consider "return type" to differentiate these methods. We must remember that a return type is not considered a part of a method signature.

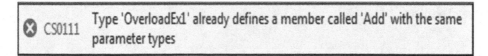

❌ CS0111   Type 'OverloadEx1' already defines a member called 'Add' with the same parameter types

Students ask:
Sir, can we have constructor overloading?

Teacher says: Definitely. You can write a similar program for constructor overloading.

Demonstration 2

```
using System;

namespace ConstructorOverloadingEx1
{
    class ConsOverloadEx
    {
        public ConsOverloadEx()
        {
            Console.WriteLine("Constructor with no argument");
        }
        public ConsOverloadEx(int a)
        {
            Console.WriteLine("Constructor with one integer argument {0}", a);
        }
        public ConsOverloadEx(int a, double b)
        {
            Console.WriteLine("You have passed one integer argument {0} and
            one double argument {1} in the constructor", a,b);
        }
    }

    class Program
    {
        static void Main(string[] args)
        {
            Console.WriteLine("***Constructor overloading Demo***\n\n");
            ConsOverloadEx ob1 = new ConsOverloadEx();
            ConsOverloadEx ob2 = new ConsOverloadEx(25);
            ConsOverloadEx ob3 = new ConsOverloadEx(10,25.5);
            //ConsOverloadEx ob4 = new ConsOverloadEx(37.5);//Error
            Console.ReadKey();
        }
    }
}
```

Output

```
***Constructor overloading Demo***


Constructor with no argument
Constructor with one integer argument 25
You have passed one integer argument 10 and one double argument 25.5 in the constructor
```

Analysis

Students ask:

Sir, it appears that it is also method overloading. What is the difference between a constructor and a method?

Teacher clarifies: We already talked about constructors in the discussion on classes. For your reference, a constructor has the same name as a class and it has no return type. So, you can consider a constructor as a special kind of method that has the same name as a class and no return type. But there are many other differences: the main focus of a constructor is to initialize objects. We cannot call them directly.

Students ask:

Sir, can we write code like this?

Demonstration 3

```
class ConsOverloadEx
    {
        public ConsOverloadEx()
        {
            Console.WriteLine("A Constructor with no argument");
        }
        public void ConsOverloadEx()
        {
            Console.WriteLine("a method");
        }
    }
```

Teacher says: Java 8 allows this but the C# compiler will raise an error.

Output

> ❌ CS0542   'ConsOverloadEx': member names cannot be the same as their enclosing type

Students ask:

Sir, can we overload the Main() method?

Teacher says: Yes. You can consider the following program.

Demonstration 4

```
using System;

namespace OverloadingMainEx
{
    class Program
    {
        static void Main(string[] args)
        {
            Console.WriteLine("***Testing Overloaded version of
            Main()***");
            Console.WriteLine("I am inside Main(string[] args) now");
            Console.WriteLine("Calling overloaded version\n");
            Main(5);
            //Console.WriteLine("***Concept of method Overloading***\n\n");
            Console.ReadKey();
        }
```

```
    static void Main(int a)
    {
        Console.WriteLine("I am inside Main(int a) now");
    }
  }
}
```

Output

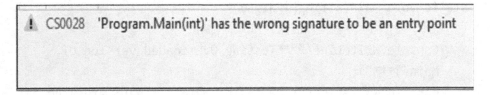

```
C:\CSharpProgs\CSharpBasicsProgs\InteractiveCSharpSolution\OverloadingMainEx\bin\Debug\OverloadingMainEx.exe
***Testing Overloaded version of Main()***
I am inside Main(string[] args) now
Calling overloaded version

I am inside Main(int a) now
```

Analysis

Although you can compile and run the preceding program, the compiler will show you the following warning message:

⚠ CS0028   'Program.Main(int)' has the wrong signature to be an entry point

Students ask:

Sir, then why we are getting a compilation error for the program if we add one more method body, like in the following?

```
namespace OverloadingMainEx
{
    class Program
    {
        static void Main(string[] args)
        {
            Console.WriteLine("***Testing Overloaded version of Main()***");
            Console.WriteLine("I am inside Main(string[] args) now");
            Console.WriteLine("Calling overloaded version\n");
            Main(5);
            //Console.WriteLine("***Concept of method Overloading***\n\n");
            Console.ReadKey();
        }
        static void Main(int a)
        {
            Console.WriteLine("I am inside Main(int a) now");
        }
        static void Main()
        {
            Console.WriteLine("I am inside Main() now");
            Console.ReadKey();
        }
    }
}
```

❌ CS0017   Program has more than one entry point defined. Compile with /main to specify the type that contains the entry point.

Teacher says: As per specification, your program can have an entry point with Main(string[] args) or with the Main() method. Here both versions of the Main method are present. That is why the compiler is confused about which one to use as an entry point. So, you need to decide the entry point as the compiler suggested. If you simply remove or comment out the Main(string[] args) version, your program can be compiled successfully, and then if you run the program, you'll receive the following output:

```
I am inside Main() now
```

Quiz

Can we have multiple Main() methods in our program, like in the following?

Demonstration 5

```
using System;

namespace MultipleMainTest
{
    class Program1
    {
        static void Main(string[] args)
        {
            Console.WriteLine("I am inside Program1.Main(string[] args)
            now");
            Console.ReadKey();
        }
    }
    class Program2
    {
        static void Main()
        {
            Console.WriteLine("I am inside Program2.Main() now");
            Console.ReadKey();
        }
    }
}
```

Teacher says: You can get following error:

> ⊗ CS0017   Program has more than one entry point defined. Compile with /main to specify the type that contains the entry point.   MultipleMainTest

To avoid this error, you can set the entry point from your project properties (here we have chosen Main() from Program2).

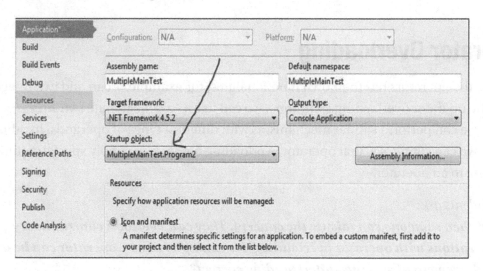

Now if you run the program, you will get following output:

```
C:\CSharpProgs\CSharpBasicsProgs\InteractiveCSharpSolution\MultipleMainTest\bin\Debug\MultipleMainTest.exe
I am inside Program2.Main() now
```

A Suggestion/Good Programming Practice

If possible, try to be consistent with parameter names and their corresponding orders for overloaded methods.

The following is an example of a **good design**:

```
public void ShowMe(int a) {..}
public void ShowMe(int a, int b){...}
```

[Note that in 2nd line, the position of int a is same as 1st case]
Bad design:
```
public void ShowMe(int a) {..}
public void ShowMe(int x, int b){...}
```

[Note that in 2nd line, we start with int x instead of int a]

Teacher continues: So far, we have tested compile-time polymorphism with method overloading. Let's test this flavor with operator overloading also.

Operator Overloading

Each of the operators has their own functionalities; for example, + can add two integers. With the operator overloading technique, we can use it to concatenate two strings; that is, we can perform similar mechanisms with different types of operands. In other words, we can simply say that operator overloading helps us to supply special/additional meaning to an operator.

Students ask:

Sir, then someone can misuse the concept. They can overload contradictory operations with operator overloading; for example, the ++ operator can be used to decrement also. Is the understanding correct?

Teacher says: Yes, we need to be careful. We should not use the ++ operator to decrement. If we do so, that will be an extremely bad design. In addition to this, we must note that C# will not allow us to overload all the operators.

MSDN provides the following guidelines.

Operators	Overloadability
+, -, !, ~, ++, --, true, false	We can overload these unary operators.
+, -, *, /, %, &, I, ^, <<, >>	We can overload these binary operators.
==, !=, <, >, <=, >=	The comparison operators can be overloaded (but see the note that follows this table).
&&, II	The conditional logical operators cannot be overloaded, but they are evaluated using & and I, which can be overloaded.
[ ]	We cannot overload the array indexing operator but we can define indexers.
(T)x	We cannot overload the cast operator but we can define new conversion operators (e.g., in the context of explicit and implicit)
+=, -=, *=, /=, %=, &=, I=, ^=, <<=, >>=	We cannot overload assignment operators but +=; for example, is evaluated using +, which can be overloaded.

(continued)

Operators	Overloadability
=, ., ?:, ??, ->, =>, f(x), as, checked, unchecked, default, delegate, is, new, sizeof,typeof	We cannot overload these operators.

Note   If overloaded, comparison operators must be overloaded in pairs; for example, if = = is overloaded, we need to overload != also. The reverse is also true and it is similar for < and > and for <= and >=.

Teacher says: Let's follow a demonstration. Here we are applying the unary operator ++ to a rectangle object to increment the length and breadth of the rectangle object.

Demonstration 6

```
using System;
namespace OperatorOverloadingEx
{
    class Rectangle
    {
        public double length, breadth;
        public Rectangle(double length, double breadth)
        {
            this.length = length;
            this.breadth = breadth;
        }
        public double AreaOfRectangle()
        {
            return length * breadth;
        }
        public static Rectangle operator ++ (Rectangle rect)
        {
            rect.length ++;
            rect.breadth++;
```

```
            return rect;
        }
    }
    class Program
    {
        static void Main(string[] args)
        {
            Console.WriteLine("***Operator Overloading Demo:Overloading ++
            operator***\n");
            Rectangle rect = new Rectangle(5, 7);
            Console.WriteLine("Length={0} Unit Breadth={1} Unit", rect.
            length,rect.breadth);
            Console.WriteLine("Area of Rectangle={0} Sq. Unit",rect.
            AreaOfRectangle());
            rect++;
            Console.WriteLine("Modified Length={0} Unit Breadth={1} Unit",
            rect.length, rect.breadth);
            Console.WriteLine("Area of new Rectangle={0} Sq. Unit", rect.
            AreaOfRectangle());
            Console.ReadKey();
        }
    }
}
```

Output

```
C:\Feluda_June12,2017Onwards\MyPrograms\CSharpProgs\CSharpBasicsProgs\InteractiveCSharpSolution\O
***Operator Overloading Demo:Overloading ++ operator***

Length=5 Unit Breadth=7 Unit
Area of Rectangle=35 Sq. Unit
Modified Length=6 Unit Breadth=8 Unit
Area of new Rectangle=48 Sq. Unit
```

Now let's overload the binary operator +.

Demonstration 7

```
using System;
namespace OperatorOverloadingEx2
{
    class ComplexNumber
    {
        public double real,imaganinary;
        public ComplexNumber()
        {
            this.real = 0;
            this.imaganinary = 0;
        }
        public ComplexNumber(double real, double imaginary )
        {
            this.real = real;
            this.imaganinary = imaginary;
        }
        //Overloading a binary operator +
        public static ComplexNumber operator +(ComplexNumber cnumber1,
        ComplexNumber cnumber2)
        {
            ComplexNumber temp = new ComplexNumber();
            temp.real = cnumber1.real + cnumber2.real;
            temp.imaganinary = cnumber1.imaganinary + cnumber2.imaganinary;
            return temp;
        }
    }
    class Program
    {
        static void Main(string[] args)
        {
            Console.WriteLine("***Operator Overloading Demo 2:Overloading
            binary operator + operator***\n");
            ComplexNumber cNumber1 = new ComplexNumber(2.1, 3.2);
```

```
        Console.WriteLine("Complex Number1: {0}+{1}i", cNumber1.
        real,cNumber1.imaganinary);
        ComplexNumber cNumber2 = new ComplexNumber(1.1, 2.1);
        Console.WriteLine("Complex Number2: {0}+{1}i", cNumber2.real,
        cNumber2.imaganinary);
        //Using the + operator on Complex numbers
        ComplexNumber cNumber3 = cNumber1 + cNumber2;
        Console.WriteLine("After applying + operator we have got:
        {0}+{1}i", cNumber3.real, cNumber3.imaganinary);
        Console.ReadKey();
    }
  }
}
```

Output

```
***Operator Overloading Demo 2:Overloading binary operator + operator***

Complex Number1: 2.1+3.2i
Complex Number2: 1.1+2.1i
After applying + operator we have got: 3.2+5.3i
```

Analysis

Students ask:

Sir, in operator overloading examples, you have used the keyword "static". Was this intentional?

Teacher says: Yes. We have to remember some key restrictions.

- The operator function must be tagged with *public* and *static*.

Otherwise, you may encounter with this kind of error:

 CS0558   User-defined operator 'ComplexNumber.operator +(ComplexNumber, ComplexNumber)' must be declared static and public

- The keyword *operator* is followed by the operator symbol.

- Function parameters are operands here and return type of the operator function that is the result of an expression.

POINTS TO REMEMBER

- The operator function must be tagged with *public* and *static*.

- The keyword *operator* is followed by the operator symbol.

Method Overriding

Teacher continues: Sometimes we want to redefine or modify the behavior of our parent class. Method overriding comes into the picture in such a scenario. Consider the following program and the output. Then go through each of the points carefully in the analysis section.

Demonstration 8

```
using System;

namespace OverridingEx1
{
    class ParentClass
    {
        public virtual void ShowMe()
        {
            Console.WriteLine("Inside Parent.ShowMe");
        }
        public void DoNotChangeMe()
        {
            Console.WriteLine("Inside Parent.DoNotChangeMe");
        }
    }
    class ChildClass :ParentClass
    {

        public override void ShowMe()
        {
            Console.WriteLine("Inside Child.ShowMe");
        }
    }

    class Program
    {
        static void Main(string[] args)
        {
```

```
        Console.WriteLine("***Method Overriding Demo***\n\n");
        ChildClass childOb = new ChildClass();
        childOb.ShowMe();//Calling Child version
        childOb.DoNotChangeMe();
        Console.ReadKey();
    }
  }
}
```

Output

```
***Method Overriding Demo***


Inside Child.ShowMe
Inside Parent.DoNotChangeMe
```

Analysis

In the preceding program, we are seeing that:

- As the name suggests, ChildClass is a derived class whose parent is ParentClass.

- A method named ShowMe() with same signature and return type is defined in both the ParentClass and the ChildClass.

- In the Main() method, we created a child class object childOb. And when we invoked the method DoNotChangeMe() through this object, it could call the method (following the inheritance property). There is no magic.

- But when we invoke the method ShowMe() through this object, it is calling the ShowMe() version defined in ChildClass; that is, the parent method version is overridden. Hence, the scenario is known as *method overriding*.

- Now notice carefully: how we have redefined the method ShowMe() in ChildClass. We have used two special keywords- virtual and override. With the keyword virtual, we meant that this method can be redefined in a child/derived class. And the override keyword is confirming that we are intentionally redefining the method of Parent class.

- If you omit the word virtual in the preceding program, you will receive the following compilation error:

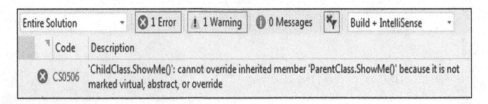

- If you use virtual keyword but omit override keyword, again you will receive the following warning message (you can run the program):

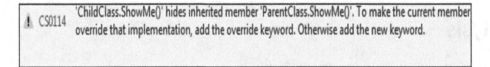

- If you omit the words *virtual* and *override* in the preceding program, you will receive the following warning message:

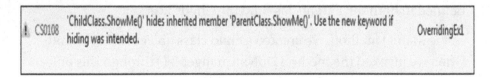

We will discuss the keyword "new" in this context shortly.

The return types, signatures and access-specifiers of virtual and overridden methods must be the same; for example, in the preceding example, if you change the accessibility from public to protected in the child class's ShowMe(), as follows:

```
protected override void ShowMe()
    {
        Console.WriteLine("Inside Child.ShowMe");
    }
```

You will receive the compilation error:

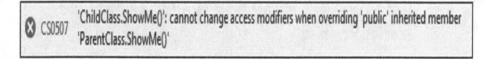

Students ask:

Sir, in method overloading, return types did not matter. But here it matters. Is this correct?

Teacher says: Yes. We must remember that signatures, return types, and accessibility should match for both virtual and overridden methods.

Students ask:

Sir, will the following program receive any compilation errors?

Demonstration 9

```
class ParentClass
    {
        public virtual int ShowMe(int i)
        {
            Console.WriteLine("I am in Parent class");
            return i;
        }
    }
    class ChildClass : ParentClass
    {
```

```
    public override void ShowMe(int i)
    {
        Console.WriteLine("I am in Child class");
    }
}
```

Teacher says: Yes. You will get following error:

Output

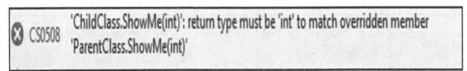

So, to overcome this, as the compiler suggested, you can change the method's (in the child class) return type to int and do some necessary changes in the method body, like in the following:

```
public override int ShowMe(int i)
    {
        Console.WriteLine("I am in Child class");
        Console.WriteLine("Incrementing i by 5");
        return i +5;//Must return  an int
    }
```

Or, you can use a method with a void return type like the following (but this time it will be treated as method overloading):

```
public void ShowMe()
    {
        Console.WriteLine("In Child.ShowMe()");
    }
```

If you use the both redefined methods in your program, you are actually implementing both method overloading and method overriding. Go through the following example.

Demonstration 10

```csharp
using System;

namespace OverridingEx2
{
    class ParentClass
    {
        public virtual int ShowMe(int i)
        {
            Console.WriteLine("I am in Parent class");
            return i;
        }
    }
    class ChildClass : ParentClass
    {
        public override int ShowMe(int i)
        {
            Console.WriteLine("I am in Child class");
            Console.WriteLine("Incrementing i by 5");
            return i + 5;//Must return  an int
        }
        public void ShowMe()
        {
            Console.WriteLine("In Child.ShowMe()");
        }
    }
    class Program
    {
        static void Main(string[] args)
        {
            Console.WriteLine("*** Overloading with Overriding Demo***\n");
            ChildClass childOb = new ChildClass();
            Console.WriteLine(childOb.ShowMe(5));//10
            childOb.ShowMe();
            Console.ReadKey();
```

```
            }
        }
    }
}
```

Output

```
*** Overloading with Overriding Demo***

I am in Child class
Incrementing i by 5
10
In Child.ShowMe()
```

Teacher says: It is said that object-oriented programmers pass through three important stages. In the first stage, they become familiar with non-object-oriented constructs/structures (e.g., they use decision statements, looping constructs, etc.). In the second stage, they start creating class and objects, and use the inheritance mechanism. And finally in the third stage, they use polymorphism to achieve late binding and make their programs flexible. So let's examine how to implement polymorphism in C# programs.

Experiment with Polymorphism

Teacher continues: Polymorphism is generally associated with one method name with multiple forms/constructs. To understand it better, we need to clear the core concepts first. So, look at the program and its corresponding output.

Demonstration 11

```
using System;

namespace BaseRefToChildObjectEx1
{
        class Vehicle
          {
```

```csharp
        public void ShowMe()
        {
            Console.WriteLine("Inside Vehicle.ShowMe");
        }
    }
    class Bus : Vehicle
    {
        public void ShowMe()
        {
            Console.WriteLine("Inside Bus.ShowMe");
        }
        public void BusSpecificMethod()
        {
            Console.WriteLine("Inside Bus.ShowMe");
        }
    }
class Program
{
    static void Main(string[] args)
    {
        Console.WriteLine("***Base Class reference to Child Class
        Object Demo***\n\n");
        Vehicle obVehicle = new Bus();
        obVehicle.ShowMe();//Inside Vehicle.ShowMe
        // obVehicle.BusSpecificMethod();//Error
        //Bus obBus = new Vehicle();//Error
        Console.ReadKey();
    }
}
}
```

Output

```
***Base Class reference to Child Class Object Demo***


Inside Vehicle.ShowMe
```

Analysis

Note the two important lines of codes in the preceding program:

```
Vehicle obVehicle = new Bus();
obVehicle.ShowMe();
```

Here we are pointing to a derived class object(Bus object) through a parent class reference(Vehicle reference) and then we are invoking the ShowMe() method. This way of invoking is allowed and we will not receive any compilation issues; that is, a base class reference can point to a derived class object.

But we cannot use either of these lines:

1. `obVehicle.BusSpecificMethod();//Error`

(Since the apparent type here is Vehicle not Bus).To remove this error, you need to downcast, as follows:

```
((Bus)obVehicle).BusSpecificMethod();
```

2. `Bus obBus = new Vehicle();//Error`

As mentioned, to remove this error, you need to downcast, as follows:

```
Bus obBus = (Bus)new Vehicle();
```

POINTS TO REMEMBER

Through a parent class reference, we can refer to a child class object but the reverse is not true. *An object reference can implicitly upcast to base class reference and explicitly downcast to a derived class reference.* We will learn about the upcasting and downcasting operations in detail in the chapter on Analysis of Some Key Comparisons (Chapter 8).

Now we will slightly modify the program using the keywords *virtual* and *override,* as follows. Notice that we have tagged the parent class (Vehicle) method with virtual and Child class (Bus) method with override.

Demonstration 12

```
using System;

namespace PloymorphismEx1
{
    class Vehicle
     {
         public virtual void ShowMe()
         {
             Console.WriteLine("Inside Vehicle.ShowMe");
         }
     }
    class Bus : Vehicle
     {
         public override void ShowMe()
         {
             Console.WriteLine("Inside Bus.ShowMe");
         }
         public void BusSpecificMethod()
         {
             Console.WriteLine("Inside Bus.ShowMe");
         }
     }
```

```
class Program
{
    static void Main(string[] args)
    {
        Console.WriteLine("***Polymorphism Example-1 ***\n\n");
        Vehicle obVehicle = new Bus();
        obVehicle.ShowMe();//Inside Bus.ShowMe
        // obVehicle.BusSpecificMethod();//Error
        //Bus obBus = new Vehicle();//Error
        Console.ReadKey();
    }
}
}
```

Output

```
***Polymorphism Example-1 ***


Inside Bus.ShowMe
```

Analysis

Notice the output. This time, the child class method is invoked (Not the parent class method!). It is because we already tagged the ShowMe() method in the Vehicle class as virtual. Now the compiler will no longer see the apparent type to call the method (i.e., the call cannot be resolved in compile-time binding). When we point a child class object's method through a base class reference, the compiler uses *the object type referenced by the base type reference* to invoke the correct object's method. In this case, the compiler can pick the ShowMe() from the Bus class because the Bus object is referenced by the base class (Vehicle) reference.

So, by marking a method in the base class as virtual, we intend to achieve polymorphism. Now we can intentionally redefine (override) the method in the child classes. In the child class, by tagging a method with the keyword *override*, we deliberately redefine the corresponding virtual method.

POINTS TO REMEMBER

- In C#, all methods are by default non-virtual. But, in Java, they are virtual by default. So, in C#, we need to tag the keyword *override* to avoid any unconscious overriding.

- C# also uses the *new* keyword to mark a method as non-overriding, which we will discuss shortly.

Students ask:
Sir, you are saying, "The parent class reference can point to a child object but the reverse is not true." Why do we support this kind of design?

Teacher says: We must agree about these facts: We can say that all Buses are Vehicles but the reverse is not necessarily true because there are other vehicles like Trains, Ships that are not definitely buses.

In the same manner, in programming terminology, all derived classes are of type base classes but the reverse is not true. For example, suppose we have a class called Rectangle and it is derived from another class called Shape. Then we can say that all Rectangles are Shapes but the reverse is not true.

And you must remember that we need to do an "is-a" test for an inheritance hierarchy and the direction of "is-a" is always straightforward.

Students ask:
Sir, you are saying that the call will be resolved at runtime for following codes?

```
Vehicle obVehicle = new Bus();
 obVehicle.ShowMe();
```

But we can clearly see that a Bus object is pointed by the parent class reference and compiler could bind ShowMe() to the Bus object during early binding (or compile-time binding). Why did it delay the process unnecessarily?

Teacher says: Looking at the preceding code, you may think like this. But let's assume that we have one more child class, Taxi, which is also inherited from the Parent class Vehicle. And at runtime, based on some situation, we need to invoke the ShowMe() method either from Bus or from Taxi. Consider a case like the following: We are generating a random number between 0 and 10 .Then we are checking whether the number is an even number or an odd number. If it is an even number, we are using Bus object, otherwise we are using the Taxi object to invoke the corresponding ShowMe() method.

Consider the following code.

Demonstration 13

```
using System;

namespace PolymorphismEx3
{
    class Vehicle
    {
        public virtual void ShowMe()
        {
            Console.WriteLine("Inside Vehicle.ShowMe");
        }
    }
    class Bus : Vehicle
    {
        public override void ShowMe()
        {
            Console.WriteLine("Inside Bus.ShowMe");
        }
    }
    class Taxi : Vehicle
    {
```

```
    public override void ShowMe()
    {
        Console.WriteLine("Inside Taxi.ShowMe");
    }
}
class Program
{
    static void Main(string[] args)
    {
        Console.WriteLine("***Polymorphism Example-3 ***\n");
        Vehicle obVehicle;
        int count = 0;
        Random r = new Random();
        while( count <5)
        {
            int tick = r.Next(0, 10);
            if(tick%2==0)
            {
                obVehicle = new Bus();

            }
            else
            {
                obVehicle = new Taxi();
            }
            obVehicle.ShowMe();//Output will be determined during
            runtime
            count++;
        }

        Console.ReadKey();
    }
}
}
```

Output

Note that the output may vary.

This is the first run:

```
***Polymorphism Example-3 ***

Inside Taxi.ShowMe
Inside Bus.ShowMe
Inside Taxi.ShowMe
Inside Taxi.ShowMe
Inside Bus.ShowMe
```

This is the second run:

```
***Polymorphism Example-3 ***

Inside Bus.ShowMe
Inside Taxi.ShowMe
Inside Taxi.ShowMe
Inside Taxi.ShowMe
Inside Taxi.ShowMe
```

And so on.

Explanation

Now you should realize why the compiler needs to delay the decision until runtime for this kind of coding and how we are achieving polymorphism.

Students ask:

There are some situations where we may want to place a restriction. A method in the parent class should not be overridden by a method of its child class. How can we achieve that?

Teacher says: In many interviews, you may face this question. *We must remember that we can prevent overriding by the use of 'static,' 'private,' or 'sealed' keywords.* But here we have discussed the use of "sealed" only.

Consider the following code. Here the compiler itself is preventing the inheritance process.

Demonstration 14

```
sealed class ParentClass
    {
        public void ShowClassName()
        {
            Console.WriteLine("Inside Parent.ShowClassName");
        }
    }
    class ChildClass : ParentClass //Error
    {
        //Some code
    }
```

We will receive following error: 'ChildClass': cannot derive from sealed type 'ParentClass'.

Output

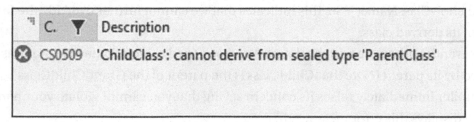

Teacher continues: The sealed keyword may not be associated with class only. We can use it with methods also. Go through the following program to understand it better.

Demonstration 15

```
class ParentClass
    {
        public virtual void ShowClassName()
```

```
    {
        Console.WriteLine("Inside Parent.ShowClassName");
    }
}
class ChildClass : ParentClass
{
    sealed public override void ShowClassName()
    {
        Console.WriteLine("Inside ChildClass.ShowClassName");
    }
}
class GrandChildClass : ChildClass
{
    public override void ShowClassName()
    {
        Console.WriteLine("Inside GrandChildClass.ShowClassName");
    }
}
```

Here we are experimenting with multilevel inheritance where (as the names suggest) ChildClass is deriving from ParentClass and GrandChildClass is deriving from ChildClass. But in ChildClass, we have used the keyword *sealed* with the overriding method ShowClassName(). So, this indicates that we cannot further override the method in any of its derived class.

But grandchildren are naughty in general. So, it tried to violate the rule that was imposed by its parent (Note that ChildClass is the parent of the GrandChildClass). So, the compiler immediately raises its concern saying that you cannot violate your parents' rule and displays this error message:

Output

	Code	Description
❌	CS0239	'GrandChildClass.ShowClassName()': cannot override inherited member 'ChildClass.ShowClassName()' because it is sealed

Teacher continues: Now consider the case of private constructors. If a class has only private constructors, it cannot be sub classed. This concept can be used to make a singleton design pattern where we prevent unnecessary objects creation in the system with the use of the new keyword; for example, the following program will give you a compilation error.

Demonstration 16

```
class ParentClass
    {
        private ParentClass() { }
        public void ShowClassName()
        {
            Console.WriteLine("Inside Parent.ShowClassName");
        }
    }
    class ChildClass : ParentClass //Error
    {
        //Some code
    }
```

Output

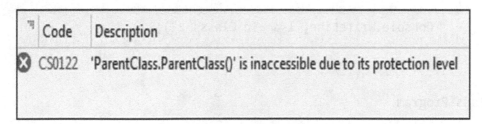

	Code	Description
❌	CS0122	'ParentClass.ParentClass()' is inaccessible due to its protection level

Quiz

Can you predict the output? Is there any compilation error?

Demonstration 17

```
using System;
namespace QuizOnSealedEx1
{
    class QuizOnSealed
    {
        public virtual void TestMe()
        {
            Console.WriteLine("I am in Class-1");
        }

    }
    class Class1: QuizOnSealed
    {
        sealed public override void TestMe()
        {
            Console.WriteLine("I am in Class-1");
        }
    }
    class Class2: QuizOnSealed
    {
        public override void TestMe()
        {
            Console.WriteLine("I am in Classs-2");
        }
    }

    class Program
    {
        static void Main(string[] args)
        {
            Console.WriteLine("***Quiz on sealed keyword usage***\n");
            Class2 obClass2 = new Class2();
            obClass2.TestMe();
            Console.ReadKey();
```

```
        }
    }
}
```

Output

The program will compile and run successfully.

```
C:\CSharpProgs\CSharpBasicsProgs\InteractiveCSharpSolution\QuizOnSealedEx1\bin\Debug\QuizOnSealedEx1.exe

***Quiz on sealed keyword usage***

I am in Classs-2
```

Explanation

We did not encounter any issue here because Class2 is not a child class of Class1. It is also derived from the same parent class, QuizOnSealed, and it has the freedom to override the TestMe() method.

POINTS TO REMEMBER

A sealed class cannot be a base class. They prevent the derivational process. This is why they cannot be abstract. MSDN states that with some runtime optimization, we can invoke sealed class members slightly faster.

Students ask:
Sir, so far, you have used the keyword *sealed* for methods and classes. Can we apply it to member variables?

Teacher says: No. We can use *readonly* or *const* in those contexts. We can declare constants like a variable but the key point is they cannot be changed after the declaration. On the other hand, we can assign a value to a readonly field during the declaration time or through a constructor. To declare a constant variable, we need to prefix the keyword *const* before the declaration. Constants are implicitly static. Comparisons between these two are covered in the chapter on Analysis of Some Key Comparisons in C# (Chapter 8).

Quiz

Will the code compile?

```
class A
{
    sealed int a = 5;
}
```

Answer

No. In C#, it is not allowed.

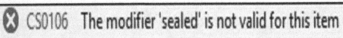

In this case, you could use readonly.

Quiz

Will the code compile?

```
class A
    {
        sealed A()
        { }
    }
```

Answer

No. In C#, it is not allowed.

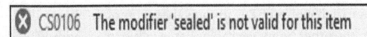

Teacher continues: The keyword *sealed* is used to prevent overriding but constructors cannot be overridden at all, as per the language specification. If we want to prevent a constructor from being called by its derived classes, we can mark it private. (Constructors aren't inherited by a child class; we need to explicitly call a base class constructor if needed).

Students ask:

Sir, to prevent inheritance, which process needs to be preferred: case 1 or case 2?

Case 1:

```
class A1
    {
       private A1() { }
       }
```

Case 2:

```
sealed class A2
    {
        //some code..
    }
```

Teacher says: First of all, we need to be aware of our requirements. We should not generalize any decision in advance. In case 1, we can add other things and then we can easily derive a new class from that. But in case 2, we cannot derive a child class. To better understand it, let's add some code to case 1 and follow this case study.

Demonstration 18

```
using System;

namespace SealedClassVsA_ClassWithPrivateCons
{
    class A1
    {
      public int x;
      private A1() { }
      public A1(int x) { this.x = x; }
```

```
    }
    sealed class A2
    {
        //some code..
    }
    class B1 : A1
    {
       public  int y;
        public B1(int x,int y):base(x)
        {
            this.y = y;
        }
    }
    //class B2 : A2 { }//Cannot derive from sealed type 'A2'

    class Program
    {
        static void Main(string[] args)
        {
           Console.WriteLine("***Case study: sealed class vs private
           constructor***\n");
           B1 obB1 = new B1(2, 3);
           Console.WriteLine("\t x={0}",obB1.x);
           Console.WriteLine("\t y={0}",obB1.y);
           Console.Read();
        }
    }
}
```

Output

```
***Case study: sealed class vs private constructor***


        x=2
        y=3
```

Analysis

We can see that we can extend the class in case 1, but notice the commented line:

```
//class B2 : A2 { }//Cannot derive from sealed type 'A2'
```

If you uncomment this, you'll get this compilation error:

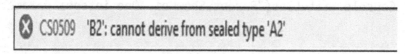

The key thing to remember is that if you use a private constructor only to prevent inheritance, then you are using the wrong approach. The private constructors are commonly used in the classes that contain only static members. When you learn about design patterns, you will see that we can use private constructors for a singleton design pattern to stop additional instantiation. And in those cases, our intent is different.

Students ask:

Sir, give us some pointers so that we can easily distinguish between method overloading and method overriding.

Teacher says: The following points can help you to brush up your knowledge:

In method overloading *all methods may reside inside the same class* (note the word '*may*' here because we can have examples where the concept of method overloading spans in two classes—both a parent and its child).

In method overriding, the inheritance hierarchy of a parent class and a child class is involved, which means that at least a parent class and its child class (i.e., minimum of two classes) are involved in case of method overriding.

Consider the following program and output.

Demonstration 19

```
using System;

namespace OverloadingWithMultipleClasses
{
    class Parent
    {
```

```
        public void ShowMe()
        {
            Console.WriteLine("Parent.ShowMe1.No parameter");
        }
        public void ShowMe(int a)
        {
            Console.WriteLine("Parent.ShowMe1. One integer parameter");
        }
    }
    class Child:Parent
    {
        //An overloaded method in child/derived class
        public void ShowMe(int a,int b)
        {
            Console.WriteLine("Child.ShowMe1. Two integer parameter");
        }
    }
    class Program
    {
        static void Main(string[] args)
        {
            Console.WriteLine("*** Overloading across multiple
            classes***\n");
            Child childOb = new Child();
            //Calling all the 3 overloaded methods
            childOb.ShowMe();
            childOb.ShowMe(1);
            childOb.ShowMe(1,2);
            Console.ReadKey();
        }
    }
}
```

Output

```
*** Overloading across multiple classes***

Parent.ShowMe1.No parameter
Parent.ShowMe1. One integer parameter
Child.ShowMe1. Two integer parameter
```

Note   Even Visual Studio will give you a clue when you are about to use these overloaded methods. You can see that the child class object can access 1+2; that is, a total of three overloaded methods in this case.

```
24    class Program
25    {
26       static void Main(string[] args)
27       {
28          Console.WriteLine("*** Overloading across multiple classes***\n");
29          Child childOb = new Child();
30          childOb.
31       }           Equals
32    }              GetHashCode
33    }              GetType
34                   ShowMe          void Child.ShowMe(int a, int b) (+ 2 overloads)
                     ToString
```

In method overloading, signatures are different. In method overriding, method signatures are same/compatible. (Though you do not need to consider the word *compatible* now. Later you may learn about covariant return type in Java and there the word 'compatible' will make sense to you. But in C#, you can ignore the word "compatible").

We can achieve compile-time (static) polymorphism through method overloading, but we can achieve runtime (dynamic) polymorphism through method overriding. For static binding/early binding/overloading, compiler gathers its knowledge at compile time, so in general, it performs faster.

```
┌─────────────────────────────────────────────────────────────┐
│                    POINTS TO REMEMBER                        │
└─────────────────────────────────────────────────────────────┘
```

All C# methods are non-virtual by default (but in Java, they are just opposite). Here we use the keyword *override* to intentionally override or redefine a method (which was marked as virtual). In addition to these two keywords, the keyword *new* comes into the picture to mark a method as non-overriding.

Teacher says: Let's finish this discussion with a simple program to demonstrate the use of '*new*' keyword in the context of overriding. Consider the following program and output.

Demonstration 20

```csharp
using System;

namespace OverridingEx3
{
    class ParentClass
    {
        public virtual void ShowMe()
        {
            Console.WriteLine("Inside Parent.ShowMe");
        }
    }
    class ChildClass : ParentClass
    {
        public new void ShowMe()
        {
            Console.WriteLine("Inside Child.ShowMe");
        }
    }
    class Program
    {
        static void Main(string[] args)
        {
```

```
Console.WriteLine("*** Use of 'new' in the context of method
Overriding ***\n");
ParentClass parentOb = new ParentClass();
parentOb.ShowMe();//Calling Parent version
ChildClass childOb = new ChildClass();
childOb.ShowMe();//Calling Child version
Console.ReadKey();
        }
    }
}
```

Output

```
*** Use of 'new' in the context of method Overriding ***

Inside Parent.ShowMe
Inside Child.ShowMe
```

Analysis

If you do not use the keyword *new* with the ShowMe() method in the Child class, you'll see a warning message:

> ⚠ CS0114   'ChildClass.ShowMe()' hides inherited member 'ParentClass.ShowMe()'. To make the current member override that implementation, add the override keyword. Otherwise add the new keyword.

If you are familiar with Java, you may find this feature interesting because it is not allowed there. The idea is simple: C# introduces the concept of marking a non-overriding method, which we do not want to use polymorphically.

Teacher continues: To understand the difference with *override* keyword, consider the following example. Here one child class is using override, another one is using new. Now compare the polymorphic behavior.

Demonstration 21

```
using System;

namespace OverridingEx4
{
    class ParentClass
    {
        public virtual void ShowMe()
        {
            Console.WriteLine("Inside Parent.ShowMe");
        }
    }
    class ChildClass1 : ParentClass
    {
        public override void ShowMe()
        {
            Console.WriteLine("Inside Child.ShowMe");
        }
    }
    class ChildClass2 : ParentClass
    {
        public new void ShowMe()
        {
            Console.WriteLine("Inside Child.ShowMe");
        }
    }

    class Program
    {
        static void Main(string[] args)
        {
            Console.WriteLine("*** Use of 'new' in the context of method
            Overriding.Example-2 ***\n");
            ParentClass parentOb;
```

```
        parentOb= new ParentClass();
        parentOb.ShowMe();
        parentOb = new ChildClass1();
        parentOb.ShowMe();//Inside Child.ShowMe
        parentOb = new ChildClass2();
        parentOb.ShowMe();//Inside Parent.ShowMe

        Console.ReadKey();
    }
  }
}
```

Output

```
*** Use of 'new' in the context of method Overriding.Example-2 ***

Inside Parent.ShowMe
Inside Child.ShowMe
Inside Parent.ShowMe
```

Analysis

We can see the impact of using *new* keyword in the last line of output. We can see that "new" member is not polymorphic (not printing Child.ShowMe).

Abstract Class

We often expect that someone else will carry out our incomplete work. A real-life example is with property purchases and remodeling. It is very common that grandparents bought a property , and then parents built a small house on that property, and later a grandchild made the house bigger or redecorated the old house. The basic idea is same: we may want someone to continue and complete the incomplete work first. We give them freedom that upon completion, they can remodel as per their needs. The concepts of an abstract class best suits in such types of scenarios in the programming world.

These are incomplete classes and we cannot instantiate objects from this type of class. The child of those classes must complete them first and then they can redefine some of the methods (by overriding).

In general, if a class contains at least one incomplete/abstract method, the class itself is an abstract class. The term *abstract method* means that the method has the declaration (or signature) but no implementation. In other words, you can think of abstract members as virtual members without a default implementation.

POINTS TO REMEMBER

A class that contains at least one abstract method must be marked as an abstract class.

The subclass must finish the incomplete task; that is, they need to provide those implementations but if they fail to provide those, they will be again marked with the abstract keyword.

So, the technique is very useful when a base/parent class wants to define a generalized form that will be shared by its subclasses. It simply passes the responsibility to fill in the details to its subclasses. Let's start with a simple demo.

Demonstration 22

```
using System;

namespace AbstractClassEx1
{
    abstract class MyAbstractClass
    {
```

```
    public abstract void ShowMe();
}
class MyConcreteClass : MyAbstractClass
{
    public override void ShowMe()
    {
        Console.WriteLine("I am from a concrete class.");
        Console.WriteLine("My ShowMe() method body is complete.");
    }
}
class Program
{
    static void Main(string[] args)
    {
        Console.WriteLine("***Abstract class Example-1 ***\n");
        //Error:Cannot create an instance of the abstract class
        // MyAbstractClass abstractOb=new MyAbstractClass();
        MyConcreteClass concreteOb = new MyConcreteClass();
        concreteOb.ShowMe();
        Console.ReadKey();
    }
}
}
```

Output

```
***Abstract class Example-1 ***

I am from a concrete class.
My ShowMe() method body is complete.
```

Teacher continues: An abstract class can contain concrete methods also. The child class may or may not override those methods.

Demonstration 23

```csharp
using System;

namespace AbstractClassEx2
{
    abstract class MyAbstractClass
    {
        protected int myInt = 25;
        public abstract void ShowMe();
        public virtual void CompleteMethod1()
        {
                    Console.WriteLine("MyAbstractClass.
                    CompleteMethod1()");
        }
        public void CompleteMethod2()
        {
            Console.WriteLine("MyAbstractClass.CompleteMethod2()");
        }

    }
    class MyConcreteClass : MyAbstractClass
    {
        public override void ShowMe()
        {
            Console.WriteLine("I am from a concrete class.");
            Console.WriteLine("My ShowMe() method body is complete.");
            Console.WriteLine("value of myInt is {0}",myInt);
        }
        public override void CompleteMethod1()
        {
            Console.WriteLine("MyConcreteClass.CompleteMethod1()");
        }
    }
```

```
class Program
{
    static void Main(string[] args)
    {
        Console.WriteLine("***Abstract class Example-2 ***\n");
        //Error:Cannot create an instance of the abstract class
        // MyAbstractClass abstractOb=new MyAbstractClass();
        MyConcreteClass concreteOb = new MyConcreteClass();
        concreteOb.ShowMe();
        concreteOb.CompleteMethod1();
        concreteOb.CompleteMethod2();
        Console.WriteLine("\n\n*** Invoking methods through parent
        class reference now ***\n");
        MyAbstractClass absRef = concreteOb;
        absRef.ShowMe();
        absRef.CompleteMethod1();
        absRef.CompleteMethod2();
        Console.ReadKey();
    }
}
}
```

Output

Explanation

The preceding example demonstrates that we can use the abstract class reference to point to the child class objects, and then we can invoke the associated methods. Later we will learn that we can get significant benefit from this kind of approach.

Students ask:

How can we implement the concept of runtime polymorphism here?

Teacher says: We used it in the previous example. Note the following portion of code:

```
Console.WriteLine("\n\n*** Invoking methods through parent class reference now ***\n");
MyAbstractClass absRef = concreteOb;
absRef.ShowMe();
absRef.CompleteMethod1();
absRef.CompleteMethod2();
Console.ReadKey();
```

Students ask:

Can an abstract class contain fields?

Teacher says: Yes. In the previous example, we used such a field; that is, myInt.

Students ask:

In the preceding example, the access modifier is public. Is it mandatory?

Teacher says: No. We can use other types also. Later you will notice that it is one of the key differences with interfaces.

Students ask:

Suppose in a class we have more than ten methods, and out of those, only one is an abstract method. Do we need to mark the class with the keyword abstract?

Teacher says: Yes. If a class contains at least one abstract method, the class itself is abstract. You can simply recognize the fact that an abstract keyword is used to represent the incompleteness. So, if your class contains one incomplete method, the class is incomplete, and hence it needs to be marked with the keyword *abstract*.

So, the simple formula is that whenever your class has at least one abstract method, the class is an abstract class.

Teacher continues: Now consider a reverse scenario. Suppose, you have marked your class abstract but there is no abstract method in it, like this:

```
abstract class MyAbstractClass
    {
        protected int myInt = 25;
        //public abstract void ShowMe();
        public virtual void CompleteMethod1()
        {
            Console.WriteLine("MyAbstractClass.CompleteMethod1()");
        }
        public void CompleteMethod2()
        {
            Console.WriteLine("MyAbstractClass.CompleteMethod2()");
        }
    }
```

Quiz

Can we compile the program?

Answer

Yes. Still it will compile but you must remember that you cannot create an object for this class. So, if you code like this:

```
MyAbstractClass absRef = new MyAbstractClass();//Error
```

The compiler will raise its concern.

> ⊗ CS0144   Cannot create an instance of the abstract class or interface 'MyAbstractClass'

Students ask:

So sir, how can we create an object from an abstract class?

Teacher says: We cannot create objects from an abstract class.

Students ask:

Sir, it appears to me that an abstract class has virtually no use if it is not extended. Is this correct?

Teacher says: Yes.

Students ask:

If a class extends an abstract class, it has to implement all the abstract methods. Is this correct?

Teacher says: The simple formula is that if you want to create objects of a class, the class needs to be completed; that is, it should not contain any abstract methods. So, if the child class cannot provide implementation (i.e., body) of all the abstract methods, it should mark itself again with the keyword *abstract*, like in the following example.

```
abstract class MyAbstractClass
    {
        public abstract void InCompleteMethod1();
        public abstract void InCompleteMethod2();
    }
    abstract class ChildClass : MyAbstractClass
    {
        public override void InCompleteMethod1()
        {
                Console.WriteLine("Making complete of
                InCompleteMethod1()");
        }
    }
```

In this case, if you forget to use the keyword *abstract*, the compiler will raise an error saying that ChildClass has not implemented InCompleteMethod2().

⊗ CS0534 'ChildClass' does not implement inherited abstract member 'MyAbstractClass.InCompleteMethod2()'

Students ask:

We can say that a concrete class is a class that is not abstract. Is this correct?

Yes.

Students ask:

Sometimes we are confused about the order of keywords; for example, in the preceding case we are using:

```
public override void InCompleteMethod1(){...}
```

Teacher says: The method must have a return type and it should be preceded by your method name. So, if you can remember this concept, you will never write something like "public void override <MethodName>", which is incorrect in C#.

Students ask:

Can we tag a method with both abstract and sealed?

Teacher says: No. It is like if you say that you want to explore C# but you will not go through any material. Similarly, by declaring abstract, you want to share some common information across the derived classes and you indicate that overriding is necessary for them; that is, the inheritance chain needs to grow but at the same time, by declaring sealed, you want to put the end marker to the derivational process, so that the inheritance chain cannot grow. So, in this case, you are trying to implement two opposite constraints simultaneously.

Quiz

Can you predict the output?

```
using System;

namespace ExperimentWithConstructorEx1
{
    class MyTestClass
    {
        //Constructors cannot be abstract or sealed
        abstract MyTestClass()//Error
        {
            Console.WriteLine("abstract constructor");
        }
    }

    class Program
    {
        static void Main(string[] args)
        {
            Console.WriteLine("***Quiz : Experiment with a
            constructor***\n");
            MyTestClass ob = new MyTestClass();
            Console.ReadKey();
        }
    }
}
```

Output

Compilation error.

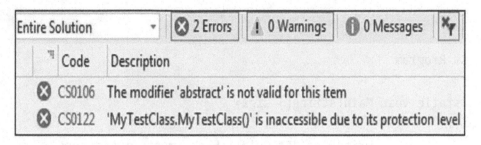

Students ask:

Sir, why can't constructors be abstract?

Teacher says: We usually use the keyword *abstract* with a class to indicate that it is incomplete and the subclass will take the responsibility to make him complete. We must remember that constructors cannot be overridden (i.e., they are sealed). Also, if you analyze the actual purpose of constructors (i.e., to initialize objects), you must agree that since we cannot create objects from abstract classes, the design perfectly suits here.

Quiz

Can you predict the output?

```
using System;

namespace ExperimentWithAccessModifiersEx1
{
    abstract class IncompleteClass
    {
        public abstract  void ShowMe();
    }
    class CompleteClass : IncompleteClass
    {
        protected override void ShowMe()
        {
```

```
            Console.WriteLine("I am complete.");
            Console.WriteLine("I supplied the method body for
            showMe()");
        }
    }

    class Program
    {
        static void Main(string[] args)
        {
            Console.WriteLine("***Quiz : Experiment with access
            specifiers***\n");
            IncompleteClass myRef = new CompleteClass();
            myRef.ShowMe();
            Console.ReadKey();
        }
    }
}
```

Output

Compiler error.

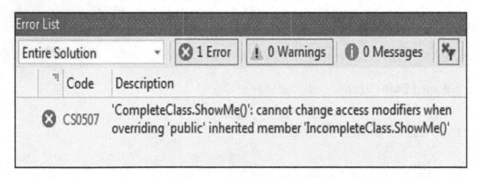

Note: We need to use the public access modifier instead of the protected access modifier in the CompleteClass. Then you can get the following output:

```
***Quiz : Experiment with access specifiers***

I am complete.
I supplied the method body for showMe().
```

Students ask:

Sir, why are we not using protected in both classes?

Teacher says: Conceptually, you can do this but then you'll encounter the compile-time error inside the Main() method. This is because a protected method access is limited to the class (in which it defined) and in its derived class instances.

```
static void Main(string[] args)
{

    Console.WriteLine("***Quiz : Experiment with access specifiers***\n");
    IncompleteClass myRef = new CompleteClass();
    myRef.ShowMe();   ⟵
    Console.ReadKey();
}
```

Summary

This chapter covered

- ✓ Method overloading
- ✓ Operator overloading
- ✓ Method overriding
- ✓ Abstract classes
- ✓ How to achieve runtime polymorphism with abstract classes
- ✓ Method signatures
- ✓ How to identify if methods are overloaded or not
- ✓ How to overload constructors
- ✓ How to overload Main() method
- ✓ How can we use multiple Main() in our program
- ✓ How to achieve compile-time polymorphism and runtime polymorphism
- ✓ Why late binding is necessary
- ✓ Use of virtual, override, sealed, and abstract keywords
- ✓ How to prevent inheritance with different techniques
- ✓ A comparison between using the *sealed* keyword in our application vs. using private constructor in our application
- ✓ A brief comparison between method overloading and method overriding
- ✓ Why constructors cannot be abstract
- ✓ 23+ complete program demonstration and outputs to cover these concepts in details

CHAPTER 5

Interfaces: An Art in OOP

Introduction to Interfaces

Teacher starts the discussion: An interface is a special type in C#. An interface contains only method signatures to define some specifications. The subtypes need to follow those specifications. When you use an interface, you may find many similarities with an abstract class.

With the interface, we declare *what we are trying to implement, but we are not specifying how we are going to achieve that.* It may also appear that an interface is similar to a class that does not include any instance variable. All of their methods are declared without a body (i.e., methods are actually abstract). The keyword *interface* is used to declare an interface type; it is preceded by your intended interface name.

POINTS TO REMEMBER

- In simple terms, interfaces helps us separate "what parts" from "how parts."

- To declare them, use the *interface* keyword.

- Interface methods do not have bodies. We simply replace the body with a semicolon like this:

```
void Show();
```

- There is no access modifier attached with an interface method.

- It is recommended that you preface the interface name with the capital letter I, such as

```
interface IMyInterface{..}
```

© Vaskaran Sarcar 2018
V. Sarcar, *Interactive C#*, https://doi.org/10.1007/978-1-4842-3339-9_5

We can support dynamic method resolution during runtime with the help of interfaces. Once defined, a class can implement any number of interfaces. As usual, let's start with a simple example.

Demonstration 1

```
using System;

namespace InterfaceEx1
{
    interface IMyInterface
    {
        void Show();
    }
    class MyClass : IMyInterface
    {
        public void Show()
        {
            Console.WriteLine("MyClass.Show() is implemented.");
        }
    }

    class Program
    {
        static void Main(string[] args)
        {
            Console.WriteLine("***Exploring Interfaces.Example-1***\n");
            MyClass myClassOb = new MyClass();
            myClassOb.Show();
            Console.ReadKey();
        }
    }
}
```

Output

```
***Exploring Interfaces.Example-1***

MyClass.Show() is implemented.
```

POINTS TO REMEMBER

If we try to implement an interface, we need to match the method signatures.

Students ask:

Sir, if these methods are incomplete, then the class that is using the interface needs to implement all the methods in the interfaces. Is this correct?

Teacher says: Exactly. If the class cannot implement all of them, it will announce its incompleteness by marking itself abstract. The following example will help you better understand this.

Here, our interface has two methods. But a class is implementing only one. So, the class itself becomes abstract.

```
interface IMyInterface
    {
        void Show1();
        void Show2();
    }
//MyClass becomes abstract. It has not implemented Show2() of
//IMyInterface
    abstract class MyClass2 : IMyInterface
    {
        public void Show1()
        {
            Console.WriteLine("MyClass.Show1() is implemented.");
        }
        public abstract void Show2();
    }
```

Analysis

The formula is same: A class needs to implement all the methods defined in the interface; otherwise, it will be an abstract class.

If you forget to implement Show2() and you do not mark your class with abstract keyword, as follows...

```
class MyClass2 : IMyInterface
{
    public void Show1()
    {
        Console.WriteLine("MyClass.Show1() is implemented.");
    }
    //public abstract void Show2();
}
```

The compiler will raise the following error.

```
CS0535   'MyClass2' does not implement interface member 'IMyInterface.Show2()'
```

Students ask:

Sir, in this case, a subclass of MyClass2 can complete the task by implementing only Show2(). Is this correct?

Teacher says: Yes. 'Demonstration 2' is the complete example.

Demonstration 2

```
using System;

namespace InterfaceEx2
{
    interface IMyInterface
    {
```

```csharp
        void Show1();
        void Show2();
    }
    //MyClass becomes abstract. It has not implemented Show2()
      of  IMyInterface
    abstract class MyClass2 : IMyInterface
    {
        public void Show1()
        {
            Console.WriteLine("MyClass.Show1() is implemented.");
        }
        public abstract void Show2();
    }
    class ChildClass : MyClass2
    {
        public override void Show2()
        {
            Console.WriteLine("Child is completing -Show2() .");
        }
    }

    class Program
    {
        static void Main(string[] args)
        {
            Console.WriteLine("***Exploring Interfaces.Example-2***\n");
            //MyClass is abstract now
            //MyClass myClassOb = new MyClass();
            MyClass2 myOb = new ChildClass();
            myOb.Show1();
            myOb.Show2();
            Console.ReadKey();
        }
    }
}
```

Output

```
***Exploring Interfaces.Example-2***

MyClass.Show1() is implemented.
Child is completing -Show2() . ←
```

Students ask:

Sir, you said earlier that interfaces could help us implement the concept of multiple inheritance. Can our class implement two or more interfaces?

Teacher says: Yes. The following example shows you how to do that.

Demonstration 3

```
using System;

namespace InterfaceEx3
{
    interface IMyInterface3A
    {
        void Show3A();
    }
    interface IMyInterface3B
    {
        void Show3B();
    }
    class MyClass3 :IMyInterface3A, IMyInterface3B
    {
        public void Show3A()
        {
            Console.WriteLine("MyClass3 .Show3A() is completed.");
        }
        public void Show3B()
        {
```

```
            Console.WriteLine("MyClass3 .Show3B() is completed.");
        }
    }
class Program
    {
        static void Main(string[] args)
        {
            Console.WriteLine("***Exploring Interfaces.Example-3***\n");
            MyClass3 myClassOb = new MyClass3();
            myClassOb.Show3A();
            myClassOb.Show3B();
            Console.ReadKey();
        }
    }
```

Output

```
***Exploring Interfaces.Example-3***

MyClass3 .Show3A() is completed.
MyClass3 .Show3B() is completed.
```

Students ask:

In the preceding program, method names are different in interfaces. But if both of the interfaces contain the same method name, how can we implement them?

Teacher says: Very good question. We need to use the concept of *explicit interface implementation*. In an explicit interface implementation, the method name is preceded by the interface name, such as ***<interfacename>.methodname (){...}.*** Let's go through the following implementation.

Demonstration 4

```csharp
using System;

namespace InterfaceEx4
{
    //Note: Both of the interfaces have the same method name //"Show()".
    interface IMyInterface4A
    {
        void Show();
    }
    interface IMyInterface4B
    {
        void Show();
    }
    class MyClass4 : IMyInterface4A, IMyInterface4B
    {
        public void Show()
        {
            Console.WriteLine("MyClass4 .Show() is completed.");
        }

        void IMyInterface4A.Show()
        {
            Console.WriteLine("Explicit interface Implementation.
            IMyInterface4A .Show().");
        }

        void IMyInterface4B.Show()
        {
            Console.WriteLine("Explicit interface Implementation.
            IMyInterface4B .Show().");
        }
    }
    class Program
    {
        static void Main(string[] args)
```

```
    {
        Console.WriteLine("***Exploring Interfaces.Example-4***\n");

        //All the 3 ways of callings are fine.
        MyClass4 myClassOb = new MyClass4();
        myClassOb.Show();

        IMyInterface4A inter4A = myClassOb;
        inter4A.Show();

        IMyInterface4B inter4B = myClassOb;
        inter4B.Show();

        Console.ReadKey();
    }
}
```

Output

```
***Exploring Interfaces.Example-4***

MyClass4 .Show() is completed.
Explicit interface Implementation.IMyInterface4A .Show().
Explicit interface Implementation.IMyInterface4B .Show().
```

POINTS TO REMEMBER

- We must note of an interesting fact. When we are implementing interface methods explicitly, we are not attaching the keyword *public* with them. But in implicit implementation, it is necessary.

- According to MSDN: "*It is a compile-time error for an explicit interface member implementation to include access modifiers, and it is a compile-time error to include the modifiers* abstract, virtual, override, or static."

- If a class (or struct) implements an interface, then the instance of it implicitly converts to the interface type. This is why we can use the following lines without any error:

  ```
  IMyInterface4A inter4A = myClassOb;
  ```

  Or

  ```
  IMyInterface4B inter4B = myClassOb;
  ```

In this example, myClassOb is an instance of the MyClass4 class, which implements both interfaces—IMyInterface4A and IMyInterface4B.

Students ask:

Can an interface inherit or implement another interface?

Teacher says: It can inherit but not implement (by definition). Consider the following example.

Demonstration 5

```
using System;

namespace InterfaceEx5
{
    interface Interface5A
    {
        void ShowInterface5A();
    }
    interface Interface5B
    {
        void ShowInterface5B();
    }
    //Interface implementing multiple inheritance
    interface Interface5C :Interface5A, Interface5B
    {
        void ShowInterface5C();
    }
```

```csharp
class MyClass5 : Interface5C
{
    public void ShowInterface5A()
    {
        Console.WriteLine("ShowInterface5A() is completed.");
    }

    public void ShowInterface5B()
    {
        Console.WriteLine("ShowInterface5B() is completed.");
    }

    public void ShowInterface5C()
    {
        Console.WriteLine("ShowInterface5C() is completed.");
    }
}

class Program
{
    static void Main(string[] args)
    {
        Console.WriteLine("***Exploring Interfaces.Example-5***");
        Console.WriteLine("***Concept of multiple inheritance through
        interface***\n");

        MyClass5 myClassOb = new MyClass5();
        Interface5A ob5A = myClassOb;
        ob5A.ShowInterface5A();

        Interface5B ob5B = myClassOb;
        ob5B.ShowInterface5B();

        Interface5C ob5C = myClassOb;
        ob5C.ShowInterface5C();

        Console.ReadKey();
    }
}
}
```

Output

```
***Exploring Interfaces.Example-5***
***Concept of multiple inheritance through interface***

ShowInterface5A() is completed.
ShowInterface5B() is completed.
ShowInterface5C() is completed.
```

Quiz

Predict the output.

```
using System;

namespace InterfaceEx6
{
    interface Interface6
    {
        void ShowInterface6();
    }
    class MyClass6 : Interface6
    {
        void Interface6.ShowInterface6()
        {
            Console.WriteLine("ShowInterface6() is completed.");
        }
    }
    class Program
    {
        static void Main(string[] args)
        {
            MyClass6 myClassOb = new MyClass6();
            myClassOb.ShowInterface6();//Error
            //Interface6 ob6 = myClassOb;
            //ob6.ShowInterface6();
```

```
        Console.ReadKey();
    }
  }
}
```

Output

There is a compilation error.

 CS1061   'MyClass6' does not contain a definition for 'ShowInterface6' and no extension method 'ShowInterface6' accepting a first argument of type 'MyClass6' could be found (are you missing a using directive or an assembly reference?)

Analysis

You can see that we have implemented the interface explicitly. According to the language specification, to access the explicit interface member, we need to use the interface type. To overcome the error, you can use following lines of codes (i.e., uncomment the two lines shown earlier):

```
Interface6 ob6 = myClassOb;
ob6.ShowInterface6();
```

Then, you will get following output:

```
ShowInterface6() is completed.
```

Alternatively, you can use the following line of code to get the same output:

```
((Interface6)myClassOb).ShowInterface6();
```

Students ask:
Can we extend from a class and implement an interface at the same time?

Teacher says: Yes. You can always extend from one class (provided it is not sealed or there is no other similar constraints). In that case, it is suggested that you use a *positional notation*. The parent class is positioned first, followed by a comma, followed by the interface name, such as in the following:

```
Class ChildClass: BaseClass,IMyinterface{...}
```

Students ask:
Why do we need explicit interface methods?

Teacher says: If you notice carefully, you will find that the real power of explicit interface is when we have same method signature in two or more different interfaces. Although their signatures are the same, the purpose may be different; for example, if we have two interfaces—ITriangle and IRectangle—and both contain a method with same signature (e.g., `BuildMe()`), you can assume that `BuildMe()` in ITriangle probably wants to build a triangle; whereas `BuildMe()` in IRectangle probably wants to build a rectangle. So, it is expected that you will invoke the appropriate `BuildMe()` method based on the situation.

Tag/Tagging/Marker Interface

Teacher continues: An empty interface is known as a Tag/Tagging/Marker interface.

```
//Marker interface example
interface IMarkerInterface
{
}
```

Students ask:
Sir, why do we need a marker interface?

Teacher says:

- We can create a common parent. (Value types cannot inherit from other value types, but they can implement interfaces. We will learn about value types shortly).

- If a class (or a structure) implements an interface, then the instance of it implicitly converts to the interface type. If a class implements a marker interface, there is no need to define a new method (because the interface itself does not have any such method).

- We can use extension methods with marker interfaces to overcome some challenges in our program.

Note   MSDN suggests that you do not use marker interface. They encourage you to use the concept of attribute. Detailed discussions of attribute and extension methods are beyond the scope of this book.

Teacher asks:

Can you tell me the difference between an abstract class and an interface?

Students say:

- An abstract class can be fully implemented or partially implemented; that is, in an abstract class, we can have concrete methods, but an interface cannot have that. An interface contains the contracts of conducts. (Although in Java, this definition is modified slightly. From Java 8 onward, we can use a default keyword in an interface to provide a default implementation of a method).

- An abstract class can have only one parent class (it can extend from another abstract class or concrete class). An interface can have multiple parent interfaces. An interface can only extend from other interface(s).

- The methods of an interface are public by default. An abstract class can have other flavors (e.g., private, protected etc.).

- In C#, fields are not allowed in an interface. An abstract class can have fields (both static and non-static with different kind of modifiers).

So, if you write something like this:

```
interface IMyInterface
    {
        int i;//Error:Cannot contain fields
    }
```

You will receive a compiler error.

 CS0525   Interfaces cannot contain fields

However, the following code is fine:

```
abstract class MyAbstractClass
    {
        public static int i=10;
        internal int j=45;
    }
```

Students ask:

Sir, how can we decide whether we should use an abstract class or an interface?

Teacher says: Good question. I believe that if we want to have centralized or default behaviors, the abstract class is a better choice. In these cases, we can provide default implementation, which are available in all child classes. On the other hand, interface implementation starts from a scratch. They indicate some kind of rules/contracts on what is to be done (e.g., you must implement the method), but they will not enforce you on the *how* part of it. Also, interfaces are preferred when we are trying to implement the concept of multiple inheritance.

But at the same time, if we need to add a new method to an interface, then we need to track down all the implementations of that interface, and we need to put the concrete implementation of that method in all of those places. An abstract class is ahead here. We can add a new method in an abstract class with a default implementation, and our existing code will run smoothly.

MSDN provides following recommendations: (You can refer this online discussion: https://stackoverflow.com/questions/20193091/recommendations-for-abstract-classes-vs-interfaces)

- If you anticipate creating multiple versions of your component, create an abstract class. Abstract classes provide a simple and easy way to version your components. By updating the base class, all inheriting classes are automatically updated with the change. Interfaces, on the other hand, cannot be changed once created. If a new version of an interface is required, you must create a completely new interface.

- If the functionality that you are creating will be useful across a wide range of disparate objects, use an interface. Abstract classes should be used primarily for objects that are closely related; whereas interfaces are best suited for providing common functionality to unrelated classes.

- If you are designing small, concise bits of functionality, use interfaces. If you are designing large functional units, use an abstract class.

- If you want to provide common, implemented functionality among all implementations of your component, use an abstract class. Abstract classes allow you to partially implement your class; whereas interfaces contain no implementation for any members.

Students ask:

Sir, can we make the interface sealed?

Teacher says: The responsibility of implementing an interface is entirely left up to the developer. So, if you make the interface sealed, then who will implement the incomplete methods of that interface? Basically, you are trying to implement two opposite constructs at the same time.

In the following declaration, Visual Studio IDE raises errors.

Demonstration 6

```csharp
using System;

namespace Test_Interface
{
    sealed interface IMyInterface
    {

      void Show();
    }
    class Program
    {
        static void Main(string[] args)
        {
            //some code
        }
    }
}
```

Output

 CS0106   The modifier 'sealed' is not valid for this item

Students ask:

Sir, can we use the keyword "abstract" before the interface method?

Teacher says: Is there any need to do that? Microsoft clearly states that interfaces can contain no implementation of methods; that is, implicitly, they are abstract. In Visual Studio IDE, you'll see a compile-time error if you write something like this:

Demonstration 7

```
interface IMyInterface
    {
        abstract void Show();
    }
```

Output

> ⊗ CS0106   The modifier 'abstract' is not valid for this item

Now remove the keyword *abstract* from the preceding example, build your program, and then open the ILcode. You can see that it is already marked virtual and abstract.

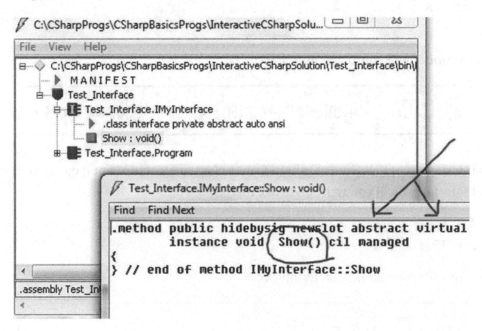

Students ask:

Sir, we understand that interfaces are very powerful. But at the same time, we have seen many restrictions associated with it. Can you please summarize the key restrictions associated with an interface?

Teacher says: The following are some of them, not including the most basic.

We cannot define any fields, constructors, or destructors in an interface. Also, you should not use access modifiers because implicitly, they are public.

Nesting of types (e.g., class, interface, enumeration, and structs) is not allowed. So, if you write code like this:

```
interface IMyInterface
    {
    void Show();
    class A { }
    }
```

The compiler will complain, as follows:

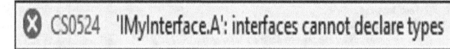

CS0524   'IMyInterface.A': interfaces cannot declare types

An interface is not allowed to inherit from a class or structure but it can inherit from another interface. So, if you write code like this:

```
class A { }
interface IB : A { }
```

The compiler will complain, as follows:

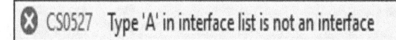

CS0527   Type 'A' in interface list is not an interface

Students ask:

Sir, can you please summarize the benefits of using interfaces?

Teacher says: In many cases, interfaces are very helpful, such as in the following:

- When we try to implement polymorphism
- When we try to implement the concept of multiple inheritance
- When we try to develop loosely coupled systems
- When we try to support parallel developments

Students ask:

Sir, why do we need the restriction that says, "An interface cannot inherit from a class"?

Teacher says: A class or structure can have some implementations. So, if we allow an interface to inherit from them, the interface may contain the implementations, which is against the core aim of an interface.

Summary

This chapter answered the following questions:

✓ What is an interface?

✓ How do you design an interface?

✓ What are the basic characteristics of an interface?

✓ How can we implement multiple interfaces?

✓ How do you deal with interfaces that have a method with same name?

✓ What are the different types of interfaces?

✓ How do you deal with explicit interface techniques?

✓ Why do we need explicit interface methods?

✓ What is a marker interface?

✓ What is the difference between an abstract class and an interface?

✓ How do we decide whether we should use an abstract class or an interface?

✓ What are the key restrictions associated with an interface?

CHAPTER 6

Encapsulation with Properties and Indexers

Overview of Properties

Teacher starts the discussion: We already know that encapsulation is one of the key characteristics in object-oriented programming. In C#, properties are very important because they help encapsulate an object state. A *property* is a member that provides a flexible mechanism to read, write, or compute the value of a private field. Initially, properties may appear similar to fields, but actually they have either get or set or both blocks attached with them. These special blocks/methods are called *accessors*. In simple terms, get blocks are used for reading purposes and set blocks are used for assigning purposes.

In the following code, we will examine how to gain complete control of getting or setting a value of private members. Apart from this type of control and flexibility, we can also impose some constraints with the properties, and these characteristics make them unique in nature.

Demonstration 1

```
using System;

namespace PropertiesEx1
{
    class MyClass
    {
```

© Vaskaran Sarcar 2018
V. Sarcar, *Interactive C#*, https://doi.org/10.1007/978-1-4842-3339-9_6

```
        private int myInt; // also called private "backing" field
        public int MyInt    // The public property
        {
            get
            {
                return myInt;
            }
            set
            {
                myInt = value;
            }
        }
    }
    class Program
    {
        static void Main(string[] args)
        {
            Console.WriteLine("***Exploring Properties.Example-1***");
            MyClass ob = new MyClass();
            //ob.myInt = 10;//Error: myInt is inaccessible
            //Setting  a new value
            ob.MyInt = 10;//Ok.We'll get 10
            //Reading the value
            Console.WriteLine("\nValue of myInt is now:{0}", ob.MyInt);
            //Setting another value to myInt through MyInt
            ob.MyInt = 100;
            Console.WriteLine("Now myInt value is:{0}", ob.MyInt);//100
            Console.ReadKey();
        }
    }
}
```

Output

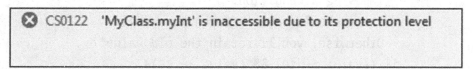

```
***Exploring Properties.Example-1***

Value of myInt is now:10
Now myInt value is:100
```

Analysis

If you use ob.myInt=10;, the compiler will raise a concern, as follows:

❌ CS0122   'MyClass.myInt' is inaccessible due to its protection level

But, you can see that with the MyInt property, we can have complete control of getting or setting the private field myInt.

- Note the naming convention: we just replaced the beginning letter of the private field's name with the corresponding capital letter (m of myInt is replaced with M, in this case) for better readability and understanding.

- Note the contextual keyword *value*. It is an implicit parameter associated with properties. We typically use it for the assignment.

- Sometimes a private field that stores the data exposed by a public property is called a *backing store* or a *backing field*. So, myInt is the private backing field in the preceding example.

- With properties, any of these modifiers can be used: public, private, internal, protected, new, virtual, abstract, override, sealed, static, unsafe, and extern.

Students ask:

Sir, how can we impose a constraint/restriction through properties?

Teacher says: Suppose, you want a constraint that the user can set a value (in the preceding program) if the intended value lies between 10 and 25. Otherwise, the system will retain the previous value. This type of constraint can be easily implemented through properties. In this case, to implement this constraint, we can modify the set block as follows:

```
set
    {
        //myInt = value;
        /*Imposing a condition:
          value should be in between 10 and 25.
          Otherwise, you'll retain the old value*/
        if ((value >= 10) && (value <= 25))
        {
            myInt = value;
        }
        else
        {
            Console.WriteLine("The new value {0} cannot be set",
            value);
            Console.WriteLine("Please choose a value between 10
            and 25");
        }
    }
```

Now if you run the program once again, you receive following output:

```
C:\Feluda_new16oct14\MyPrograms\CSharpProgs\CSharpBasicsProgs\InteractiveC

***Exploring Properties.Example-1***

Value of myInt is now: 10
 The new value 100 cannot be set
 Please choose a value between 10 and 25
Now myInt value is:10
```

Teacher continues: When we are dealing with a property where we have only get an accessor, it is known as a *read-only property.*

The following is a read-only property:

```
......
private int myInt;
public int MyInt
   {
      get
      {
         return myInt;
      }
//set accessor is absent here
   }
```

And the properties that have only set accessors are called *write-only properties.* The following is an example of a *write-only property*:

```
......
    private int myInt;
    public int MyInt
    {
        //get accessor is absent here
        set
        {
            myInt = value;
        }
    }
```

Generally, we have both accessors, and those properties are known as *read-write properties.* In Demonstration 1, we used a read-write property.

Since C# 3.0 onward, we can reduce our code size, which is associated with properties. Consider the following code:

```
//private int myInt;
public int MyInt
{
    //get
```

```
//{
//    return myInt;
//}
//set
//{
//    myInt = value;
//}
get;set;
}
```

We replaced the nine lines that were used in Demonstration 1 with a single line. This declaration is known as an *automatic property* declaration. The compiler will input the intended code for us in this case to make our lives easier.

Reduce the Code Size

Suppose that you have a read-only property like this:

```
class MyClass
    {
        private double radius = 10;
        public double Radius
        {
            get { return radius; }

        }
    }
```

You can reduce the code size by using *expression-bodied properties* (which was introduced in C# 6.0), like in the following:

```
class MyClass
    {
        private double radius = 10;
        //Expression bodied properties (C#6.0 onwards)
        public double Radius => radius;
    }
```

You can see that the *two braces* and the keywords *get* and *return* are replaced by this symbol '=>'.

If you open the IL code, you'll see that these property accessors internally transformed to get_MethodName() and set_MethodName(). You can check their return types; for example, here we get methods such as

```
public int get_MyInt() {...}
```

and

```
public void set_MyInt(){...}
```

Consider the following code and corresponding IL code.

Demonstration 2

```
using System;
namespace Test4_Property
{
    class MyClass
    {
        //private int myInt;
        public int MyInt
        {
            //automatic property declaration
            get;set;
        }
    }
    class Program
    {
        static void Main(string[] args)
        {
            Console.WriteLine("***Exploring Properties.Example-1***");
            MyClass ob = new MyClass();
            //ob.myInt = 1;//Error:myInt is inaccessible
            //Setting  a new value
```

```
        ob.MyInt = 106;//Ok.We'll get 106
        //Reading the value
        Console.WriteLine("\nValue of myInt is now:" + ob.MyInt);
        Console.ReadKey();
    }
}
}
```

IL Code

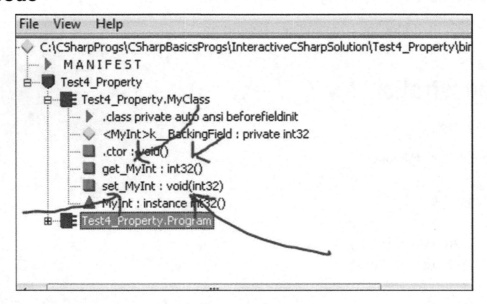

POINTS TO REMEMBER

From C# 6 onward, we can use property initializers like following:

```
public int MyInt2
    {
        //automatic property declaration
        get; set;
    } = 25;//Automatic initialization
```

This implies that MyInt2 was initialized with the value 25. We can also make it read-only by removing the set accessor.

In C# 7.0, we can further reduce our code, as follows:

```
class MyClass
{
    private int myInt; // also called as private "backing" field
    //public int MyInt //The public property
    //{
    //    get
    //    {
    //        return myInt;
    //    }
    //    set
    //    {
    //        myInt = value;
    //    }
    //}
    //C#7.0 onwards
    public int MyInt
    {
        get => myInt;
        set => myInt = value;
    }
}
```

You must check that the compiler version is set to version 7. If your compiler is set to C#6.0 or below, for that code block, you'll get these errors:

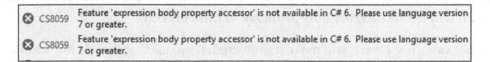

| ❌ CS8059 | Feature 'expression body property accessor' is not available in C# 6. Please use language version 7 or greater. |
| ❌ CS8059 | Feature 'expression body property accessor' is not available in C# 6. Please use language version 7 or greater. |

At the time of this writing, I do not need to make any changes because for me, C# 7.0 was set by default.

To check your language version, you can go to **Project Properties** then **Build** then **Advanced Build Settings** and then **Language version**. You can also refer to the following screenshot for your reference.

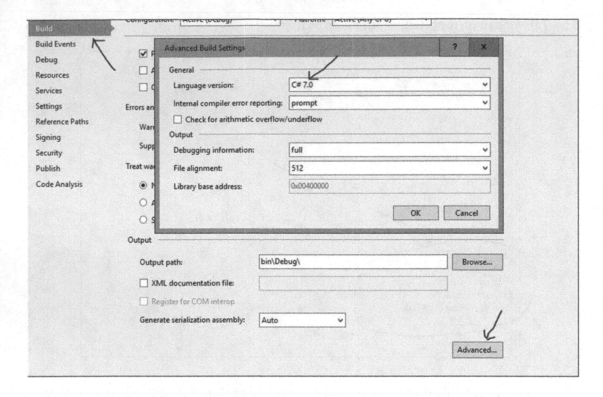

Students ask:

Sir, it appears that if we have a set accessor, we can make it private, and in that case, it will act like a read-only property. Is this correct?

Teacher says: Yes. Even if you make it protected, it means that you do not want to expose it to other types.

Students ask:

Sir, why should we prefer public properties rather than public fields?

Teacher says: With this approach, you can promote encapsulation, which is one of the key features of OOP.

Students ask:

Sir, when should we use read-only properties?

Teacher says: To create immutable types.

Virtual Property

Teacher continues: We said earlier that we can create different type of properties with different type of modifiers. Here we are picking two of them. Consider the following code.

Demonstration 3

```
using System;

namespace VirtualPropertyEx1
{
  class Shape
    {
        public virtual double Area
        {
            get
            {
                return 0;
            }
        }
    }
    class Circle : Shape
    {
        int radius;
        public Circle(int radius)
        {
            this.radius = radius;
        }
        public int Radius
        {
            get
            {
                return radius;
            }
        }
```

155

```csharp
        public override double Area
        {
            get
            {
                return 3.14 * radius * radius;
            }
        }
    }
    class Program
    {
        static void Main(string[] args)
        {
            Console.WriteLine("***Case study with a virtual Property***");
            Circle myCircle = new Circle(10);
            Console.WriteLine("\nRadius of the Cricle is {0} Unit",
            myCircle.Radius);
            Console.WriteLine("Area of the Circle is {0} sq.
            Unit",myCircle.Area);
            Console.ReadKey();
        }
    }
}
```

Output

C:\CSharpProgs\CSharpBasicsProgs\InteractiveCSharpSolution\VirtualPropertyEx1\bin\Debug\VirtualPropertyEx1

```
***Case study with a virtual Property***

Radius of the Cricle is 10 Unit
Area of the Circle is 314 sq. Unit
```

Abstract Property

If you replace the Shape class in VirtualPropertyEx1 with the following code:

```
abstract class Shape
    {
      public abstract double Area
        {
            get;
        }
    }
```

And run the program again, you'll get the same output. But this time you are using an abstract property.

POINTS TO REMEMBER

We have already used inheritance modifiers such as abstract, virtual, and override, with examples of properties. We can use other inheritance modifiers also, such as new and sealed.

Apart from these, properties can be associated with all access modifiers (public, private, protected, and internal); static modifiers (static); and unmanaged code modifiers (unsafe, extern).

Quiz

Can you predict the output?

```
using System;

namespace QuizOnPrivateSetProperty
{
    class MyClass
    {
        private double radius = 10;
        public double Radius => radius;
        public double Area => 3.14 * radius * radius;
    }
```

```
    class Program
    {
        static void Main(string[] args)
        {
            Console.WriteLine("***Quiz on Properties***");
            MyClass ob = new MyClass();
            Console.WriteLine("Area of the circle is {0} sq. unit",
            ob.Area);
            Console.ReadKey();
        }
    }
}
```

Output

```
C:\Feluda_new16oct14\MyPrograms\CSharpProgs\CSharpBasicsProgs\InteractiveCSharpSolution\Quizon...
***Quiz on Properties***
Area of the circle is 314 sq. unit
```

Analysis

You can see that here we have used expression-bodied properties (which is available C#
6.0 onward).

Quiz

Can you predict the output?

```
using System;
namespace QuizOnPrivateSet
{
    class MyClass
    {
        private double radius = 10;
        public double Radius
```

```
    {
        get
        {
            return radius;
        }
         private set
        {
            radius = value;
        }
    }
    public double Area => 3.14 * radius * radius;
}
class Program
{
    static void Main(string[] args)
    {
        Console.WriteLine("***Quiz on Properties***");
        MyClass ob = new MyClass();
        ob.Radius = 5;
        Console.WriteLine("Radius of the circle {0} unit", ob.Radius);
        Console.WriteLine("Area of the circle is {0} sq. unit",
        ob.Area);
        Console.ReadKey();
    }
}
}
```

Output

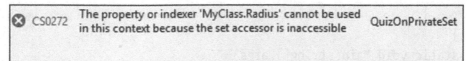

❌ CS0272   The property or indexer 'MyClass.Radius' cannot be used
in this context because the set accessor is inaccessible   QuizOnPrivateSet

Analysis

Note that the set accessor is preceded by the keyword *private*.

Indexers

Consider the following program and output.

Demonstration 4

```
using System;

namespace IndexerEx1
{
    class Program
    {
        class MySentence
        {
            string[] wordsArray;
            public MySentence( string mySentence)
            {
                wordsArray = mySentence.Split();
            }
            public string this[int index]
            {
                get
                {
                    return wordsArray[index];
                }
                set
                {
                    wordsArray[index] = value;
                }
            }
        }
        static void Main(string[] args)
        {
            Console.WriteLine("***Exploring Indexers.Example-1***\n");
            string mySentence = "This is a nice day.";
            MySentence sentenceObject = new MySentence(mySentence);
```

```
        for (int i = 0; i < mySentence.Split().Length; i++)
        {
            Console.WriteLine("\t sentenceObject[{0}]={1}",i,sentence
            Object[i]);
        }
        Console.ReadKey();
    }
  }
}
```

Output

```
 C:\CSharpProgs\CSharpBasicsProgs\InteractiveCSharpSolution\IndexerEx1\bin\Debug\IndexerEx1.exe

***Exploring Indexers.Example-1***

        sentenceObject[0]=This
        sentenceObject[1]=is
        sentenceObject[2]=a
        sentenceObject[3]=nice
        sentenceObject[4]=day.
```

Analysis

We are seeing some interesting characteristics of the program.

- The program is similar to properties, but the key difference is that the name of property is *this*.

- We used index arguments just like arrays. These are called *indexers*. We can treat the instances of a class or struct or an interface as arrays. The *this* keyword is used to refer the instances.

POINTS TO REMEMBER

- All the modifiers—private, public, protected, internal—can be used for indexers (just like properties).

- The return type may be any valid C# data type.

- We can create a type with multiple indexers, each with different types of parameters.

- As usual, we can create read-only indexers by eliminating the set accessor. But though it is syntactically correct, it is recommended that you use a method in those scenarios (e.g., it is always good to use a method to retrieve employee information corresponding to the employee ID). So, you should avoid this:

```
//NOT a recommended style
Class Employee{
   //using indexers to get employee details
           public string this[int empId]
           {
               get
               {
                   //return Employee details
               }
           }
}
```

Teacher continues: Let us examine another demonstration. In the following program, we have used a dictionary to hold some employee name with their salaries. Then we are trying to see the upper limit of their salaries. If an employee is not found in our dictionary, we will say that the record is not found.

To use a Dictionary class, we need to include the following line in our program because the class is defined there:

```
using System.Collections.Generic;
```

```
⊞Assembly mscorlib, Version=4.0.0.0, Culture=neutral, PublicKeyToken=b77a5c561934e089

⊞using ...

⊟namespace System.Collections.Generic
  {
⊞      ...public class Dictionary<TKey, TValue> : IDictionary<TKey, TValue>, ICollection<KeyValuePair<TKey
       {
⊞          ...public Dictionary();
⊞          ...public Dictionary(int capacity);
⊞          ...public Dictionary(IEqualityComparer<TKey> comparer);
⊞          ...public Dictionary(IDictionary<TKey, TValue> dictionary);
⊞          ...public Dictionary(int capacity, IEqualityComparer<TKey> comparer);
⊞          ...public Dictionary(IDictionary<TKey, TValue> dictionary, IEqualityComparer<TKey> comparer);
⊞          ...protected Dictionary(SerializationInfo info, StreamingContext context);

⊞          ...public TValue this[TKey key] { get; set; }

⊞          ...public ValueCollection Values { get; }
⊞          ...public KeyCollection Keys { get; }
⊞          ...public int Count { get; }
⊞          ...public IEqualityComparer<TKey> Comparer { get; }

⊞          ...public void Add(TKey key, TValue value);
```

A dictionary is a collection and a <key, value> pair. It uses a hash-table data structure to store a key with its corresponding values. The mechanism is very fast and efficient. It is recommended that you learn more about dictionaries. You should first understand that

```
employeeWithSalary = new Dictionary<string, double>();
employeeWithSalary.Add("Amit",20125.87);
```

In the preceding two lines of code, we created a dictionary and then used its Add method. In this dictionary, whenever we want to add data, the first parameter should be a string and the second one should be a double. So, we can add an Employee Amit (a string variable) with the salary (a double variable) as a dictionary element. We follow the same procedure for the remaining elements in the dictionary.Go through the program and then analyse the output.

Demonstration 5

```
using System;
using System.Collections.Generic;

namespace IndexerQuiz1
{
    class EmployeeRecord
    {
```

```
Dictionary<string, double> employeeWithSalary;
public EmployeeRecord()
{
    employeeWithSalary = new Dictionary<string, double>();
    employeeWithSalary.Add("Amit",20125.87);
    employeeWithSalary.Add("Sam",56785.21);
    employeeWithSalary.Add("Rohit",33785.21);
}
public bool this[string index, int predictedSalary]
{
    get
    {
        double salary = 0.0;
        bool foundEmployee = false;
        bool prediction = false;
        foreach (string s in employeeWithSalary.Keys)
        {
            if (s.Equals(index))
            {
                foundEmployee = true;//Employee found
                salary = employeeWithSalary[s];//Employees
                //actual salary
                if( salary>predictedSalary)
                {
                    //Some code
                    prediction = true;
                }
                else
                {
                    //Some code
                }
             break;
            }
        }
```

```csharp
            if(foundEmployee == false)
            {
                Console.WriteLine("Employee {0} Not found in our
                database.", index);
            }
            return prediction;
        }
    }
}

class Program
{
    static void Main(string[] args)
    {
        Console.WriteLine("***Quiz on Indexers***\n");
        EmployeeRecord employeeSalary = new EmployeeRecord();
        Console.WriteLine("Is Rohit's salary is more than 25000$ ?- {0}",
        employeeSalary["Rohit",25000]);//True
        Console.WriteLine("Is Amit's salary is more than 25000$ ?- {0}",
        employeeSalary["Amit",25000]);//False
        Console.WriteLine("Is Jason's salary is more than 10000$ ?-{0}",
        employeeSalary["Jason",10000]);//False
        Console.ReadKey();
    }
}
}
```

Output

```
C:\CSharpProgs\CSharpBasicsProgs\InteractiveCSharpSolution\IndexerQuiz1\bin\Debug\IndexerQuiz1.exe

***Quiz on Indexers***

Is Rohit's salary is more than 25000$ ?- True
Is Amit's salary is more than 25000$ ?- False
Employee Jason Not found in our database.
Is Jason's salary is more than 10000$ ?-False
```

Analysis

I have introduced this program to show that we can use indexers with different types of parameters.

Students ask:
Sir, can we have multiple indexers in the same class?

Teacher says: Yes. But in that case, the method signatures must be different from each other.

Students ask:
Sir, then indexers can be overloaded?

Teacher says: Yes.

Students ask:
Sir, so far, indexers look like arrays. What are the differences between an array and an indexer?

Teacher says: Yes. Even sometimes developers describe indexers as virtual arrays. But here are some key differences:

- Indexers can take non-numeric subscripts. We have already tested this.

- Indexers can be overloaded but arrays cannot.

- An indexer value is not classified as a variable. So, they cannot be used as ref or out parameters, whereas arrays can be.

Interface Indexer

Students ask:
Sir, how can we use indexers with interfaces?

Teacher says: Next is an example where we are implementing an interface implicitly with indexers. Before we proceed, we need to remember the key distinction between an interface indexer and a class indexer.

- An interface indexer does not have a body. (Notice that the presence of get and set with only a semicolon in the following demonstration.)

- An interface indexer does not have modifiers.

Demonstration 6

```
using System;

namespace IndexerEx2
{
    interface IMyInterface
    {
        int this[int index] { get; set; }
    }
    class MyClass : IMyInterface
    {
        //private int[] myIntegerArray;
        private int[] myIntegerArray = new int[4];
        public int this[int index]
        {
            get
            {
                return myIntegerArray[index];
            }
            set
            {
                myIntegerArray[index] = value;
            }
        }
    }
    class Program
    {
        static void Main(string[] args)
        {
```

```
        Console.WriteLine("***Exploring Indexers with
        interfaces***\n");
        MyClass obMyClass = new MyClass();
        //Initializing 0th, 1st and 3rd element using indexers
        obMyClass[0] = 10;
        obMyClass[1] = 20;
        obMyClass[3] = 30;
        for (int i = 0; i <4; i++)
        {
            // Console.WriteLine("\t obMyClass[{0}]={1}", i,
            obMyClass[i]);
            System.Console.WriteLine("Element #{0} = {1}", i,
            obMyClass[i]);
        }
        Console.ReadKey();
    }
  }
}
```

Output

```
C:\Feluda_new16oct14\MyPrograms\CSharpProgs\CSharpBasicsProgs\InteractiveCSharpSolution\Indexer...
***Exploring Indexers with interfaces***

Element #0 = 10
Element #1 = 20
Element #2 = 0
Element #3 = 30
```

Quiz

Will the code compile?

```
using System;

namespace IndexerQuiz2
{
```

```
interface IMyInterface
    {
        int this[int index] { get; set; }
    }
class MyClass : IMyInterface
{
    private int[] myIntegerArray = new int[4];
    //Explicit interface implementation
    int IMyInterface.this[int index]
    {
        get => myIntegerArray[index];
        set => myIntegerArray[index] = value;
    }
}
class Program
    {
        static void Main(string[] args)
        {
        Console.WriteLine("***Quiz on Indexers with explicit interface
        technique***\n");
        MyClass obMyClass = new MyClass();
        IMyInterface interOb = (IMyInterface)obMyClass;
        //Initializing 0th, 1st and 3rd element using indexers
        interOb[0] = 20;
        interOb[1] = 21;
        interOb[3] = 23;
        for (int i = 0; i < 4; i++)
        {
            Console.WriteLine("\t obMyClass[{0}]={1}", i,interOb[i]);
        }
        Console.ReadKey();
        }
    }
}
```

Answer

Yes. Here is the output:

```
C:\Feluda_new16oct14\MyPrograms\CSharpProgs\CSharpBasicsProgs\InteractiveCSharpSolution\Indexer...
***Quiz on Indexers with explicit interface technique***

        obMyClass[0]=20
        obMyClass[1]=21
        obMyClass[2]=0
        obMyClass[3]=23
```

Analysis

Here is an example where we are implementing an interface explicitly with indexers. In this example, we used latest C# 7.0 features (Notice the get, set bodies).

We are accessing the elements.

```
MyClass obMyClass = new MyClass();
IMyInterface interOb = (IMyInterface)obMyClass;          ⟵
//Initializing 0th, 1st and 3rd element using indexers
interOb[0] = 20;
interOb[I] = 21;
interOb[3] = 23;
```

An explicit implementation of an indexer is nonpublic (also nonvirtual; i.e., cannot be overridden). So, instead of an interface object, if we tried using the MyClass object, obMyClass, like in the previous demonstration, we will get compilation errors.

POINTS TO REMEMBER

- An interface indexer does not have a body.

- An interface indexer does not have modifiers.

- Since C# 7.0, we can write codes like this:

```
public int MyInt
 {
    get => myInt;
    set => myInt = value;
 }
```

- An explicit implementation of an indexer is non-public and non-virtual.

Summary

This chapter covered

- ✓ Different types of properties

- ✓ Automatic properties

- ✓ Expression-bodied properties with the latest C# 7.0features

- ✓ Virtual and abstract properties

- ✓ Why we should prefer public properties over public fields

- ✓ How properties are different from arrays

- ✓ How to impose a constraint/restriction through properties

- ✓ When to use read-only properties and when to avoid them

- ✓ Indexers.

- ✓ How indexers differ from properties

- ✓ How to use indexers with explicit and implicit interfaces and the restrictions to keep in mind

- ✓ How interface indexers are different from class indexers

Understanding Class Variables

Teacher starts the discussion: Sometimes we do not want to operate through instances of a type. Instead, we prefer to work on the type itself. The concept of class variables or class methods comes to mind in these scenarios. They are commonly known as *static variables* or *static methods*. In C#, the class itself can be static. In general, when we tag the keyword *static* to a class, it is a static class; when it is tagged with a method, it is called a static method; and when we associate it with a variable, it is known as a static variable.

Class Variables

Let's begin with a simple example.

Demonstration 1

```
using System;

namespace StaticClassEx1
{
    static class Rectangle
    {
        public static double Area(double len, double bre)
        {
            return len * bre;
        }
    }
```

© Vaskaran Sarcar 2018
V. Sarcar, *Interactive C#*, https://doi.org/10.1007/978-1-4842-3339-9_7

```
class Program
{
    static void Main(string[] args)
    {
        Console.WriteLine("***Exploring class variables.Example--
        1***\n");
        double length = 25;
        double breadth = 10;
        Console.WriteLine("Area of Rectangle={0} sq. unit", Rectangle.
        Area(length, breadth));
        Console.ReadKey();
    }
}
}
```

Output

C:\CSharpProgs\CSharpBasicsProgs\InteractiveCSharpSolution\StaticClassEx1\bin\Debug\StaticClassEx1.e.

```
***Exploring class variables.Example-1***

Area of Rectangle=250 sq. unit
```

Analysis

You can see that we have invoked the Area (..) method of the Rectangle class through the class name. We did not make any instance of the Rectangle class here.

Students ask:

Can we also create an instance of the Rectangle class and then invoke the Area (..) method?

Teacher says: No. It is not allowed here. If it is allowed, then is there any need to introduce the concept of static class? So, if you are coding in Visual Studio and you try to introduce a line like this:

```
Rectangle rect = new Rectangle();//Error
```

You will get following compilation error.

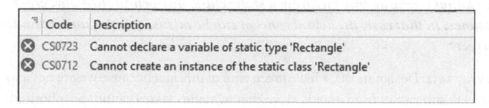

	Code	Description
❌	CS0723	Cannot declare a variable of static type 'Rectangle'
❌	CS0712	Cannot create an instance of the static class 'Rectangle'

Students ask:

But if we have a non-static method inside the Rectangle class, how can we access that method? This time, we need an instance to access the method.

Teacher says: This is why static classes have restrictions: they can contain only static members. So, if you try to put a non-static method, let's say ShowMe(), in our Rectangle class like this:

```
static class Rectangle
{
    public static double Area(double len, double bre)
    {
        return len * bre;
    }
    //Error:Cannot declare instance members in a static class
    public void ShowMe()
    {
        Console.WriteLine("Rectangle.ShowMe()");
    }
}
```

You will get following compilation error.

❌	CS0708	'ShowMe': cannot declare instance members in a static class

Students ask:

We cannot create an instance from a static class. But a child class may create an instance. In that case, the actual concept can be misused. Is this understanding correct?

Teacher says: Designers of C# have taken care of this fact because we are not allowed to create subclasses from a static class; that is, static classes cannot be inherited. So, in our previous example, if you try to create a non-static derived class (e.g., ChildRectangle) in the following manner:

```
static class Rectangle
{
    public static double Area(double len, double bre)
    {
        return len * bre;
    }
}
//Error:cannot derive from static class 'Rectangle'
class ChildRectangle:Rectangle
{ }
```

You will get a compilation error.

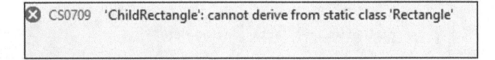

CS0709   'ChildRectangle': cannot derive from static class 'Rectangle'

Students ask:

Then static classes are sealed. Is this correct?

Teacher says: Yes. If you open the IL code, you will see this:

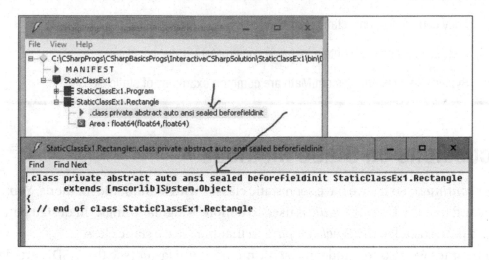

Teacher continues: You may also have noticed that we used the Console class in nearly every place. This class is also a static class. If you right-click on Console and then press "Go to Definition" (or press F12), you will see this:

```
┌─────────────────────────────────────────────────────────┐
│                   POINTS TO REMEMBER                     │
└─────────────────────────────────────────────────────────┘
```

- Static classes are sealed (i.e., they cannot be inherited or instantiated).

- They can contain only static members.

- A static class cannot contain instance constructors.

- System.Console and System.Math are common examples of static classes.

Discussions on Static Methods

Teacher continues: So far, we have seen static classes with some static methods. You understand that the keyword *static* is used to denote "singular things." In design patterns, there is a pattern called the *Singleton pattern* that may use a static class.

Sometimes we also conclude that static methods are faster (see the MSDN article at `https://msdn.microsoft.com/en-us/library/ms973852.aspx` for more information). But, the key thing is that they cannot be part of any instance. This is why our `Main()` method is static.

And if you notice the `Main()` method, you can see that it is contained in a non-static class (Program). So, it is apparent that a non-static class can contain static methods. To explore this in detail, let's go through the following program, where we have a non-static class that contains a static and a non-static method.

Demonstration 2

```csharp
using System;

namespace StaticMethodsEx1
{
    class NonStaticClass
    {
        //a static method
        public static void StaticMethod()
        {
            Console.WriteLine("NonStaticClass.StaticMethod");
```

```
    }
    //a non-static method
    public void NonStaticMethod()
    {
        Console.WriteLine("NonStaticClass.NonStaticMethod");
    }
}

class Program
{
    static void Main(string[] args)
    {
        Console.WriteLine("***Exploring static methods.Example--
        1***\n");
        NonStaticClass anObject = new NonStaticClass();
        anObject.NonStaticMethod();//Ok
        //anObject.StaticMethod();//Error
        NonStaticClass.StaticMethod();
        Console.ReadKey();
    }
}
}
```

Output

```
C:\CSharpProgs\CSharpBasicsProgs\InteractiveCSharpSolution\StaticMethodsEx1\bin\Debug\StaticMeth...

***Exploring static methods.Example-1***

NonStaticClass.NonStaticMethod
NonStaticClass.StaticMethod
```

If you uncomment the following line:

```
//anObject.StaticMethod();
```

You will receive the following error:

> ❌ CS0176   Member 'NonStaticClass.StaticMethod()' cannot be accessed with an instance reference; qualify it with a type name instead

Now consider the modified program. I have introduced one static variable and an instance variable here to analyze them with the static and instance methods.

Demonstration 3

```csharp
using System;

namespace StaticMethodsEx2
{
    class NonStaticClass
    {
        static int myStaticVariable = 25;//static variable
        int myInstanceVariable = 50;//instance variable
        //a static method
        public static void StaticMethod()
        {
            Console.WriteLine("NonStaticClass.StaticMethod");
            Console.WriteLine("myStaticVariable = {0}",
            myStaticVariable);//25
            //Console.WriteLine("StaticMethod->instance variable = {0}",
            myInstanceVariable);//error
        }
        //a non-static method
        public void NonStaticMethod()
        {
            Console.WriteLine("NonStaticClass.NonStaticMethod");
            Console.WriteLine("NonStaticMethod->static variable = {0}",
            myStaticVariable);//25 Ok
```

```csharp
            //Console.WriteLine("myStaticVariable = {0}", this.
            myStaticVariable);//Error
            Console.WriteLine("myInstanceVariable = {0}",
            myInstanceVariable);//50
        }
    }

    class Program
    {
        static void Main(string[] args)
        {
            Console.WriteLine("***Exploring static methods.Example--
            2***\n");
            NonStaticClass anObject = new NonStaticClass();
            anObject.NonStaticMethod();//Ok
            //anObject.StaticMethod();//Error
            NonStaticClass.StaticMethod();
            Console.ReadKey();
        }
    }
}
```

Output

```
C:\CSharpProgs\CSharpBasicsProgs\InteractiveCSharpSolution\StaticMethodEx2\bin\Debug\StaticMetho...

***Exploring static methods.Example-2***

NonStaticClass.NonStaticMethod
NonStaticMethod->static variable = 25
myInstanceVariable = 50
NonStaticClass.StaticMethod
myStaticVariable = 25
```

181

Analysis

Note the commented lines. Each of them can cause compilation error. For example, if you uncomment this line:

```
//Console.WriteLine("myStaticVariable = {0}", this.myStaticVariable);//Error
```

It causes the following error:

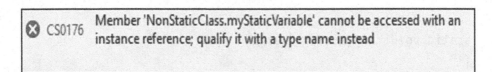

Because *this* is also an instance reference here.

Teacher continues: Later you will learn that in C#, we have extension methods. (We can extend an existing type with new methods without affecting the definition of the type.) These are basically static methods but invoked with instance method syntax, so that you can treat static methods as instance methods. They are most commonly used in the context of LINQ's query operators. However, a detailed discussion on these topics is beyond the scope of this book.

Discussions on Static Constructors

We can use a static constructor to initialize any static data or to perform such an action that needs to run only once. We cannot call a static constructor directly (i.e., we do not have any direct control when the static constructor will be executed). But we know that it will be called automatically in either of these scenarios:

- Before the creation of an instance of a type.

- When we reference a static member in our program.

Consider the following program and output.

Demonstration 4

```
using System;

namespace StaticConstructorEx1
{
    class A
    {
        static int StaticCount=0,InstanceCount=0;
        static A()
        {
            StaticCount++;
            Console.WriteLine("Static constructor.Count={0}",StaticCount);
        }
        public A()
        {
            InstanceCount++;
            Console.WriteLine("Instance constructor.Count={0}",
            InstanceCount);
        }
    }
    class Program
    {
        static void Main(string[] args)
        {
            Console.WriteLine("***Exploring static constructors***\n");
            A obA = new A();//StaticCount=1,InstanceCount=1
            A obB = new A();//StaticCount=1,InstanceCount=2
            A obC = new A();//StaticCount=1,InstanceCount=3
            Console.ReadKey();
        }
    }
}
```

Output

```
***Exploring static constructors***

Static constructor.Count=1
Instance constructor.Count=1
Instance constructor.Count=2
Instance constructor.Count=3
```

Analysis

From the program and output, we see that static constructors executes only once (not per instance)

If you introduce this code:

```
static A(int A){ }
```

You will get a compile-time error.

> ⊗ CS0132 'A.A(int)': a static constructor must be parameterless

If you introduce this code:

```
public static A(){...}
```

You will get the following compile-time error:

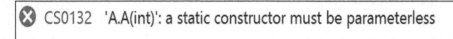

Code	Description
⊗ CS0515	'A.A()': access modifiers are not allowed on static constructors

---

POINTS TO REMEMBER

- Static constructors execute only once per type. We do not have any direct control over when the static constructor will be executed. But we know that an automatic call to a static constructor happens when we try to instantiate a type or when we try to access a static member in the type.

- A type can have only one static constructor. It must be parameterless and it does not accept any access modifier.

- Static field initializers run prior to a static constructor in the declaration order.

- In the absence of a static constructor, field initializers execute just before the type is used or anytime earlier, at the whim of the runtime.

Students ask:

When should we use static constructors?

Teacher says: It can be useful to write log entries. They are also used to create wrapper classes for unmanaged code.

Summary

This chapter covered

- ✓ Static class concepts
- ✓ Static method and static variable concepts
- ✓ Static constructor concepts
- ✓ How these concepts can be implemented in C# and the restrictions associated with them
- ✓ When and how to use these concepts

CHAPTER 8

Analysis of Some Key Comparisons in C#

Teacher says: In this chapter, we discuss some common comparisons in C#. Let's start.

Implicit Casting vs. Explicit Casting

With casting, we can convert one data type to another. Sometimes we call this process *type conversion*. Basically, there are two types of casting: implicit and explicit. As the name suggests, implicit casting is automatic and we do not need to worry about it. But, we need cast operators for explicit casting. In addition to these, there are two other types of conversions: conversion with helper classes and user-defined conversion. In this chapter, we will focus on implicit and explicit conversions. Let's go through them now.

In implicit casting, the conversion path follows small to large integral types, or derived types to base types.

The following segment of code will compile and run perfectly:

```
int a = 120;
//Implicit casting
double b = a;//ok- no error
```

With explicit casting, consider the reverse case. If you write something like this:

```
int c = b;//Error
```

The compiler will complain.

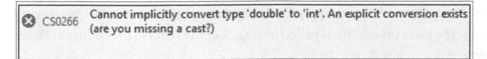

CS0266   Cannot implicitly convert type 'double' to 'int'. An explicit conversion exists (are you missing a cast?)

© Vaskaran Sarcar 2018
V. Sarcar, *Interactive C#*, https://doi.org/10.1007/978-1-4842-3339-9_8

So, you need to write something like this:

```
//Explicit casting
int c = (int)b;//Ok
```

POINTS TO REMEMBER

Casting can be applicable if one type is convertible to another type; that is, you cannot assign a string to an integer. You will always encounter errors with those kinds of attempts; for example, you will always get an error, even if you try to apply cast to it.

```
int d = ( int)"hello";//error
```

 CS0030   Cannot convert type 'string' to 'int'

There are some basic differences between implicit and explicit casting.Implicit casting is type safe (there is no loss of data because we are traveling from a small container to a large container and we have sufficient spaces). Explicit conversion is not type safe (because in this case the data is moving from a large container to a small container).

Students ask:
Sir, how to handle casting exceptions when we deal with reference types?

Teacher says: We will use either "is" or "as" operators in those scenarios. We will discuss them later.

Boxing vs. UnBoxing

Teacher continues: Now let's discuss another important topic: boxing and unboxing. Here we need to deal with value types and reference types.

Object (System.Object) is the ultimate base class for all types. Since Object is a class, it is a reference type. When we apply casting to convert a value type to object type (i.e., reference type), the procedure is called *boxing,* and the reverse procedure is known as *unboxing.*

With boxing, a value type allocates an object instance on the heap and then boxes (stores) the copied value into that object.

Here is an example of boxing:

```
int i = 10;
object o = i;//Boxing
```

Now consider the reverse scenario. If you try to write code like this:

```
object o = i;//Boxing
int j = o;//Error
```

You will face a compilation error.

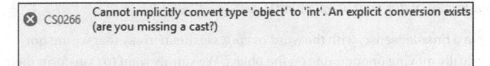

To avoid this, we need to use unboxing, like this:

```
object o = i;
int j = (int)o; //Unboxing
```

Students asks:
Which conversion is implicit: boxing or unboxing?

Teacher says: Boxing. Note that we do not need to write code like this:

```
int i = 10;
object o = (object)i;
//object o=i; is fine since Boxing is implicit.
```

Students asks:

It seems like boxing, unboxing, and typecasting operations are similar. Is this true?

Teacher says: Sometimes it may appear confusing but if you focus on the primary rule, you can easily avoid the confusion. With these operations (upcasting/downcasting, boxing/unboxing), we are trying to covert one thing into another. This is basically their similarity. Now focus on the specialties of boxing and unboxing. Boxing and unboxing are transformations between value types and object types (i.e., reference types). With boxing, a copy of value type from the stack is moved to a heap and unboxing does the reverse operation. So, you can basically say, with boxing, we are casting a value type to a reference type (and obviously, unboxing is the counterpart of this kind of operation).

But in a broader sense, with the word *casting*, we mean to say that we are not physically moving or operating on the object. We simply want to transform their apparent types only.

Students asks:

Sir, what is the common part of unboxing and downcasting (explicit casting)?

Both can be unsafe and they can throw InvalidCastException. Basically, explicit casting is always dangerous. Consider a case when an operation is unsafe. Suppose you want to transform a long into an int and you have written code like that in the following demonstration.

Demonstration 1

```
#region invalid casting
    long myLong = 4000000000;
    int myInt = int.MaxValue;
    Console.WriteLine(" Maximum value of int is {0}", myInt);
    //Invalid cast:Greater than maximum value of an integer
    myInt = (int) myLong;
     Console.WriteLine(" Myint now={0}", myInt);
  #endregion
```

Output

```
C:\CSharpProgs\CSharpBasicsProgs\InteractiveCSharpSolution\CastingEx1\bin\Debug\CastingEx1.exe

***Experiment with casting***

Maximum value of int is 2147483647
Myint now=-294967296
```

Analysis

You can see that you have not received any compilation error but the ultimate value of the integer myInt is undesirable. So, this conversion is unsafe.

Students asks:

"Boxing and unboxing can hit the performance of a program." Is this true?

Teacher says: Yes. They can significantly hit the performance of a program. Here we have introduced two programs to analyze. Demonstration 2 analyzes the performance of casting and Demonstration 3 analyzes the performance of boxing. Notice the time taken by casting or boxing operations always hits the performance of a program, and they become significant if we keep increasing the number of interations inside the for loop construct.

Demonstration 2

```csharp
using System;
using System.Diagnostics;

namespace CastingPerformanceComparison
{
    class Program
    {
        static void Main(string[] args)
        {
            Console.WriteLine("***Analysis of casting performance***\n");
            #region without casting operations
            Stopwatch myStopwatch1 = new Stopwatch();
```

```
        myStopwatch1.Start();
        for (int i = 0; i < 100000; i++)
        {
            int j = 25;
            int myInt = j;
        }
        myStopwatch1.Stop();
        Console.WriteLine("Time taken without casting : {0}",
        myStopwatch1.Elapsed);
        #endregion
        #region with casting operations
        Stopwatch myStopwatch2 = new Stopwatch();
        myStopwatch2.Start();
        for ( int i=0;i<100000;i++)
        {
            double myDouble = 25.5;
            int myInt = (int)myDouble;
        }
        myStopwatch2.Stop();
        Console.WriteLine("Time taken with casting: {0}", myStopwatch2.
        Elapsed);
        #endregion
        Console.ReadKey();
    }
  }
}
```

Output

```
***Analysis of casting performance***

Time taken without casting : 00:00:00.0002691
Time taken with casting: 00:00:00.0003089
```

Analysis

See the time difference? In casting operations, the time taken is much longer. The difference varies when we vary the number of iterations. (In your machine, you can see the similar difference but the values may differ slightly in each individual run.)

Demonstration 3

Note   We have used a simple concept of generic programming here. So, once you understand the concepts of generics, you can come back to this program.

```
using System;
using System.Collections.Generic;
using System.Diagnostics;//For Stopwatch

namespace PerformanceOfBoxing
{
    class Program
    {
        static void Main(string[] args)
        {
            Console.WriteLine("***Performance analysis in Boxing ***");
            List<int> myInts = new List<int>();
            Stopwatch myStopwatch1 = new Stopwatch();
            myStopwatch1.Start();
            for (int i = 0; i < 1000000; i++)
            {
            //Adding an integer to a list of Integers. So, there is no need
            of boxing.(Advantage of Generics)
                myInts.Add(i);
            }
            myStopwatch1.Stop();
            Console.WriteLine("Time taken without Boxing: {0}",
            myStopwatch1.Elapsed);
```

```
//Now we are testing :Boxing Performance

List<object> myObjects = new List<object>();
Stopwatch myStopwatch2 = new Stopwatch();
myStopwatch2.Start();
for (int i = 0; i < 1000000; i++)
{
    //Adding an integer to a list of Objects. So, there is need
    of boxing.
    myObjects.Add(i);
}
myStopwatch2.Stop();
Console.WriteLine("Time taken with    Boxing :{0}",
myStopwatch2.Elapsed);
Console.ReadKey();
        }
    }
}
```

Analysis

Again, notice the time difference. In boxing, the time taken is much longer. The difference also varies when we vary the number of iterations(loop).

Output

```
***Performance analysis in Boxing ***
Time taken without Boxing: 00:00:00.0098125
Time taken with    Boxing :00:00:00.0913263
```

Upcasting vs. Downcasting

With type casting, we try to change the apparent type of an object. In an inheritance chain, we can travel either from the bottom to the top or in the reverse direction.

With upcasting, we are creating a base class reference from a child class reference; with downcasting, we do the reverse.

We have already seen that all footballers (a special type of player) are players but the reverse is not necessarily true because there are tennis players, basketball players, hockey players, and so forth. And we have also seen that a parent class reference can point to a child class object; that is, we can write something like

```
Player myPlayer=new Footballer();
```

(As usual, we are assuming that Player class is the base class and the Footballer class is derived from that). This is in the direction of upcasting. In upcasting, we can have following comments:

- It is simple and implicit.

- When we create a base reference from a child class reference, that base class reference can have a more restrictive view on the child object.

To understand these points clearly, let's go through the following example.

Demonstration 4

```
using System;

namespace UpVsDownCastingEx1
{
    class Shape
    {
        public void ShowMe()
        {
            Console.WriteLine("Shape.ShowMe");
        }
    }
```

```csharp
    class Circle:Shape
    {
        public void Area()
        {
            Console.WriteLine("Circle.Area");
        }
    }
    class Rectangle:Shape
    {
        public void Area()
        {
            Console.WriteLine("Rectangle.Area");
        }
    }
    class Program
    {
        static void Main(string[] args)
        {
            Console.WriteLine("***Upcasting Example***\n");
            Circle circleOb = new Circle();
            //Shape shapeOb = new Circle();//upcasting
            Shape shapeOb = circleOb;//Upcasting
            shapeOb.ShowMe();
            //shapeOb.Area();//Error
            circleOb.Area();//ok
            Console.ReadKey();
        }
    }
}
```

Output

```
C:\CSharpProgs\CSharpBasicsProgs\InteractiveCSharpSolution\UpVsDownCasting\bin\Debug\UpVsDow...
***Upcasting Example***

Shape.ShowMe
Circle.Area
```

Analysis

Notice that we have implemented upcasting using these lines of code:

```
Shape shapeOb = circleOb;//Upcasting
shapeOb.ShowMe();
```

And you can see that although both shapeOb and circleOb point to the same object, shapeOb doesn't have access to the Area() method of circle (i.e., it has a restrictive view of that object). But circleOb can easily access its own method.

Students ask:
Sir, why does the parent reference have the restrictive view in this design?

Teacher says: When the Parent class was created, it had no idea about its child classes and the new methods it was going to add. So, it makes sense that a parent class reference should not access the specialized child class methods.

Teacher continues: If you write something like the following, you are downcasting.

```
Circle circleOb2 = (Circle)shapeOb;//Downcast
```

Because now you are creating a subclass reference from a base class reference.

But downcasting is explicit and unsafe, and we can encounter InvalidCastException with this kind of conversion.

Quiz

Let's modify the Main() method as follows. (We are keeping the remaining parts the same; that is, all three classes—Shape, Circle, and Rectangle—are as in the preceding program). Now predict the output.

```
static void Main(string[] args)
{
        Console.WriteLine("***Downcasting is unsafe demo***\n");
        Circle circleOb = new Circle();
        Rectangle rectOb = new Rectangle();
        Shape[] shapes = { circleOb, rectOb };
        Circle circleOb2 = (Circle)shapes[1];//Incorrect
        //Circle circleOb2 = (Circle)shapes[0];//Correct
        circleOb2.Area();
        Console.ReadKey();
}
```

Output

A runtime exception will be thrown.

```
39          Circle circleOb2 = (Circle)shapes[1];//Incorrect  ⊗
40          //Circle circleOb2 = (C
41          circleOb2.Area();              Exception Unhandled                    ⊣ ✕
42          Console.ReadKey();
43      }                                  System.InvalidCastException: 'Unable to cast object of type
44    }                                    'DowncastingIsUnsafeDemo.Rectangle' to type
45  }                                      'DowncastingIsUnsafeDemo.Circle'.'
46

                                           View Details | Copy Details
                                           ▷ Exception Settings
```

Analysis

This is an example where we can encounter InvalidCastException() at runtime. Shape[1] was a Rectangle object , not a Circle object. So, if you use downcasting, you need to be careful.

198

is vs. as

In some cases, we frequently need to dynamically check the type of an object, and these two keywords play an important role there.

The keyword *is* compares with a given type and returns true if casting is possible, otherwise, it will return false. On the other hand, *as* can cast the given object to the specified type if it is cast able; otherwise, it will return null.

So, we can say that with the *as* keyword, we can do both the cast-ability check and the conversion/transformation.

Demonstration 5: The Use of the "is" Keyword

Here we have modified the program slightly and instead of two different shapes, we have used three different shapes: triangle, rectangle, and circle. We are storing the different shapes in an array, and then counting the total in each category.

```
using System;

namespace IsOperatorDemo
{
    class Shape
    {
        public void ShowMe()
        {
            Console.WriteLine("Shape.ShowMe");
        }
    }
    class Circle : Shape
    {
        public void Area()
        {
            Console.WriteLine("Circle.Area");
        }
    }
    class Rectangle : Shape
    {
```

```
        public void Area()
        {
            Console.WriteLine("Rectangle.Area");
        }
    }
    class Triangle : Shape
    {
        public void Area()
        {
            Console.WriteLine("Triangle.Area");
        }
    }

    class Program
    {
        static void Main(string[] args)
        {
            Console.WriteLine("***is operator demo***\n");
            //Initialization-all counts are 0 at this point
            int noOfCircle = 0, noOfRect = 0, noOfTriangle = 0;

            //Creating 2 different circle object
            Circle circleOb1 = new Circle();
            Circle circleOb2 = new Circle();
            //Creating 3 different rectangle object
            Rectangle rectOb1 = new Rectangle();
            Rectangle rectOb2 = new Rectangle();
            Rectangle rectOb3 = new Rectangle();
            //Creating 1 Triangle object
            Triangle triOb1 = new Triangle();
            Shape[] shapes = { circleOb1, rectOb1,circleOb2,
            rectOb2,triOb1,rectOb3 };
            for(int i=0;i<shapes.Length;i++)
            {
                if( shapes[i] is Circle)
                {
                    noOfCircle++;
```

```
        }
        else if (shapes[i] is Rectangle)
        {
            noOfRect++;
        }
        else
        {
            noOfTriangle++;
        }
    }
    Console.WriteLine("No of Circles in shapes array is {0}",
    noOfCircle);
    Console.WriteLine("No of Rectangles in shapes array is {0}",
    noOfRect);
    Console.WriteLine("No of Triangle in shapes array is {0}",
    noOfTriangle);

    Console.ReadKey();
    }
  }
}
```

Output

```
C:\CSharpProgs\CSharpBasicsProgs\InteractiveCSharpSolution\IsOperatorDemo\bin\Debug\IsOperatorD...
***is operator demo***

No of Circles in shapes array is 2
No of Rectangles in shapes array is 3
No of Triangle in shapes array is 1
```

Analysis

Look at these code segments:

```
if( shapes[i] is Circle)
{
    noOfCircle++;
}
else if (shapes[i] is Rectangle)
{
    //r.Area();//error
    noOfRect++;
}
else
{
    noOfTriangle++;
}
```

We are not blindly processing objects in the shapes array. Once we go through each of them, we can manipulate whether they are a Circle, a Rectangle, or a Triangle object. If it is not our intended type, the "if condition" will be false and we can avoid runtime surprises.

So, you can always test the simple fact that *all circles are shapes, but the reverse is not true* with the following lines of code:

```
Console.WriteLine("*****");
Shape s = new Shape();
Circle c = new Circle();

Console.WriteLine("Any Circle is a Shape?{0}", c is Shape);//True
Console.WriteLine("Any Shape is a Circle? {0}", (s is Circle));//False
```

Output

```
*****
Any Circle is a Shape?True
Any Shape is a Circle? False
```

Demonstration 6: The Use of the "as" Keyword

Now go through a similar program. But this time, we have used the *as* keyword instead of the *is* keyword.

```csharp
using System;
namespace asOperatorDemo
{
    class Program
    {
        class Shape
        {
            public void ShowMe()
            {
                Console.WriteLine("Shape.ShowMe");
            }
        }
        class Circle : Shape
        {
            public void Area()
            {
                Console.WriteLine("Circle.Area");
            }
        }
        class Rectangle : Shape
        {
            public void Area()
            {
```

```csharp
            Console.WriteLine("Rectangle.Area");
        }
    }
    static void Main(string[] args)
    {
        Console.WriteLine("***as operator demo***\n");
        Shape shapeOb = new Shape();
        Circle circleOb = new Circle();
        Rectangle rectOb = new Rectangle();
        circleOb = shapeOb as Circle; //no exception
        if( circleOb!=null)
        {
            circleOb.ShowMe();
        }
        else
        {
            Console.WriteLine("'shapeOb as Circle' is prodcuing null ");
        }
        shapeOb = rectOb as Shape;
        if (shapeOb != null)
        {
            Console.WriteLine("'rectOb as Shape' is NOT prodcuing null ");
            shapeOb.ShowMe();
        }
        else
        {
            Console.WriteLine(" shapeOb as Circle is prodcuing null ");
        }
        Console.ReadKey();
    }
  }
}
```

Output

```
 C:\CSharpProgs\CSharpBasicsProgs\InteractiveCSharpSolution\asOperatorDemo\bin\Debug\asOperator...
***as operator demo***

'shapeOb as Circle' is prodcuing null
'rectOb as Shape' is NOT prodcuing null
Shape.ShowMe
```

Analysis

The operator *as* does the conversion automatically if the operation is cast-able; otherwise, it returns null.

POINTS TO REMEMBER

The *as* operator will do the downcast operation successfully or it will evaluate to null (if the downcast fails). So, the way through which we did the null check in the preceding program is very common in C# programming.

Passing Value Types by Value vs. Passing Value Types by Reference (with ref vs. out)

Teacher continues: We are already aware that a value type variable directly contains its data, and a reference type variable contains a reference to its data.

So, passing a value type variable to a method by value means that we are actually passing a copy to the method. So, if the method makes any change on that copied parameter, it has no effect on the original data. If you wish that the change made by the caller method reflects back to original data, you need to pass it by reference with either a *ref* keyword or an *out* keyword.

Let's go through the program.

Demonstration 7: Passing Value Type by Value

```csharp
using System;

namespace PassingValueTypeByValue
{
    class Program
    {

        static void Change(int x)
        {
            x = x * 2;
            Console.WriteLine("Inside Change(), myVariable is {0}", x);//50
        }
        static void Main(string[] args)
        {
            Console.WriteLine("***Passing Value Type by Value-Demo***");
            int myVariable = 25;
            Change(myVariable);
            Console.WriteLine("Inside Main(), myVariable={0}",
            myVariable);//25
            Console.ReadKey();
        }
    }
}
```

Output

C:\CSharpProgs\CSharpBasicsProgs\InteractiveCSharpSolution\PassingValueTypeByValue\bin\Debug\Pas...

```
***Passing Value Type by Value-Demo***
Inside Change(), myVariable is 50
Inside Main(), myVariable=25
```

206

Analysis

Here we made a change inside the Change() method. But this changed value is not reflected outside the Change() method, because inside the Main() method, we are seeing that the value of the myVariable is 25. This is because actually the change made was on the copy of myVariable (or in other words, the effect was only on the local variable x).

The ref Parameter vs. the out Parameter

Teacher continues: Now consider the same program with a minor modification, as follows (highlighted with the arrow).

Demonstration 8

```
using System;

namespace PassingValueTypeUsingRef
{
    class Program
    {
        static void Change(ref int x)
        {
            x = x * 2;
            Console.WriteLine("Inside Change(), myVariable is {0}", x);//50
        }
        static void Main(string[] args)
        {
            Console.WriteLine("***Passing Value Type by Reference using ref-Demo***");
            int myVariable = 25;
            Change(ref myVariable);
            Console.WriteLine("Inside Main(), myVariable={0}", myVariable);//50
            Console.ReadKey();
        }
    }
}
```

Output

```
***Passing Value Type by Reference using ref-Demo***
Inside Change(), myVariable is 50
Inside Main(), myVariable=50
```

Analysis

Here we made a change inside the Change() method. And this changed value is reflected outside the Change() method. Here the *ref* keyword has done the trick. With *ref int x*, we did not mean an integer parameter, rather we meant a reference to an int (which is myVariable in this case).

POINTS TO REMEMBER

We need to initialize myVariable before passing it into the ChangeMe() method; otherwise, we'll encounter a compilation error.

 CS0165   Use of unassigned local variable 'myVariable'

Teacher continues: Now consider a very similar program. This time we are showing the use of an *out* parameter.

Demonstration 9 : The Use of the "out" Parameter

```csharp
using System;

namespace PassingValueTypeUsingOut
{
    class Program
    {
        static void Change(out int x)
        {
            x = 25;
            x = x * 2;
            Console.WriteLine("Inside Change(), myVariable is {0}", x);//50
        }
        static void Main(string[] args)
        {
```

```
Console.WriteLine("***Passing Value Type by Reference using
out-Demo***");
//Need to be initialized ,if you use 'ref'
int myVariable;
Change(out myVariable);
Console.WriteLine("Inside Main(), myVariable={0}",
myVariable);//50
Console.ReadKey();
    }
  }
```

Output

```
***Passing Value Type by Reference using out-Demo***
Inside Change(), myVariable is 50
Inside Main(), myVariable=50
```

Analysis

Here we have achieved a similar result (like ref, the change is reflected in both Main() and ChangeMe()). But if you carefully notice, you will see that in this program, we did not initialize myVariable before it was passed to the ChangeMe() method. For the out parameter, this initialization is not mandatory (but for *ref*, it is a must). You will also notice that we needed to assign a value before it came out of the function; for the *out* parameter, it is required.

POINTS TO REMEMBER

For the *out* parameter, this initialization is not mandatory (but for ref, it is a must). On the other hand, we need to assign a value before it comes out of the function.

Quiz

Suppose we have modified the Change() method, as follows:

```
static void Change(out int x)
    {
        //x = 25;
        int y = 10;
        x = x * 2;
        Console.WriteLine("Inside Change(), myVariable is {0}", x);
    }
```

Will the preceding code compile?

Answer

No. We'll get a compilation error.

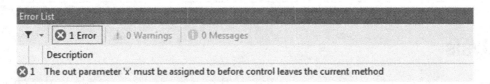

Analysis

As we mentioned earlier, we need to assign some value to x before we leave the method Change().In this case , you have assigned a value(10) to another variable y which have no use here.

Students ask:
Sir, by default, how are the arguments passed: by value or by reference?

Teacher says: They are passed by value.

Students ask:
Sir, can we pass a reference type as value (or vice versa)?

Teacher says: Yes. In the PassingValueTypeUsingRef (Demonstration 8) example, we passed a value type with the *ref* keyword. Now consider a reverse scenario. Here we are passing a reference type (string) as a value type.

210

Demonstration 10: Passing a Reference Type as Value

```csharp
using System;

namespace PassReferenceTypeUsingValue
{
    class Program
    {
        static void CheckMe(string s)
        {
            s = "World";
            Console.WriteLine("Inside CheckMe(), the string value is
            {0}", s);//World
        }
        static void Main(string[] args)
        {
            string s = "Hello";
            Console.WriteLine("Inside Main(), Initially the  string value
            is {0}", s);//Hello
            CheckMe(s);
            Console.WriteLine("Inside Main(), finally the  string value is
            {0}", s);//Hello
            Console.ReadKey();
        }
    }
}
```

Output

We can observe that the change made by CheckMe() has not reflected back inside Main().

```
Inside Main(), Initially the  string value is Hello
Inside CheckMe(), the  string value is World  <--
Inside Main(), finally the  string value is Hello <--
```

Students ask:

Sir, so it appears that we cannot modify the value once we pass a reference type as a value. Is this understanding correct?

Teacher says: Not at all. It depends on how you are using it; for example, consider the following program. Here we are changing the first two elements of an array using this mechanism.

Demonstration 11: A Case Study with Array Elements

```
using System;

namespace PassReferenceTypeUsingValueEx2
{
    class Program
    {
        static void CheckMe(int[] arr)
        {
            arr[0] = 15;
            arr[1] = 25;
            arr = new int[3] { 100, 200,300};
            Console.WriteLine("********");
            Console.WriteLine("Inside CheckMe(),arr[0]={0}", arr[0]);//100
            Console.WriteLine("Inside CheckMe(),arr[1]={0}", arr[1]);//200
            Console.WriteLine("Inside CheckMe(),arr[2]={0}", arr[2]);//300
            Console.WriteLine("********");
        }
        static void Main(string[] args)
        {
            Console.WriteLine("***Passing reference Type by value.Ex-2***");
            int[] myArray= { 1, 2, 3 };
            Console.WriteLine("At the beginning,myArray[0]={0}",
            myArray[0]);//1
            Console.WriteLine("At the beginning,myArray[1]={0}",
            myArray[1]);//2
```

```
        Console.WriteLine("At the beginning,myArray[2]={0}",
        myArray[2]);//3
        CheckMe(myArray);
        Console.WriteLine("At the end,myArray[0]={0}", myArray[0]);//15
        Console.WriteLine("At the end,myArray[1]={0}", myArray[1]);//25
        Console.WriteLine("At the end,myArray[2]={0}", myArray[2]);//3
        Console.ReadKey();
    }
  }
}
```

Output

```
***Passing reference Type by value.Ex-2***
At the beginning,myArray[0]=1
At the beginning,myArray[1]=2
At the beginning,myArray[2]=3
********
Inside CheckMe(),arr[0]=100
Inside CheckMe(),arr[1]=200
Inside CheckMe(),arr[2]=300
********
At the end,myArray[0]=15
At the end,myArray[1]=25
At the end,myArray[2]=3
```

Analysis

In the CheckMe() method, once we created a new array, the reference array started pointing to a new array. So, after that, no change is imposed in the original array, which was created inside Main(). Actually, after that operation, we were dealing with two different arrays.

Quiz

Will the code compile?

```
class Program
    {
        static void ChangeMe( int x)
        {
            x = 5;
            Console.WriteLine("Inside Change() the value is {0}", x);
        }
        static void ChangeMe(out int x)
        {
            //out parameter must be assigned before it leaves the function
            x = 5;
            Console.WriteLine("Inside ChangeMe() the value is {0}", x);
        }
        static void ChangeMe(ref int x)
        {
            x = 5;
            Console.WriteLine("Inside ChangeMe() the value is {0}", x);
        }
        static void Main(string[] args)
        {
            Console.WriteLine("***ref and out Comparison-Demo***");
            //for ref, the variable need to be initialized
            int myVariable3=25;
            Console.WriteLine("Inside Main(),before call, the value is {0}",
            myVariable3);
            ChangeMe( myVariable3);
            ChangeMe(ref myVariable3);
            ChangeMe(out myVariable3);
            Console.WriteLine("Inside Main(),after call, the value is {0}",
            myVariable3);
        }
```

Output

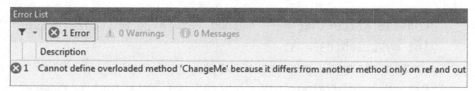

Analysis

We can have either ChangeMe(out myVariable3) or ChangeMe(ref myVariable3) with ChangeMe(myVariable3). They are not allowed together. If you comment out ChangeMe(out myVariable3) and its associated call, you receive output like this:

```
***ref and out Comparison-Demo***
Inside Main(),before call, the value is 25
Inside Change() the value is 5
Inside ChangeMe() the value is 5
Inside Main(),after call, the value is 5
```

Students ask:

Can a method (function) return multiple values in C#?

Teacher says: Yes, it can. Many of us prefer KeyValuePair in this context. But just now we have learned the use of *out* and it can help us to implement a similar concept. Consider the following program.

Demonstration 12: A Method Returning Multiple Values

```
class Program
    {
static void RetunMultipleValues(int x, out double area, out double
perimeter)
        {
            area = 3.14 * x * x;
            perimeter = 2 * 3.14 * x;
        }
```

```
static void Main(string[] args)
{
    Console.WriteLine("***A method returning multiple values***");
    int myVariable3 = 3;
    double area=0.0,perimeter=0.0;
    RetunMultipleValues(myVariable3, out area, out perimeter);
    Console.WriteLine("Area of the circle is  {0} sq. unit", area);
    Console.WriteLine("Peremeter  of the Cicle is  {0} unit",
    perimeter);
}
}
```

Output

```
***A method returning multiple values***
Area of the circle is  28.26 sq. unit
Peremeter  of the Cicle is  18.84 unit
```

A Brief Comparison of C# Types

Teacher says: C# types can be broadly classified as

- Value types

- Reference types

- Pointer types

- Generic types

Let's explore the top three in this section. The fourth one (i.e., generic types) will be covered in the PART II of this book. So, let's begin with value types and reference types.

Value Types and Reference Types

Some examples of value types are common built-in data types (e.g., int, double, char, bool, etc.), enum types, and user-defined structures. (One exception is String, which is a built-in data type but also a reference type.)

Some of the examples of reference types are class (objects), interface, arrays, and delegates.

Built-in reference types include object, dynamic, and string.

The fundamental difference between the two types is the way they are handled inside memory.

Let's start with the key differences between them.

Value types	Reference Types
• As per MSDN, the data type that holds data within its own memory location is a value type.	• On the other hand, reference types contains a pointer to another memory location that actually contains the data. (You can simply think it of two parts: an object and a reference to that object.)
• Assignment of a value type always causes a copy of the instance.	• Assignment of a reference type causes it to copy the reference only, not the actual object.
• Common examples include built-in data types except Strings (e.g., int, double, char, bool, etc.), enum types, user-defined structures.	• Common examples include: Class (Objects),interface, arrays, delegates, and a special built-in data type string (alias System.String).
• In general, a value type does not have a null value.	• A reference type can point to null (i.e., it is not pointing to any object).

Students ask:

Sir, how can we check that class is a reference type and structure is a value type in C#?

Teacher says: Consider the following program and output.

Demonstration 13: Value Types vs. Reference Types

```
using System;

namespace ImportantComparison
{
    struct MyStruct
    {
        public int i;
    }
    class MyClass
    {
        public int i;
    }
    class Program
    {
        static void Main(string[] args)
        {
            Console.WriteLine("***Test-valueTypes vs Reference Types***\n");
            MyStruct struct1, struct2;
            struct1=new MyStruct();
            struct1.i = 1;
            struct2 = struct1;

            MyClass class1, class2;
            class1= new MyClass();
            class1.i = 2;
            class2 = class1;

            Console.WriteLine("struct1.i={0}", struct1.i);//1
            Console.WriteLine("struct2.i={0}", struct2.i);//1
            Console.WriteLine("class1.i={0}", class1.i);//2
            Console.WriteLine("class2.i={0}", class2.i);//2

            Console.WriteLine("***Making changes to strcut1.i(10) and
            class1.i (20)***");
            struct1.i = 10;
            class1.i = 20;
```

```
Console.WriteLine("***After the changes, values are :***");
Console.WriteLine("struct1.i={0}", struct1.i);//10
Console.WriteLine("struct2.i={0}", struct2.i);//1
Console.WriteLine("class1.i={0}", class1.i);//20
Console.WriteLine("class2.i={0}", class2.i);//20

Console.ReadKey();
    }
  }
}
```

Output

```
***Test-valueTypes vs Reference Types***

struct1.i=1
struct2.i=1
class1.i=2
class2.i=2
***Making changes to strcut1.i(10) and class1.i (20)***
***After the changes, values are :***
struct1.i=10
struct2.i=1
class1.i=20
class2.i=20
```

Analysis

We can see that both class objects—class1 and class2—have updated their instance variable i when we made the change in class1. But the same did not happen for structures. struct2.i is keeping the old value 1, even if struct1.i changed to 10.

When we wrote struct2 = struct1;

The struct2 structure becomes an independent *copy* of struct1, with its own separate fields.

When we wrote class2 = class1;

We are copying the *reference*, which is pointing to the same object.

Students ask:
Sir, when should we prefer value types to reference types?

Teacher says:
In general, stack can be used efficiently than heap. So, the choice of data structure is important.

In a reference type, memory is not reclaimed when our methods finish the execution. To reclaim memory, the garbage collection mechanism needs to be called. It is not always dependable and straightforward.

Students ask:
Sir, when should we prefer reference types to value types?

Teacher says:
For value types, lifetime is a big concern. Memory is reclaimed when a method finishes its execution.

These are not suitable for sharing data across different classes.

Pointer Types

In C#, pointers are supported but in an unsafe context. We need to mark the block of code with the "unsafe" keyword. You also need to compile the code with the /unsafe option. So basically, by using the "unsafe" tag, you are allowed to do C++ style coding with pointers. The purpose is the same: a pointer can hold the address of a variable and can cast to other pointer types (obviously these operations are not safe).

Note

- The most common pointer operators are *, &, and - >.

- We can treat any of the following types as a pointer type: *byte, sbyte, short, ushort, int, uint, long, ulong, float, double, decimal, bool, char,* any *enum* type, any *pointer* type, or a user-defined *struct* type with unmanaged type fields only.

The following are some of the basic pointer type declarations:

- int *p Means p is a pointer to an integer

- int **p Means that p is a pointer to a pointer to an integer

- char* p Means that p is a pointer to a char

- void* p Means that p is a pointer to an unknown type (although it is allowed, it is advised to use with special care)

Consider the following example.

Demonstration 14: Pointer Types

```
using System;

namespace UnsafeCodeEx1
{
    class A
    {
    }
    class Program
    {
        static unsafe void Main(string[] args)
        {
            int a = 25;
            int* p;
            p = &a;
            Console.WriteLine("***Pointer Type Demo***");
            Console.WriteLine("*p is containing:{0}", *p);

            A obA = new A();
            //Error:Cannot take the address of, get the size of, or declare a
            pointer to a managed type ('A')
            //A* obB = obA;
            Console.ReadKey();
        }
    }
}
```

Output

```
***Pointer Type Demo***
*p is containing:25
```

Analysis

In Visual Studio 2017, you need to allow unsafe code by enabling the checkbox like following:

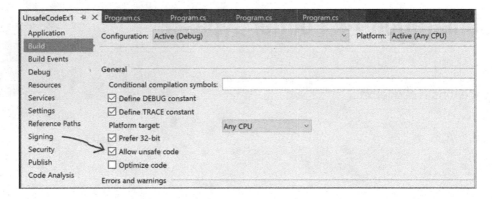

Otherwise, you will encounter this error:

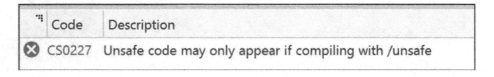

	Code	Description
❌	CS0227	Unsafe code may only appear if compiling with /unsafe

Students ask:
Sir, when do we use pointers in the context of C#?

Teacher says: One basic purpose is interoperability with C APIs. Apart from this, sometimes we may want to access memory outside our managed heap boundaries to handle some critical issues. Also as Microsoft states: *"Interfacing with the underlying operating system, accessing a memory-mapped device, or implementing a time-critical algorithm may not be possible or practical without access to pointers."*

POINTS TO REMEMBER

- We cannot convert between a pointer type and an object. Pointers do not inherit from objects.

- To declare multiple pointers at the same place, the * is written with the underlying type, such as

```
int* a, b, c; //ok
```

But if we write something like this, we encounter a compiler error.

```
int *a,*b,*c;//Error
```

- Later we'll learn about garbage collections, which basically operate on references. The garbage collector can collect the object references during the cleanup process, even if some pointer points to them. This is why a pointer cannot point to a reference (or any structure that contains a reference).

const vs. readonly

Teacher continues: C# supports two special keywords: *const* and *readonly*. The common part is that both of them try to prevent the modification of a field. Still, they have some different characteristics. We will validate those through some program segments.

POINTS TO REMEMBER

We can declare constants like a variable but the key point is they cannot be changed after the declaration. On the other hand, we can assign a value to a readonly field during the declaration or through a constructor.

To declare a constant variable, we need to prefix the keyword *const* before the declaration. We must remember that constants are implicitly static.

Demonstration 15: The Use of the "const" Keyword

```
using System;

namespace ConstantsEx1
{
    class Program
    {
        static void Main(string[] args)
        {
            Console.WriteLine("***Quiz : Experiment with a
            constructor***\n");
            const int MYCONST = 100;
            //Following line will raise error
            MYCONST=90;//error
            Console.WriteLine("MYCONST={0}", MYCONST);
            Console.ReadKey();
        }
    }
}
```

Output

> ⊗ CS0131   The left-hand side of an assignment must be a variable, property or indexer

Similarly, for readonly, we will get errors for these lines:

```
public   readonly int myReadOnlyValue=105;
//Following line will raise error
myReadOnlyValue=110;//error
```

Quiz

Will the code compile?

```
Class ReadOnlyEx
{
  public static readonly int staticReadOnlyValue;
      static ReadOnlyEx()
      {
         staticReadOnlyValue = 25;
      }
  //Some other code e.g. Main Method() etc..
}
```

Answer

Yes.

Quiz

Will the code compile?

```
Class ReadOnlyEx
{
  public  readonly int nonStaticReadOnlyValue;
      public  ReadOnlyEx(int x)
      {
         nonStaticReadOnlyValue = x;
      }
      //Some other code e.g.Main method() etc..
}
```

Answer

Yes.

Quiz

Will the code compile?

```
Class ReadOnlyEx
{
public   readonly int myReadOnlyValue=105;
        public int TrytoIncreaseNonStaticReadOnly()
        {
         myReadOnlyValue++;
        }
//Some other code e.g.Main method() etc..
}
```

Answer

No. In this case, you can change the value through a constructor only.
(TrytoIncreaseNonStaticReadOnly() is not the constructor here)

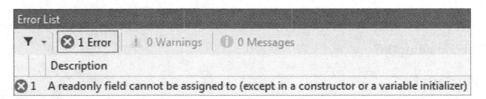

Quiz

Will the code compile?

```
public static const int MYCONST = 100;
```

Answer

No. Constants are implicitly *static*. We are not allowed to mention the keyword *static* here.

Quiz

What will the output be?

```
class TestConstants
{
 public const int MYCONST = 100;
}

class Program
{
static void Main(string[] args)
{
TestConstants tc = new TestConstants();
Console.WriteLine(" MYCONST is {0}",  tc.MYCONST);
Console.ReadKey();
}
}
```

Answer

We will encounter a compile-time error. We have already mentioned that constants are implicitly *static*. So, we cannot access them through an instance reference.

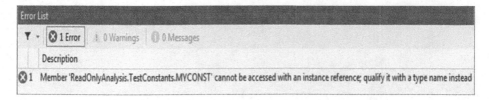

We should use the class name here. So, the following line of code will work fine:

```
Console.WriteLine(" MYCONST is {0}", TestConstants.MYCONST);
```

Students ask:
What are the advantages of using constants in the program?

Teacher says: They are easy to read and modify. We can modify a single place to reflect the changes across the program. Otherwise, we may need to find out each occurrence of the variable across the program. That method is definitely error prone.

Students ask:
When should we prefer readonly over const?

Teacher says: When we want a value of variable should not be changed but this value will be known only at runtime; for example, we may need to do some calculation prior to set an initial value.

We will also note that readonly values can be both static and non static whereas constants are always static. So, different instance of a class can have different values. A very common use of *'readonly'* can be setting out a type of software license.

POINTS TO REMEMBER

- The readonly values can be both static and non-static; whereas constants are always static.

- A very common use of readonly can be setting out a type of software license.

Summary

This chapter covered

- ✓ Comparisons between implicit and explicit casting

- ✓ Comparisons between boxing and unboxing

- ✓ Comparisons between boxing and casting

- ✓ Comparisons between upcasting and downcasting

- ✓ Use of is and as keywords

- ✓ Passing value types by value vs. passing value types by reference

- ✓ Comparisons between ref vs. out parameters

- ✓ How can we pass a reference type as value (or vice versa)?

- ✓ How can a method return multiple values in C#?

- ✓ Value types vs Reference types

- ✓ How can we check that class is a reference type and structure is a value type in C#?

- ✓ When should we prefer value types to reference types and vice versa.

- ✓ Overview of pointer types.

- ✓ Comparisons between *const* and *readonly*

CHAPTER 9

A Quick Recap of OOP Principles in C#

Teacher starts the discussion: Welcome to the final part of the object-oriented programming in C#.Let's review the core principles that we already covered in this book.

- Classes and objects
- Polymorphism
- Abstraction
- Encapsulation
- Inheritance

We can add two more.

- Message passing
- Dynamic binding

Quiz

Can you recall how these topics are covered with basic building blocks of C#?

Answers

- Class and objects: Throughout the book, in almost every example, we have used different types of classes and objects. In the examples of static classes, we did not create objects. We can access the static fields through the class names.

© Vaskaran Sarcar 2018
V. Sarcar, *Interactive C#*, https://doi.org/10.1007/978-1-4842-3339-9_9

231

- Polymorphism: Both types of polymorphism were covered. Compile-time polymorphism was covered through method overloading (and operator overloading), and runtime polymorphism was covered through method overriding techniques with the use of virtual and override keywords.

- Abstraction: This feature was tested through abstract classes and interfaces.

- Encapsulation: In addition to access modifiers, we used the concepts of properties and indexers.

- Inheritance: We explored different types of inheritance over two chapters.

- Message passing: This feature is commonly observed in a multithreaded environment. But we can consider runtime polymorphisms in this category.

- Dynamic binding: Runtime polymorphisms through method overriding examples can fall into this category. #

Students ask:

Sir, can you please summarize the difference between abstraction and encapsulation?

Teacher says: The process of wrapping up the data and codes into a single entity is known as *encapsulation*. With this technique, we prevent arbitrary and unsecured access. We used different kinds of access modifiers and the examples of properties with get and set accessors to implement the concept of encapsulation.

In abstraction, we show the essential features but hide the detailed implementation from the user; for example, when we use a remote control to switch on a television, we do not care about the internal circuits of that device. We are absolutely OK with the device as long as images come out of the television after the button is pressed.

You can revisit the Chapter 1 for these definitions.

Students ask:

In general, which one is faster—compile-time polymorphism or runtime polymorphism?

Teacher says: I indicated that if the call can be resolved early, in general, it is faster. This is why, we can conclude that compile-time binding is faster than run time binding (or polymorphism)—*because you know in advance which method to call.*

Students ask:

Sir, you told us earlier that inheritance might not always provide the best solution. Can you please elaborate?

Teacher says: In some cases, composition can provide a better solution. But to understand the composition, you need to know these concepts:

- Association

- Aggregation

Association can be one way or both ways. When you see this kind of UML diagram, it means ClassA knows about ClassB, but the reverse is not true.

The following diagram indicates a two-way association because both of the classes know each other.

Consider an example. In a college, a student can learn from multiple teachers, and a teacher can teach multiple students. There is no dedicated *ownership* in this kind of relationship. So, when we represent them with classes and objects in programming, we can say that both kinds of objects can be created and deleted independently.

Aggregation is a stronger type of association. It is widely represented as follows.

Consider an example of in this category. Suppose that Professor X submits his resignation letter because he has decided to join a new institution. Although both Professor X and his former institution can survive without each other, ultimately

Professor X needs to associate himself with a department in an institution. In a similar situation in the programming world, we'd say that the department is the owner of this relationship and the department has professors.

Similarly, we can say that a car has seats, a bike has tires, and so forth.

Note

A department has a professor. This is why an association relationship is also termed as "has a" relationship. (We must remember the key difference with inheritance here. Inheritance is associated with "is a" relationship.

Composition is a stronger form of aggregation, and this time we have a filled diamond in place.

A department in a college cannot exist without the college. The college only creates or closes its departments. (You can argue that if there is no department at all, a college cannot exist, but we do not need to complicate things by considering this type of corner case.) In other words, the lifetime of a department entirely depends on its college. This is also known as a *death relationship* because if we destroy the college, all of its departments are destroyed automatically.

To show the power of composition, let's revisit the diamond problem that we discussed in Chapter 3, and then analyze the following program.

Our Existing Code

```
using System;

namespace CompositionEx1
{
    class Parent
    {
        public virtual void Show()
        {
```

```
            Console.WriteLine("I am in Parent");
        }
    }
class Child1 : Parent
{
    public override void Show()
    {
        Console.WriteLine("I am in Child-1");
    }
}
class Child2 : Parent
{
    public override void Show()
    {
        Console.WriteLine("I am in Child-2");
    }
}
```

Let's say that the Grandchild derives from both Child1 and Child2 but it has not overridden the Show() method.

Therefore, our intended UML diagram may look like this:

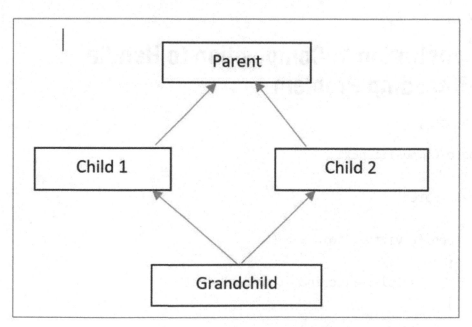

We now have ambiguity now. From which class will Grandchild call the Show() method—Child1 or Child2? To remove this type of ambiguity, C# does not support multiple inheritance through classes. This is known as the *diamond problem*.

So, if you code like this:

```
class GrandChild : Child1, Child2//Error: Diamond Effect
{
    public void Show()
    {
        Console.WriteLine("I am in Child-2");
    }
}
```

The C# compiler will complain with this error:

Code	Description
❌ CS1721	Class 'GrandChild' cannot have multiple base classes: 'Child1' and 'Child2'

Now let's see how we can handle this situation with composition. Consider the following code.

Demonstration 1: Composition to Handle the Preceding Problem

```
using System;

namespace CompositionEx1
{
    class Parent
    {
        public virtual void Show()
        {
            Console.WriteLine("I am in Parent");
        }
    }
```

```csharp
class Child1 : Parent
{
    public override void Show()
    {
        Console.WriteLine("I am in Child-1");
    }
}
class Child2 : Parent
{
    public override void Show()
    {
        Console.WriteLine("I am in Child-2");
    }
}
//class GrandChild : Child1, Child2//Error: Diamond Effect
//{
//}
class Grandchild
{
    Child1 ch1 = new Child1();
    Child2 ch2 = new Child2();
    public void ShowFromChild1()
    {
        ch1.Show();
    }
    public void ShowFromChild2()
    {
        ch2.Show();
    }
}

class Program
{
    static void Main(string[] args)
    {
```

```
        Console.WriteLine("***Composition to handle the Diamond
        Problem***\n");
        Grandchild gChild = new Grandchild();
        gChild.ShowFromChild1();
        gChild.ShowFromChild2();
        Console.ReadKey();
    }
  }
}
```

Output

```
***Composition to handle the Diamond Problem***

I am in Child-1
I am in Child-2
```

Analysis

You can see that both Class1 and Class2 have overridden their parent Show() method. And the Grandchild class doesn't have its own Show() method. Still, we can call those class-specific methods through the Grandchild's object.

The Grandchild is creating the objects from both Class1 and Class2 inside its body. So, if Grandchild objects are not present in our application (e.g., if those are garbage collected), we can say that there is no Class1 or Class2 objects reside inside the system. You can also place some restrictions on users so that they are not able to create objects for Class1 and Class2 directly inside the application; but for simplicity, we have ignored that part.

Demonstration 2: An Aggregation Example

Suppose that you want to be little liberal in the preceding case. You want to avoid the death relationship between the Grandchild and the Child classes. You can use aggregation to implement a program where other classes can effectively use the references to Class1 and Class2.

```csharp
using System;

namespace AggregationEx1
{
    class Parent
    {
        public virtual void Show()
        {
            Console.WriteLine("I am in Parent");
        }
    }
    class Child1 : Parent
    {
        public override void Show()
        {
            Console.WriteLine("I am in Child-1");
        }
    }
    class Child2 : Parent
    {
        public override void Show()
        {
            Console.WriteLine("I am in Child-2");
        }
    }
    //class GrandChild : Child1, Child2//Error: Diamond Effect
    //{
    //}
    class Grandchild
    {
        Child1 ch1;
        Child2 ch2;
        public Grandchild(Child1 ch1, Child2 ch2)
        {
            this.ch1 = ch1;
```

```
            this.ch2 = ch2;
        }
        public void ShowFromChild1()
        {
            ch1.Show();
        }
        public void ShowFromChild2()
        {
            ch2.Show();
        }
    }

    class Program
    {
        static void Main(string[] args)
        {
            Console.WriteLine("***Aggregation to handle the Diamond
            Problem***\n");
            Child1 child1 = new Child1();
            Child2 child2 = new Child2();
            Grandchild gChild = new Grandchild(child1,child2);
            gChild.ShowFromChild1();
            gChild.ShowFromChild2();
            Console.ReadKey();
        }
    }
}
```

Output

```
***Aggregation to handle the Diamond Problem***

I am in Child-1
I am in Child-2
```

Analysis

In this case, Child1 and Child2 objects can survive without Grandchild objects. This is why we say that composition is a stronger form of aggregation.

Note

You are aware of generalization, specialization, and realization. We have used these concepts in our applications. When our class extends another class (i.e., inheritance), we use the concepts of generalization and specialization; for example, a footballer (a.k.a. a soccer player) is a special kind (specialization) of athlete. Or we can say that both a footballer and basketball player are athletes (generalization). And when our class implemented an interface, we used the concept of realization.

Students ask:

What are the challenges and drawbacks of OOP?

Teacher says: Many experts believe that, in general, the size of object-oriented programs are larger. Due to the larger size, we may need more storage (But nowadays, these issues hardly matter.)

Some developers find difficulties in object-oriented programming style. They may still prefer other approaches, such as structured programming. So, if they are forced to work in such an environment, life becomes tough for them.

In addition, we cannot model each real-world problem in object-oriented style. Overall, however, I personally like object-oriented programming style because I believe that its merits are greater than its demerits.

Summary

This chapter included the following:

- ✓ A quick review of the core OOP principles in this book

- ✓ How to differentiate abstraction from encapsulation

- ✓ How to implement the concept of composition and aggregation in our C# application

- ✓ The challenges and drawbacks associated with OOP

PART II

Get Familiar with Some Advanced Concepts

This section's highlights:

- A pathway to advanced C# programming
- Five evergreen and advanced concepts of C#

CHAPTER 10

Delegates and Events

Introduction to Delegates

Teacher starts the discussion: Delegates are one of the most important topics in C#
programming, and they have made C# very powerful. Delegates are reference types
derived from System.Delegate. They are similar to object references but the key
distinction is that they point to methods. We can achieve type safety with the use of
delegates. For this reason, sometimes we refer to them as *type-safe function pointers.*

POINTS TO REMEMBER

- An object reference points to a particular type of object (e.g., when we write A
  ob=new A(); we mean that ob is a reference to an A type object); whereas a
  delegate points to a particular type of method.

- A delegate is an object that knows how to invoke the method associated with it.
  With a delegate type, you know which kind of method is invoked by its instances.

- We can write plug-in methods with delegates.

Suppose that we have a method called Sum with two integer parameters, like this:

```
public static int Sum(int a, int b)
{
  return a+b;
}
```

© Vaskaran Sarcar 2018
V. Sarcar, *Interactive C#*, https://doi.org/10.1007/978-1-4842-3339-9_10

We can declare a delegate to point to the Sum method, as follows:

```
Mydel del = new Mydel(Sum);
```

But before that, we need to define the Mydel delegate, which must have the same signature, as follows:

```
public delegate int Mydel(int x, int y);
```

The return type, parameters, and their corresponding order are the same for both the Sum method and the Mydel delegate. (Remember that method names are not part of a signature.)

Note that Mydel is compatible with any method that has an integer return type(int) and that is taking a two-integer parameter, like the Sum (int a, int b) method.

A Formal Definition

A delegate is a reference type derived from System.Delegate, and its instances are used to call methods with matching signatures. The general definition of a delegate is "a representative." Therefore, we can say that our delegates must represent methods with matching signatures.

The following example illustrates the use of delegates.

Case 1 is a method call that does not use a delegate.

Case 2 is a method that calls a delegate.

Demonstration 1

```
using System;

namespace DelegateEx1
{
    public delegate int Mydel(int x, int y);

    class Program
    {
        public static int Sum(int a, int b) { return a + b; }

        static void Main(string[] args)
        {
```

```
Console.WriteLine("***Delegate Example -1: A simple delegate
demo***");
int a = 25, b = 37;
//Case-1
Console.WriteLine("\n Calling Sum(..) method without using a
delegate:");
Console.WriteLine("Sum of a and b is : {0}", Sum(a,b));

Mydel del = new Mydel(Sum);
Console.WriteLine("\n Using delegate now:");
//Case-2
Console.WriteLine("Calling Sum(..) method with the use of a
delegate:");
//del(a,b) is shorthand for del.Invoke(a,b)
Console.WriteLine("Sum of a and b is: {0}", del(a, b));
//Console.WriteLine("Sum of a and b is: {0}", del.Invoke(a, b));
Console.ReadKey();
        }
    }
}
```

Output

```
***Delegate Example -1: A simple delegate demo***

 Calling Sum(..) method without using a delegate:
Sum of a and b is : 62

 Using delegate now:
Calling Sum(..) method with the use of a delegate:
Sum of a and b is: 62
```

Make Your Code Size Short

We can make the code size in the preceding example shorter.

Replace this line :

```
Mydel del = new Mydel(Sum);
```

with this line:

```
Mydel del = Sum;
```

Note the commented lines. del(a,b) is shorthand for

```
del.Invoke(a,b)
```

Students ask:

Suppose in our program, Sum() method is overloaded. Then the compiler may be confused if we write Mydel del=Sum;. Is this correct?

Teacher says: Not at all. The compiler can bind the correct overloaded method. Let's test this with a simple example. (In the previous example, we tested static methods with delegates, so we are intentionally using non-static methods this time to cover both cases.)

Demonstration 2

```
using System;

namespace Quiz1OnDelegate
{
    public delegate int Mydel1(int x, int y);
    public delegate int Mydel2(int x, int y,int z);

    class A
    {
        //Overloaded non static Methods
        public int Sum(int a, int b) { return a + b; }
        public int Sum(int a, int b,int c) { return a + b+ c; }
    }

    class Program
    {
        static void Main(string[] args)
```

```
        {
            Console.WriteLine("***Quiz on Delegate***");
            int a = 25, b = 37, c=100;
            A obA1 = new A();
            A obA2 = new A();

            Mydel1 del1 = obA1.Sum;
            Console.WriteLine("del1 is pointing Sum(int a,int b):");
            //Pointing Sum(int a, int b)
            Console.WriteLine("Sum of a and b is: {0}", del1(a, b));

            Mydel2 del2 = obA1.Sum;//pointing Sum(int a, int b, int c)
            Console.WriteLine("del2 is pointing Sum(int a,int b,int c):");
            //Pointing Sum(int a, int b, int c)
            Console.WriteLine("Sum of a, b and c is: {0}", del2(a, b,c));
            //same as
            //Console.WriteLine("Sum of a, b and c is: {0}", del2.Invoke
            (a, b, c));
            Console.ReadKey();
        }
    }
}
```

Output

```
***Quiz on Delegate***
del1 is pointing Sum(int a,int b):
Sum of a and b is: 62
del2 is pointing Sum(int a,int b,int c):
Sum of a, b and c is: 162
```

Analysis

The compiler is choosing the correct overloaded method. You'll always receive a compile-time error if you mistakenly code like this:

del1(a,b,c)

 CS1593   Delegate 'Mydel1' does not take 3 arguments

Or, if you code like this:

del2(a,b)

 CS7036   There is no argument given that corresponds to the required formal parameter 'z' of 'Mydel2'

 CS0219   The variable 'c' is assigned but its value is never used

Students ask:
Why are delegates often referred to as a type-safe function pointers?

Teacher says: When we want to pass any method to a delegate, the delegate signature and the method signature need to match. For this reason, they are often called *type -safe function pointers*.

Quiz

Will the code compile?

```
using System;

namespace Test1_Delegate
{
    public delegate int MultiDel(int a, int b);
    class A : System.Delegate//Error
    { ..}

}
```

Answer

No. We cannot derive from the Delegate class.

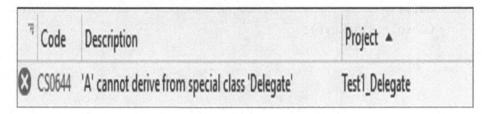

Code	Description	Project ▲
❌ CS0644	'A' cannot derive from special class 'Delegate'	Test1_Delegate

Multicast Delegates/Chaining Delegates

Teacher continues: When a delegate is used to encapsulate more than one method of a matching signature, we call it a *multicast delegate*. These delegates are subtypes of System.MulticastDelegate, which is a subclass of System.Delegate. The following is an example of a multicast delegate.

Demonstration 3

```
using System;

namespace MulticastDelegateEx1
{
    public delegate void MultiDel();

    class Program
    {
        public static void show1() { Console.WriteLine("Program.Show1()"); }
        public static void show2() { Console.WriteLine("Program.Show2()"); }
        public static void show3() { Console.WriteLine("Program.Show3()"); }
        static void Main(string[] args)
        {
            Console.WriteLine("***Example of a Multicast Delegate***");
```

```
            MultiDel md = new MultiDel(show1);
            md += show2;
            md += show3;
            md();
            Console.ReadKey();
        }
    }
}
```

Output

```
■ C:\CSharpProgs\CSharpBasicsProgs\InteractiveCSharpSolution\Multi

***Example of a Multicast Delegate***
Program.Show1()
Program.Show2()
Program.Show3()
```

Students ask:

In the preceding example, the return type of our multicast delegate is void. What is the intention behind this?

Teacher says: In general, for a multicast delegate, we have multiple methods in the invocation list. However, a single method or delegate invocation can return only a single value, so the multicast delegate type should have a void return type. If you still want to experiment with a nonvoid return type, you will receive the return value from the last method only. The preceding methods will be called but the return values will be discarded. Go through the following quiz for a clear understanding.

Quiz

Suppose that we have written the following program, where we the multicast delegate and the methods associated with it have return types. Will the program compile?

```
using System;

namespace MulticastDelegateEx2
{
    public delegate int MultiDel(int a, int b);

    class Program
    {
        public static int Sum(int a, int b)
        {
            Console.Write("Program.Sum->\t");
            Console.WriteLine("Sum={0}", a+b);
            return a + b;
        }
        public static int Difference(int a, int b)
        {
            Console.Write("Program.Difference->\t");
            Console.WriteLine("Difference={0}", a - b);
            return a - b;
        }
        public static int Multiply(int a, int b)
        {
            Console.Write("Program.Multiply->\t");
            Console.WriteLine("Multiplication={0}", a * b);
            return a * b;
        }

        static void Main(string[] args)
        {
            Console.WriteLine("***Testing a Multicast Delegate***");
            MultiDel md = new MultiDel(Sum);
            md += Difference;
            md += Multiply;
```

```
            int c = md(10, 5);
            Console.WriteLine("Analyzing the value of c");
            Console.WriteLine("c={0}", c);
            Console.ReadKey();
        }
    }
}
```

Output

Yes, the program will compile and the output will be as follows:

```
***Testing a Multicast Delegate***
Program.Sum->    Sum=15
Program.Difference->     Difference=5
Program.Multiply->       Multiplication=50
Analyzing the value of c
c=50
```

Analysis

Note the value of c. To compile and run, it is not necessary that we have a void return type for the multicast delegate. But if we have return types for those methods and we do code like this, then we get the value from the last invoked method in the invocation/calling chain. All other values are discarded in between but there will be no alert for this. Therefore, it is suggested that you experiment multicast delegate with void return type.

Students ask:

Therefore, even if we use a nonvoid return type with a multicast delegate, we will not see any compilation error. Is this understanding correct?

Teacher says: Yes. In that scenario, you are going to receive the return value from the last method only. So, just think if it makes sense to you.

Students ask:
Can we use delegates to define callback methods?

Yes. It is one of the key purposes of using delegates.

Students ask:
What is the invocation list of a multicast delegate?

Teacher says: A multicast delegate maintains a linked list of delegates. This list is called the *invocation list* that consists of one or more elements. When we call a multicast delegate, the delegates in the invocation list are called synchronously in the order in which they appear. If any error occurs during the execution, it throws an exception.

Covariance and Contravariance in Delegates

When we instantiate a delegate, we can assign it a method that has a "more derived return type" than the "originally specified return type." This support is available in C# 2.0 onward. On the other hand, contravariance allows a method with parameter types that are less derived than in the delegate type. The concept of covariance has supported arrays since C#1.0, and so we can write this:

```
Console.WriteLine("***Covariance in arrays(C#1.0 onwards)***");
//ok, but not type safe
object[] myObjArray = new string[5];
```

But this is not type safe, because this kind of line

```
myObjArray[0] = 10;//runtime error
```

will encounter runtime errors.

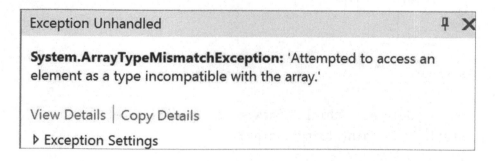

```
Exception Unhandled                                    �📌 ✕

System.ArrayTypeMismatchException: 'Attempted to access an
element as a type incompatible with the array.'

View Details | Copy Details
▷ Exception Settings
```

Covariance in Delegates/Method Group Variance

Covariance and contravariance has been supported by delegates since C# 2.0. Support for generic type parameters, generic interfaces, and generic delegates began with C#4.0. Until now, I have not discussed generic types. So,this section deals with non-generic delegates and starts with covariance.

Demonstration 4

```
using System;

namespace CovarianceWithDelegatesEx1
{
    class Vehicle
    {
        public Vehicle ShowVehicle()
        {
            Vehicle myVehicle = new Vehicle();
            Console.WriteLine(" A Vehicle created");
            return myVehicle;
        }
    }
    class Bus:Vehicle
    {
        public Bus ShowBus()
        {
            Bus myBus = new Bus();
            Console.WriteLine(" A Bus created");
            return myBus;
        }
    }

    class Program
    {
        public delegate Vehicle   ShowVehicleTypeDelegate();
        static void Main(string[] args)
        {
```

```
Vehicle vehicle1 = new Vehicle();
Bus bus1 = new Bus();
Console.WriteLine("***Covariance in delegates(C# 2.0
onwards)***");
ShowVehicleTypeDelegate del1 = vehicle1.ShowVehicle;
del1();
//Note that it is expecting a Vehicle(i.e. a basetype) but
received a Bus(subtype)
//Still this is allowed through Covariance
ShowVehicleTypeDelegate del2 = bus1.ShowBus;
del2();
Console.ReadKey();
        }
    }
}
```

Output

```
***Covariance in delegates(C# 2.0 onwards)***
A Vehicle created
A Bus created
```

Analysis

In the preceding program, we can see that compiler did not complain about this line:

```
ShowVehicleTypeDelegate del2 = bus1.ShowBus;
```

Although our delegate return type was Vehicle, its del2 object received a derived type "Bus" object.

Contravariance in Delegates

Contravariance is related to parameters. Suppose that a delegate can point to a method that accepts a derived type parameter. With the help of contravariance, we can use the same delegate to point to a method that accepts a base type parameter.

Demonstration 5

```
using System;

namespace ContravariancewithDelegatesEx1
{
    class Vehicle
    {
        public void ShowVehicle(Vehicle myV)
        {
            Console.WriteLine(" Vehicle.ShowVehicle");
        }
    }
    class Bus : Vehicle
    {
        public void ShowBus(Bus myB)
        {
            Console.WriteLine("Bus.ShowBus");
        }
    }
    class Program
    {
        public delegate void TakingDerivedTypeParameterDelegate(Bus v);
        static void Main(string[] args)
        {
            Vehicle vehicle1 = new Vehicle();//ok
            Bus bus1 = new Bus();//ok
            Console.WriteLine("***Exploring Contravariance with C#
            delegates***");
            //General case
            TakingDerivedTypeParameterDelegate del1 = bus1.ShowBus;
            del1(bus1);
            //Special case:
            //Contravariance:
```

```
/*Note that the delegate expected a method that accepts a
bus(derived) object parameter but still it can point to the
method that accepts vehicle(base) object parameter*/
TakingDerivedTypeParameterDelegate del2 = vehicle1.ShowVehicle;
del2(bus1);
//Additional note:you cannot pass vehicle object here
//del2(vehicle1);//error
Console.ReadKey();
        }
    }
}
```

Output

```
***Exploring Contravariance with C# delegates***
Bus.ShowBus
Vehicle.ShowVehicle
```

Analysis

Go through the program and the supported commented line to understand
the code better. We can see from the preceding example that our delegate,
TakingDerivedTypeParameterDelegate, expects a method that accepts a bus (derived)
object parameter, yet it can point to a method that accepts vehicle as a (base) object
parameter.

Events

Teacher says: Events are used to notify or signal that a state of an object is changed. This information is useful for the clients of that object (e.g., a mouse-click or a key press in a GUI application are very common example of events).

In a real-world scenario, consider a social media platform such as Facebook. Whenever we update any of our information on Facebook, our friends are notified immediately. (This is a very common example of an observer design pattern). So, you can assume that when you make some changes to your Facebook page, internally, some events are fired so that your friends can get those updates. These updates are received by only those people who are already on our friend list (i.e., we have accepted them as our friends). In programming terminology, we say that these people are registered in our friend list. If someone does not want to get updates, he/she can simply unregister from that friend list. Therefore, the terms "register and unregister" are associated with events.

Before we go forward, we must remember the following points:

- Events are associated with delegates. To understand events, you should learn delegates first. When an event occurs, the delegates given to it by its clients are invoked.

- In .NET, events are implemented as multicast delegates.

- A publisher-subscriber model is followed here. A publisher (or broadcaster) publishes a notification (or information) and the subscriber receives this notification. But subscribers have the freedom when to start listening and when to stop listening (in programming terms, when to register and when to unregister).

- Publisher is the type that contains the delegate. Subscribers register themselves by using += on the publisher's delegate and unregister themselves by using -= on that delegate. So, when we apply += or -= to an event, they have a special meaning (in other words, they are not shortcuts for assignments in these cases).

- Subscribers do not talk to each other. Actually ,these are the key goals of supporting an event architecture:

  - Subscribers cannot communicate with each other.

  - We can make a loosely coupled system.

- If we use Visual Studio IDE, it makes our life extremely easy when we deal with events. But I believe that these concepts are the core of C#, and so it's better to learn from the basics.

- The .NET framework provides a generic delegate that supports the standard event design patterns, as follows:

```
public delegate void EventHandler<TEventArgs>(object sendersource,
TEventArgs e) where TEventArgs : EventArgs;
```

Until now, you have not learned about C# generics. To support backward compatibility, most of the events in the .NET framework follow the *non-generic custom delegate* pattern that we have used here.

Steps to Implement a Simple Event in C#

(Here we will try to follow the most widely accepted naming conventions.)

Step 1: Create a Publisher class

> #1.1. Create a delegate. (First, choose a name for your event, let's say JobDone. Then create a delegate with a name like JobDoneEventHandler).

> #1.2. Create the event (using the event keyword) based on the delegate.

> #1.3. Raise the event. (The standard pattern requires that the method should be tagged with protected virtual. Also, the name must match the name of the event and be prefixed with On).

Step 2: Create a Subscriber class.

> #2.1.Write an event handler method. The name of the event handler method starts with On by convention.

Let's go through the program.

Demonstration 6

```
using System;

namespace EventEx1
{
    //Step1-Create a publisher
    class Publisher
    {
        //Step1.1-Create a delegate.Delegate name should be
        //"yourEventName"+EventHandler
        public delegate void JobDoneEventHandler(object sender, EventArgs
        args);
        //Step1.2-Create the event based on the delgate
        public event JobDoneEventHandler JobDone;
        public void ProcessOneJob()
        {
            Console.WriteLine("Publisher:One Job is processed");
            //Step1.3-Raise the event
            OnJobDone();
        }
        /*The standard pattern requires that the method should be tagged
        with protected virtual. Also the name must match name of the event
        and it will be prefixed with "On".*/
        protected virtual void OnJobDone()
        {
            if (JobDone != null)
                JobDone(this, EventArgs.Empty);
        }

    }
    //Step2-Create a subscriber
    class Subscriber
    {
        //Handling the event
        public void OnJobDoneEventHandler(object sender, EventArgs args)
        {
```

```
            Console.WriteLine("Subscriber is notified");
        }
    }
    class Program
    {
        static void Main(string[] args)
        {
            Console.WriteLine("***A simple event demo***");
            Publisher sender = new Publisher();
            Subscriber receiver = new Subscriber();
            sender.JobDone += receiver.OnJobDoneEventHandler;
            sender.ProcessOneJob();

            Console.ReadKey();
        }
    }
}
```

Output

```
***A simple event demo***
Publisher:One Job is processed
 Subscriber is notified
```

Students ask:

Sir, can we subscribe multiple event handlers to a single event?

Teacher says: Yes. Events are implemented as multicast delegates in C#, so we can associate multiple event handlers to a single event. Suppose we have two subscribers: Subscriber1 and Subscriber2, and both of them want to get notification from the Publisher. The following codes will work fine:

```
Publisher sender = new Publisher();
Subscriber1 receiver = new Subscriber1();
Subscriber2 receiver2 = new Subscriber2();
sender.JobDone += receiver.OnJobDoneEventHandler;
sender.JobDone += receiver2.OnJobDoneEventHandler;
sender.ProcessOneJob();
```

POINTS TO REMEMBER

In real world coding, you have to be careful about these subscriptions (e.g., in your application you are only doing the registrations through events, and then after some period of time you observe memory leaks as a side effect. As a result, your application will be slow (it could crash). Garbage collectors cannot recollect these memories if you do not put unsubscribe operations in the proper places.

Passing Data with Event Arguments

If you look at the preceding program once again, you'll see that we did not pass anything specific with the event argument.

```
    * Also the name must match name of the even
protected virtual void OnJobDone()
{
    if (JobDone != null)
        JobDone(this, EventArgs.Empty);
}
```

In real-world programming, we need to pass more information than EventArgs. Empty (or null). And in those scenarios, we need to follow these steps:

1. Create a subclass of System.EventArgs.

2. Encapsulate the intended data with the event. In the following example, we have used a property.

3. Create an instance of this class and pass it with the event.

To better demonstrate, I have slightly modified the earlier program.

Demonstration 7

```
using System;

namespace EventEx2
{
    //Step-a. Create a subclass of System.EventArgs
    public class JobNoEventArgs : EventArgs
    {
        //Step-b.Encapsulate your intended data with the event. In the
        below example, we have used a property.
        private int jobNo;
        public int JobNo
        {
            get
            {
                return jobNo;
            }
            set
            {
                JobNo = value;
            }
        }
        public JobNoEventArgs(int jobNo)
        {
            this.jobNo = jobNo;
        }
    }
    //Step1-Create a publisher
    class Publisher
    {
        //Step1.1-Create a delegate.Delegate name should be
        "yourEventName"+EventHandler
        //public delegate void JobDoneEventHandler(object sender, EventArgs
        args);
```

```csharp
        public delegate void JobDoneEventHandler(object sender,
        JobNoEventArgs args);
        //Step1.2-Create the event based on the delgate
        public event JobDoneEventHandler JobDone;
        public void ProcessOneJob()
        {
            Console.WriteLine("Publisher:One Job is processed");
            //Step1.3-Raise the event
            OnJobDone();
        }
        /*The standard pattern requires that the method should be tagged
        with protected virtual.
        Also the name must match name of the event and it will be
        prefixed with "On".*/
        protected virtual void OnJobDone()
        {
            if (JobDone != null)
                //Step-c. Lastly create an instance of the event generator
                class and pass it with the event.
                JobDone(this,new JobNoEventArgs(1));
        }
    }
    //Step2-Create a subscriber
    class Subscriber
    {
        //Handling the event
        public void OnJobDoneEventHandler(object sender, JobNoEventArgs args)
        {
            Console.WriteLine("Subscriber is notified.Number of job
            processed is :{0}",args.JobNo);
        }
    }

    class Program
    {
        static void Main(string[] args)
```

```
    {
        Console.WriteLine("*** Event example 2:Passing data with
        events***");
        Publisher sender = new Publisher();
        Subscriber receiver = new Subscriber();
        sender.JobDone += receiver.OnJobDoneEventHandler;
        sender.ProcessOneJob();
        Console.ReadKey();
    }
  }
}
```

Output

```
*** Event example 2:Passing data with events***
Publisher:One Job is processed
 Subscriber is notified.Number of job processed is :1
```

Analysis

Now we can see that by following the preceding mechanism, we can get additional information (the number of jobs processed) when we are raising the event.

Event Accessors

Go back to our first program on events (EventEx1), where we declared the event as

```
public event JobDoneEventHandler JobDone;
```

The compiler converts this with a private delegate field and supplies two event accessors: add and remove.

The following codes will produce the equivalent behavior:

```
//public event JobDoneEventHandler JobDone;
#region custom event accessors
private JobDoneEventHandler _JobDone;
public event JobDoneEventHandler JobDone
{
  add
  {
   _JobDone += value;
  }
 remove
  {
   _JobDone -= value;
  }
}
#endregion
```

If you use these codes in this program, you need to modify our OnJobDone() method, like this:

```
protected virtual void OnJobDone()
{
    //if (JobDone != null)
    //    JobDone(this, EventArgs.Empty);
    //for custom event accessor
    if (_JobDone != null)
        _JobDone(this, EventArgs.Empty);
}
```

If you want to verify our claim, you can simply refer to the IL code.

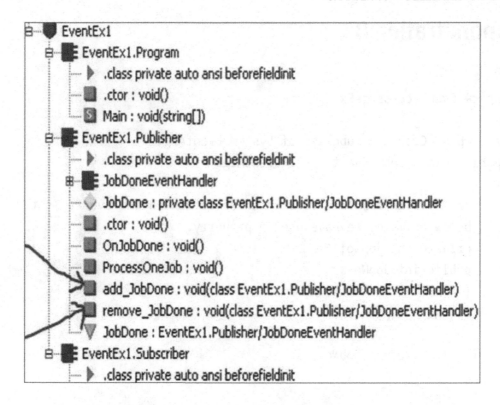

From the IL code, we can see that add and remove parts are compiled to add_<EventName> and remove_<EventName>.

If the compiler is doing everything for us, then why do we need to bother with these details? The simple answers are

- We define these accessors ourselves to take additional control (e.g., we may want to place some special type of validations or we may want to log more information, etc.)

- Sometimes we need to implement an interface explicitly and that interface may contain one or more events.

Now modify our EventEx2 program slightly. In this case, we are using custom accessor and logging some additional information. Let's go through the following program and output.

Demonstration 8

```
using System;

namespace EventAccessorsEx1
{
    //Step-a. Create a subclass of System.EventArgs
    public class JobNoEventArgs : EventArgs
    {
        //Step-b.Encapsulate your intended data with the event. In the
        below example, we have used a property.
        private int jobNo;
        public int JobNo
        {
            get
            {
                return jobNo;
            }
            set
            {
                JobNo = value;
            }
        }
        public JobNoEventArgs(int jobNo)
        {
            this.jobNo = jobNo;
        }
    }
    //Step1-Create a publisher
    class Publisher
    {
        //Step1.1-Create a delegate.Delegate name should be
        "yourEventName"+EventHandler
        //public delegate void JobDoneEventHandler(object sender, EventArgs
        args);
```

```csharp
public delegate void JobDoneEventHandler(object sender,
JobNoEventArgs args);
//Step1.2-Create the event based on the delgate
//public event JobDoneEventHandler JobDone;
#region custom event accessors
private JobDoneEventHandler _JobDone;
public event JobDoneEventHandler JobDone
{
    add
    {
        Console.WriteLine("Inside add accessor-Entry");
        _JobDone += value;
    }
    remove
    {
        _JobDone -= value;
        Console.WriteLine("Unregister completed-Exit from remove
        accessor");
    }
}
#endregion
public void ProcessOneJob()
{
    Console.WriteLine("Publisher:One Job is processed");
    //Step1.3-Raise the event
    OnJobDone();
}
/*The standard pattern requires that the method should be tagged
with protected virtual.
 * Also the name must match name of the event and it will be
 prefixed with "On".*/
protected virtual void OnJobDone()
{
    if (_JobDone != null)
        //Step-c. Lastly create an instance of the event generator
        class and pass it with the event.
```

271

```csharp
                _JobDone(this, new JobNoEventArgs(1));
        }
    }
    //Step2-Create a subscriber
    class Subscriber
    {
        //Handling the event
        public void OnJobDoneEventHandler(object sender, JobNoEventArgs args)
        {
            Console.WriteLine(" Subscriber is notified.Number of job
            processed is :{0}", args.JobNo);
        }
    }

    class Program
    {
        static void Main(string[] args)
        {
            Console.WriteLine("*** Testing custom event accessors***");
            Publisher sender = new Publisher();
            Subscriber receiver = new Subscriber();
            //Subscribe/Register
            sender.JobDone += receiver.OnJobDoneEventHandler;
            sender.ProcessOneJob();
            //Unsubscribe/Unregister
            sender.JobDone -= receiver.OnJobDoneEventHandler;
            Console.ReadKey();
        }
    }
}
```

Output

```
*** Testing custom event accessors***
Inside add accessor-Entry ←
Publisher:One Job is processed
 Subscriber is notified.Number of job processed is :1
Unregister completed-Exit from remove accessor ←
```

When you apply a custom event accessor, it is suggested that you implement the locking mechanism also; that is, we could write it like this:

```csharp
#region custom event accessors
private JobDoneEventHandler _JobDone;
public object lockObject = new object();
public event JobDoneEventHandler JobDone
{
    add
    {
        lock (lockObject)
        {
            Console.WriteLine("Inside add accessor-Entry");
            _JobDone += value;
        }
    }
    remove
    {
        lock (lockObject)
        {
            _JobDone -= value;
            Console.WriteLine("Unregister completed-Exit from remove accessor");
        }
    }
}
```

In general, locking operations are expensive. To make our example simple, I have ignored that suggestion here.

Students ask:

Sir, what type of modifiers are allowed for events?

Teacher says: Since we have used virtual keyword already, you can guess that overridden events are allowed. Events can be abstract, sealed, or static too.

Summary

This chapter covered

- ✓ Delegates and their importance

- ✓ How delegates can be used in our program

- ✓ Why delegates are type safe

- ✓ Multicast delegates

- ✓ How to achieve covariance and contravariance using delegates

- ✓ Events and how to use them

- ✓ How to pass data with event arguments

- ✓ Event accessors and how to use them

CHAPTER 11

Flexibilities with Anonymous Functions

Anonymous Methods and Lamda Expressions

Teacher starts the discussion: Let's go back to our delegate program (DelegateEx1). I have added few lines of code to that program to generate the same output. To help you to understand the differences among invocations, I have kept the old stuffs as it is.

Notice the additional stuff. These additional blocks of code can help you better understand anonymous methods and lambda expressions. Anonymous methods were introduced in C# 2.0 and lambda expressions were introduced in C# 3.0.

As the name suggests, a method without a name is an anonymous method in C#. The main goal of an anonymous method is to complete an action quickly, even if we write less code. It is a block of code that can be used as a delegate's parameter.

Similarly, a lambda expression is a method without a name. It is used in place of a delegate instance. The compiler can covert these expressions to either a delegate instance or an expression tree. (The discussion of expression trees is beyond the scope of this book.)

In the following demonstration, two additional blocks of code have been added: one for the anonymous method and one for lambda expressions. Each of these generates the same output.

© Vaskaran Sarcar 2018
V. Sarcar, *Interactive C#*, https://doi.org/10.1007/978-1-4842-3339-9_11

Demonstration 1

```
using System;

namespace LambdaExpressionEx1
{
    public delegate int Mydel(int x, int y);

    class Program
    {
        public static int Sum(int a, int b) { return a + b; }

        static void Main(string[] args)
        {
            Console.WriteLine("*** Exploring Lambda Expression***");
            //Without using delgates or lambda expression
            int a = 25, b = 37;
            Console.WriteLine("\n Calling Sum method without using a
            delegate:");
            Console.WriteLine("Sum of a and b is : {0}", Sum(a, b));

            //Using Delegate( Initialization with a named method)
            Mydel del = new Mydel(Sum);
            Console.WriteLine("\n Using delegate now:");
            Console.WriteLine("Calling Sum method with the use of a
            delegate:");
            Console.WriteLine("Sum of a and b is: {0}", del(a, b));

            //Using Anonymous method(C# 2.0 onwards)
            Mydel del2 = delegate (int x, int y) { return x + y; };
            Console.WriteLine("\n Using Anonymous method now:");
            Console.WriteLine("Calling Sum method with the use of an
            anonymous method:");
            Console.WriteLine("Sum of a and b is: {0}", del2(a, b));

            //Using Lambda expression(C# 3.0 onwards)
            Console.WriteLine("\n Using Lambda Expresson now:");
            Mydel sumOfTwoIntegers = (x1, y1) => x1 + y1;
```

```
        Console.WriteLine("Sum of a and b is: {0}", sumOfTwoIntegers(a,
        b));
        Console.ReadKey();
    }
  }
}
```

Output

```
*** Exploring Lambda Expression***

 Calling Sum method without using a delegate:
Sum of a and b is : 62

 Using delegate now:
Calling Sum method with the use of a delegate:
Sum of a and b is: 62

 Using Anonymous method now:
Calling Sum method with the use of an anonymous method:
Sum of a and b is: 62

 Using Lambda Expresson now:
Sum of a and b is: 62
```

Analysis

The following are the key characteristics of a lambda expression:

- It is an anonymous method (or unnamed methods), written instead of a delegate instance.

- It can contain expressions or statements to create delegates or an expression tree (LINQ queries and expression trees are beyond the scope of this book).

Notice that we have the following delegate:

```
public delegate int Mydel(int x, int y);
```

And we have assigned and invoked a lambda expression as

```
(x1, y1) => x1 + y1
```

So, you can see that each parameter of the lambda expression corresponds to delegate parameters (x1 to x, y1 to y in this case) and the type of the expression (x+y is an *int* in this case) corresponds to return the type of the delegate.

- Lambda operator => (pronounced *goes to*) is used in lambda expressions. It has the right associativity and its precedence is same as the assignment (=) operator.

- The input parameters are specified on the left side of the lambda operator, and the expression or statement is specified on the right side of the lambda operator.

- We can omit parentheses if our lambda expression has only one parameter; for example, we can write something like this to calculate the square of a number:

  x=>x*x

POINTS TO REMEMBER

- Anonymous methods were introduced in C# 2.0 and lambda expressions were introduced in C# 3.0.They are similar, but lambda expressions are more concise and experts suggest that if your application is targeting .NET Framework version 3.5 or above, you should prefer lambda expressions to anonymous methods in general. These two features are known as anonymous functions in C#.

- You should avoid using unsafe code and jump statements such as *break, goto* and *continue* inside the body of an anonymous method.

Students ask:

Then we should always try to use anonymous method because it is faster and code size is smaller. Is this correct?

Teacher says: No. See the restrictions associated with anonymous methods. Also, if you need to write similar functionalities multiple times, you must avoid anonymous methods.

Func, Action, and Predicate Delegates

Author's Note: Now we will quickly cover three important generic delegates. I am placing the topic here because they easily relate to lambda expression and anonymous methods. We are going to discuss on generics shortly. So, if you already have a basic idea about generic programming, you can continue; otherwise, return here once you learn more about them.

Func Delegates

There are many forms of the Func delegate. They can take 0 to 16 input parameters but always have one return type. Consider the following method:

```
private static string ShowStudent(string name, int rollNo)
 {
  return string.Format("Student Name is :{0} and  Roll Number is :{1}",
  name, rollNo);
 }
```

To invoke this method using a delegate, we need to follow these steps:

Step 1. Define a delegate something like this:

```
public delegate string Mydel(string n, int r);
```

Step 2. Attach the method with the delegate like this:

```
Mydel myDelOb = new Mydel (ShowStudent);
```

Or in short,

```
Mydel myDelOb = ShowStudent;
```

Step 3. Now, you can invoke the method like this:

```
myDelOb.Invoke ("Jon", 5);
```

Or simply with

```
myDelOb ("Jon", 5);
```

But we can make the code simpler and shorter using the readymade/inbuilt delegate Func in this case, as shown here:

```
Func<string, int, string> student = new Func<string, int,
string>(ShowStudent);
Console.WriteLine(ShowStudent("Amit", 1));
```

So, you can predict that this Func delegate is perfectly considering both input types—string and int—with the return type string. If you move your cursor on this, in Visual Studio, you can see that last parameter is considered as the return type of the function, and the others are considered input type.

```
Func<string, int, string> student = new Func<string, int, string>(ShowStudent);
```

delegate TResult System.Func<in T1, in T2, out TResult>(T1 arg1, T2 arg2)
Encapsulates a method that has two parameters and returns a value of the type specified by the TResult parameter.

T1 is string
T2 is int
TResult is string

Students ask:

Sir, we have different kinds of methods that can take a different number of input parameters. How can we use Func in functions that consider more than or less than two input parameters, unlike the preceding method?

Teacher says: Func delegates can consider 0 to 16 input parameters. So, we can use any of these forms:

```
Func<T, TResult>
Func<T1, T2, TResult>
Func<T1, T2, T3, TResult>
.....
Func<T1, T2, T3..., T15, T16, TResult>
```

Action Delegates

Action delegates can take 1 to 16 input parameters but do not have a return type. So, suppose we have a SumOfThreeNumbers method that takes three input parameters and whose return type is void, as follows:

```
private static void SumOfThreeNumbers(int i1, int i2, int i3)
    {
        int sum = i1 + i2 + i3;
        Console.WriteLine("Sum of {0},{1} and {2} is: {3}", i1, i2, i3,
        sum);
    }
```

We can use an action delegate to get the sum of three integers, as follows:

```
Action<int, int, int> sum = new Action<int, int, int>(SumOfThreeNumbers);
        sum(10, 3, 7);
```

Predicate Delegates

Predicate delegates are used to evaluate something. For example, a method defines some criteria and we need to check whether an object can meet the criteria. Consider the following method:

```
private static bool GreaterThan100(int myInt)
    {
        return myInt > 100 ? true : false;
    }
```

We can see that this method evaluates whether an input is greater than 100 or not. We can use a predicate delegate to perform the same test, as follows:

```
Predicate<int> isGreater = new Predicate<int>(GreaterThan100);
Console.WriteLine("125 is greater than 100? {0}", isGreater(125));
Console.WriteLine("60 is greater than 100? {0}", isGreater(60));
```

The following program demonstrates all of these concepts with a simple program.

Demonstration 2

```csharp
using System;

namespace Test1_FuncVsActionVsPredicate
{
    class Program
    {
        static void Main(string[] args)
        {
            Console.WriteLine("***Testing Func vs Action vs Predicate***");
            //Func
            Console.WriteLine("<---Using Func--->");
            Func<string, int, string> student = new Func<string, int,
            string>(ShowStudent);
            Console.WriteLine(ShowStudent("Amit", 1));
            Console.WriteLine(ShowStudent("Sumit", 2));
            //Action
            Console.WriteLine("<---Using Action--->");
            Action<int, int, int> sum = new Action<int, int,
            int>(SumOfThreeNumbers);
            sum(10, 3, 7);
            sum(5, 10, 15);

            //Predicate
            Console.WriteLine("<---Using Predicate--->");
            Predicate<int> isGreater = new Predicate<int>(GreaterThan100);
            Console.WriteLine("125 is greater than 100? {0}",
            isGreater(125));
            Console.WriteLine("60 is greater than 100? {0}",
            isGreater(60));

            Console.ReadKey();
        }
```

```csharp
    private static string ShowStudent(string name, int rollNo)
    {
        return string.Format("Student Name is :{0} and  Roll Number is
        :{1}", name, rollNo);
    }
    private static void SumOfThreeNumbers(int i1, int i2, int i3)
    {
        int sum = i1 + i2 + i3;
        Console.WriteLine("Sum of {0},{1} and {2} is: {3}", i1, i2, i3,
        sum);
    }
    private static bool GreaterThan100(int myInt)
    {
        return myInt > 100 ? true : false;
    }
    }
}
```

Output

```
***Testing Func vs Action vs Predicate***
<---Using Func--->
Student Name is :Amit and  Roll Number is :1
Student Name is :Sumit and  Roll Number is :2
<---Using Action--->
Sum of 10,3 and 7 is: 20
Sum of 5,10 and 15 is: 30
<---Using Predicate--->
125 is greater than 100? True
60 is greater than 100? False
```

Summary

This chapter discussed the following:

- ✓ Anonymous methods
- ✓ Lambda expressions
- ✓ Func, action, and predicate delegates
- ✓ How these concepts can be used effectively in a C# application

CHAPTER 12

Generics

Comparison between Generic and Non-Generic Programs

Teacher starts the discussion: Generics are one of the key concepts of C#. They came in C# 2.0, and since then, they have expanded with additional features.

To understand the power of generics, we will start with a non-generic program and then write a generic program. Later, we will do a comparative analysis and then we will try to discover the advantages of generic programming. Consider the following program and the output.

Demonstration 1: A Non-Generic Program

```
using System;

namespace NonGenericEx
{
    class NonGenericEx
    {
        public int ShowInteger(int i)
        {
            return i;
        }
        public string ShowString(string s1)
        {
            return s1;
        }
    }
```

© Vaskaran Sarcar 2018
V. Sarcar, *Interactive C#*, https://doi.org/10.1007/978-1-4842-3339-9_12

```
    class Program
    {
        static void Main(string[] args)
        {
            Console.WriteLine("***A non-generic program example***");
            NonGenericEx nonGenericOb = new NonGenericEx();
            Console.WriteLine("ShowInteger returns :{0}", nonGenericOb.
            ShowInteger(25));
            Console.WriteLine("ShowString returns :{0}", nonGenericOb.
            ShowString("Non Generic method called"));
            Console.ReadKey();
        }
    }
}
```

Output

```
***A non-generic program example***
ShowInteger returns :25
ShowString returns :Non Generic method called
```

Now let's try to introduce a generic program. Before we start, these are the key points:

- The angle brackets <> are used to create generic classes.

- We can define a class with placeholders for the type of its methods, fields, parameters etc. and in a generic program; these placeholders will be replaced with the particular type.

- Microsoft states: "Generic classes and methods combine reusability, type safety, and efficiency in a way that their non-generic counterparts cannot. Generics are most frequently used with collections and the methods that operate on them. Version 2.0 of the .NET Framework class library provides a new namespace, System.Collections.Generic, which contains several new generic-based collection classes. It is recommended that all applications that target the .NET Framework 2.0 and later use the new generic collection classes instead of the older non-generic counterparts such as ArrayList." (See https://docs.microsoft.com/en-us/dotnet/ csharp/programming-guide/generics/introduction-to-generics.)

Let's start with the following program.

Demonstration 2: A Generic Program

```
using System;

namespace GenericProgrammingEx1
{
    class MyGenericClass<T>
    {
        public T Show(T value)
        {
            return value;
        }
    }
    class Program
    {
        static void Main(string[] args)
        {
            Console.WriteLine("***Introduction to Generics***");
            MyGenericClass<int> myGenericClassIntOb = new
            MyGenericClass<int>();
            Console.WriteLine("Show returns :{0}", myGenericClassIntOb.
            Show(100));
            MyGenericClass<string> myGenericClassStringOb = new
            MyGenericClass<string>();
            Console.WriteLine("Show returns :{0}", myGenericClassStringOb.
            Show("Generic method called"));
            MyGenericClass<double> myGenericClassDoubleOb = new
            MyGenericClass<double>();
```

```
        Console.WriteLine("Show returns :{0}", myGenericClassDoubleOb.
        Show(100.5));

        Console.ReadKey();
    }
  }
}
```

Output

```
***Introduction to Generics***
Show returns :100
Show returns :Generic method called
Show returns :100.5
```

Analysis

We can do a comparative analysis of Demonstration 1 and Demonstration 2 now. We have seen the following characteristics:

- For non-generic methods, we need to specify methods like `ShowInteger()` and `ShowString()` to handle the particular data types. For the generic version, on the other hand, `Show()`is sufficient. In general, there are fewer lines of code in generic versions (i.e., code size is smaller).

- Inside `Main()` in Demonstration 1, we encounter a compile-time error in the second line, as follows:

```
Console.WriteLine("ShowDouble returns :{0}", nonGenericOb.
ShowDouble(25.5));//error
```

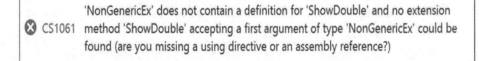

> ⊗ CS1061   'NonGenericEx' does not contain a definition for 'ShowDouble' and no extension method 'ShowDouble' accepting a first argument of type 'NonGenericEx' could be found (are you missing a using directive or an assembly reference?)

The reason for this is : In this example, we did not define a `'ShowDouble(double d)'` method. So, to avoid this error, we need to include an additional method in the class, NonGenericEx, as follows:

```
class NonGenericEx
{
    public int ShowInteger(int i)
    {
        return i;
    }
    public string ShowString(string s1)
    {
        return s1;
    }
    public double ShowDouble(double d)
    {
        return d;
    }
}
```

Further Analysis

The code size of our NonGenericEx class increases with this addition. We needed to increase the code size because we are now trying to process a different data type "double."

Now look at to Demonstration 2, where we are getting the double data type without modifying our MyGenericClass. As a result, we can conclude that the generic version is more flexible.

Note

In general, generic programming is more flexible than non-generic programming and requires fewer lines of codes.

Consider the following program.

Demonstration 3

```
using System;
using System.Collections;

namespace GenericEx2
{
    class Program
    {
        static void Main(string[] args)
        {
            Console.WriteLine("***Use Generics to avoid runtime error***");
            ArrayList myList = new ArrayList();
            myList.Add(10);
            myList.Add(20);
            myList.Add("Invalid");//No compile time error but will cause
            //runtime error
            foreach (int myInt in myList)
            {
                Console.WriteLine((int)myInt); //downcasting
            }
            Console.ReadKey();
        }
    }

}
```

Output

The program will not raise any compile-time errors.

```
========== Build: 1 succeeded, 0 failed, 0 up-to-date, 0 skipped ==========
```

But at runtime, we encounter this error:

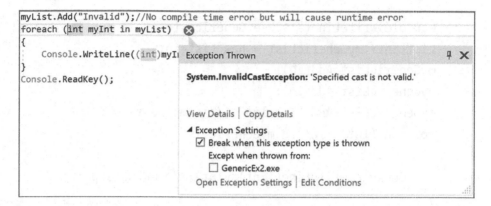

This is because the third element (i.e., myList [2] in our ArrayList) is not an integer (it is a string). During compile time, we did not encounter any issues because it was stored as an object. Notice the snapshot taken from visual studio:

> myList.Add("Invalid");
>
> int ArrayList.Add(**object value**)
> Adds an object to the end of the System.Collections.ArrayList.
> **value:** *The System.Object to be added to the end of the System.Collections.ArrayList. The value can be null.*

Analysis

In this type of programing, we may face performance overhead due to boxing and downcasting.

Now consider the following program.

Demonstration 4

```
using System;
using System.Collections.Generic;

namespace GenericEx3
{
    class Program
    {
```

```
        static void Main(string[] args)
        {
            Console.WriteLine("***Use Generics to avoid runtime error***");
            List<int> myGenericList = new List<int>();
            myGenericList.Add(10);
            myGenericList.Add(20);
            myGenericList.Add("Invalid");// compile time error
            foreach (int myInt in myGenericList)
            {
                Console.WriteLine((int)myInt);//downcasting
            }
            Console.ReadKey();
        }
    }
}
```

Output

> ❌ CS1503   Argument 1: cannot convert from 'string' to 'int'

In this case, we cannot add a string in myGenericList because it was intended to hold integers only. The error is caught during compile time; we do not need to wait until runtime to get this error.

Analysis

By comparing Demonstration 3 and Demonstration 4, we can say that

- To avoid runtime errors, we should prefer the generic version of code to the non-generic version.

- If we use generic programming, we can avoid penalties caused by boxing/unboxing.

- We can use List<string> myGenericList2 = new List<string>();
  to create a list that will hold the strings. The List<T> version is more
  flexible and usable than ArrayList, the non-generic version.

Demonstration 5: Exercise on Self-Referenced Generic Types

Let's suppose that in your employee class you have employee IDs and department names. Write a simple program to decide whether two employees are the same or not. But the constraint for you is that your class should derive from a generic interface that defines the specification for this comparison method.

The following demonstration can be treated as a sample implementation for the requirement.

```
using System;

namespace GenericEx4
{
    interface ISameEmployee<T>
    {
        string CheckForIdenticalEmployee(T obj);
    }
    class Employee : ISameEmployee<Employee>
    {
        string deptName;
        int employeeID;
        public Employee(string deptName, int employeeId)
        {
            this.deptName = deptName;
            this.employeeID = employeeId;
        }
        public string CheckForIdenticalEmployee(Employee obj)
        {
            if (obj == null)
            {
                return "Cannot Compare with a Null Object";
```

```
            }
            else
            {
                if (this.deptName == obj.deptName && this.employeeID ==
                obj.employeeID)
                {
                    return "Same Employee";
                }
                else
                {
                    return "Different Employee";
                }
            }
        }
    }
    class Program
    {
        static void Main(string[] args)
        {
            Console.WriteLine("**Suppose, we have an  Employee class that
            contains deptName and employeeID***");
            Console.WriteLine("***We need to check whether 2 employee
            objects are same or not.***");
            Console.WriteLine();
            Employee emp1 = new Employee("Maths", 1);
            Employee emp2 = new Employee("Maths", 2);
            Employee emp3 = new Employee("Comp. Sc.", 1);
            Employee emp4 = new Employee("Maths", 2);
            Employee emp5=null;
            Console.WriteLine("Comparing Emp1 and Emp3 :{0}", emp1.CheckFor
            IdenticalEmployee(emp3));
            Console.WriteLine("Comparing Emp2 and Emp4 :{0}", emp2.CheckFor
            IdenticalEmployee(emp4));
```

```
        Console.WriteLine("Comparing Emp3 and Emp5 :{0}", emp3.CheckFor
        IdenticalEmployee(emp5));
        Console.ReadKey();
      }
    }
}
```

Output

```
**Suppose, we have an  Employee class that contains deptName and employeeID***
***We need to check whether 2 employee objects are same or not.***

Comparing Emp1 and Emp3 :Different Employee
Comparing Emp2 and Emp4 :Same Employee
Comparing Emp3 and Emp5 :Cannot Compare with a Null Object
```

Analysis

This is an example of where a type names itself as a concrete type (in other words, it is an example of a self-referenced generic type).

A Special Keyword Default

We are familiar with the use of the *default* keyword in switch statements, where *default* is used to refer to a default case. In the context of generics, it has a special meaning. Here we use *default* to initialize generic types with their default values (e.g., the default value for a reference type is null and the default value of a value type is bitwise zero).

Consider the following example.

Demonstration 6

```
using System;
namespace CaseStudyWithDefault
{
    class Program
    {
```

```
    static void Main(string[] args)
    {
        Console.WriteLine("***Case study- default keyword***");
        Console.WriteLine("default(int) is {0}", default(int));//0
        bool b1 = (default(int) == null);//False
        Console.WriteLine("default(int) is null ?Answer: {0}", b1);
        Console.WriteLine("default(string) is {0}", default(string));
        //null
        bool b2 = (default(string) == null);//True
        Console.WriteLine("default(string) is  null ? Answer:{0}", b2);
        Console.ReadKey();
    }
  }
}
```

Output

```
***Case study- default keyword***
default(int) is 0
default(int) is null ?Answer: False
default(string) is
default(string) is  null ? Answer:True
```

Analysis

We must remember that int is a value type and string is a reference type. So, you can now check their default values with the preceding program and output.

Demonstration 7: Assignment

Let's suppose that you have a storehouse where you can store up to three objects. To store these objects, you can use an array. Write a generic program through which you can store/retrieve different types in that storehouse. Use the concept of the *default* keyword to initialize the array with its respective types.

The following demonstration can be treated as a sample implementation for the requirement.

```csharp
using System;

namespace Assignment
{
    public class MyStoreHouse<T>
    {
        T[] myStore = new T[3];
        int position = 0;
        public MyStoreHouse()
        {
            for (int i = 0; i < myStore.Length; i++)
            {
                myStore[i] = default(T);
            }
        }
        public void AddToStore(T value)
        {
            if (position < myStore.Length)
            {
                myStore[position] = value;
                position++;
            }
            else
            {
                Console.WriteLine("Store is full already");
            }
        }

        public void RetrieveFromStore()
        {
            foreach (T t in myStore)
            {
                Console.WriteLine(t);
            }
```

```
            //Or Use this block
            //for (int i = 0; i < myStore.Length; i++)
            //{
            //     Console.WriteLine(myStore[i]);
            //}

        }
    }
    class Program
    {
        static void Main(string[] args)
        {
            Console.WriteLine("***Use case-default keyword in generic
            programming:***");
            Console.WriteLine("***\nCreating an Integer store:***");
            MyStoreHouse<int> intStore = new MyStoreHouse<int>();
            intStore.AddToStore(45);
            intStore.AddToStore(75);
            Console.WriteLine("***Integer store at this moment:***");
            intStore.RetrieveFromStore();

            Console.WriteLine("***\nCreating an String store:***");
            MyStoreHouse<string> strStore = new MyStoreHouse<string>();
            strStore.AddToStore("abc");
            strStore.AddToStore("def");
            strStore.AddToStore("ghi");
            strStore.AddToStore("jkl");//Store is full already
            Console.WriteLine("***String store at this moment:***");
            strStore.RetrieveFromStore();
            Console.ReadKey();
        }
    }

}
```

Output

```
***Use case-default keyword in generic programming:***
***
Creating an Integer store:***
***Integer store at this moment:***
45
75
0
***
Creating an String store:***
Store is full already
***String store at this moment:***
abc
def
ghi
```

Generic Constraints

Consider the following program and output, and then follow the analysis.

Demonstration 8

```csharp
using System;
using System.Collections.Generic;

namespace GenericConstraintEx
{
    interface IEmployee
    {
        string Position();
    }
    class Employee : IEmployee
    {
        public string Name;
        public int yearOfExp;
        public Employee(string name, int years)
        {
            this.Name = name;
```

```csharp
            this.yearOfExp = years;
        }
        public string Position()
        {
            if (yearOfExp < 5)
            {
                return " A Junior Employee";
            }
            else
            {
                return " A Senior Employee";
            }
        }
    }
    class EmployeeStoreHouse<Employee> where Employee : IEmployee
    //class EmployeeStoreHouse<Employee>//error
    {
        private List<Employee> MyStore = new List<Employee>();
        public void AddToStore(Employee element)
        {
            MyStore.Add(element);
        }
        public void DisplaySore()
        {
            Console.WriteLine("The store contains:");
            foreach (Employee e in MyStore)
            {
                Console.WriteLine(e.Position());
            }
        }
    }

    namespace Generic.Constraint_1
    {
        class Program
        {
```

```csharp
static void Main(string[] args)
{
    Console.WriteLine("***Example of Generic Constraints***");
    //Employees
    Employee e1 = new Employee("Amit", 2);
    Employee e2 = new Employee("Bob", 5);
    Employee e3 = new Employee("Jon", 7);

    //Employee StoreHouse
    EmployeeStoreHouse<Employee> myEmployeeStore = new Employee
    StoreHouse<Employee>();
    myEmployeeStore.AddToStore(e1);
    myEmployeeStore.AddToStore(e2);
    myEmployeeStore.AddToStore(e3);

    //Display the Employee Positions in Store
    myEmployeeStore.DisplaySore();
    Console.ReadKey();
}
    }
  }

}
```

Output

```
***Example of Generic Constraints***
The store contains:
 A Junior Employee
 A Senior Employee
 A Senior Employee
```

Note

In this example, we have examined- how can we place constraints in our application. Without the use of *'where Employee:IEmployee'* statement, we encounter this issue:

```
public void DisplaySore()
{
    foreach (Employee e in MyStore)
    {
        Console.WriteLine(e.Position());
    }
}
```

```
100 %
Error List
      1 Error        0 Warnings        0 Messages
Description
  1   'Employee' does not contain a definition for 'Position' and no extension method 'Position' accepting a first argument of type 'Employee' could
      be found (are you missing a using directive or an assembly reference?)
```

The contextual keyword 'where' helps us to place constraints in our application. In general, we can have the following constraints:

- where T: struct means that type T must be a value type. (Remember that struct is a value type.)

- where T: class means that type T must be a reference type. (Remember class is a reference type.)

- where T: IMyInter means that type T must implement the IMyInter interface.

- where T: new() means that type T must have a default (parameterless) constructor. (If you use it with other constraints, place it at last position.)

- where T: S means that type T must be derived from another generic type S. It is sometimes referred to as *naked type constraint.*

Quiz

Students ask:

Can we write a more generic form of the EmployeeStoreHouse?

Answer

Teacher says: Yes, we can. Consider the following code.

```
class EmployeeStoreHouse<T> where T : IEmployee
{
    private List<T> MyStore = new List<T>();
    public void AddToStore(T element)
    {
        MyStore.Add(element);
    }
    public void DisplaySore()
    {
        foreach (T e in MyStore)
        {
            Console.WriteLine(e.Position());
        }
    }
}
```

Covariance and Contravariance

In the discussion on delegates in Chapter 10, you learned that covariance and contravariance support in delegates started from C# 2.0. Starting in C# 4.0, these concepts can be applied to generic type parameters, generic interfaces, and generic delegates. Chapter 10 also explored these concepts with non-generic delegates.

In this chapter, we continue to explore these concepts with additional cases.

Before going forward, recall the following points:

- Covariance and contravariance deal with type conversion with arguments and return types.

- Covariance and contravariance have been used in our coding of different types of objects/arrays etc.

- .NET 4 supports generic delegates and generic interfaces. (In earlier versions, we will encounter compilation errors with generic delegates or generic interfaces).

- Contravariance is generally defined an adjustment or modification. When we try to implement these concepts in the coding world, we also try to accept the following truth (or similar truth):

  - All footballers (a.k.a. soccer players) are athletes, but the reverse is not true (because there are many athletes who play golf, basketball, hockey, etc.) Similarly, we can say that all buses are vehicles, but the reverse is not true.

  - In programming terminology, all derived classes are of type base classes but the reverse is not true. For example, suppose that we have a class called Rectangle and it is derived from a class called Shape. Then we can say that all Rectangles are Shapes, but the reverse is not true.

- As per MSDN, the concepts of covariance and contravariance deals with implicit reference conversion for array, delegate and generic types. Covariance preserves assignment compatibility and contravariance reverses it.

Students ask:

What does "assignment compatibility" mean?

Teacher says: It means that you can assign a more specific type to a compatible less-specific type. For example, the value of an integer variable can be stored in an object variable, like this:

```
int i = 25;
object o = i;//ok: Assignment Compatible
```

Let's try to understand the meaning of covariance, contravariance, and invariance from a mathematical point of view.

Let's suppose that we are only considering a domain of integers.

Case 1: We define our function, $f(x) = x + 2$ for all x.

If $x \leq y$, then we can also say $f(x) \leq f(y)$ for all x. The projection (function f) is preserving the direction of size.

Case 2: We define our $f(x) = -x$ (for all x belongs to the integer).

Now, we can see $10 \leq 20$ but $f(10) \geq f(20)$ (since $f(10) = -10$, $f(20) = -20$ and $-10 > -20$). So, our direction of size is reversed.

Case 3: We define our function, $f(x) = x*x$.

Now, we can see $-1 \leq 0$ and $f(-1) > f(0)$, but $1 < 2$ and $f(1) < f(2)$. So the projection (function f) neither always preserves the direction of size nor reverses the direction of size.

In case 1, function f is *covariant*; in case 2, function f is *contravariant*; and in case 3, function f is *invariant*.

POINTS TO REMEMBER

You can always refer to Microsoft's simple definitions at `https://docs.microsoft.com/en-us/dotnet/standard/generics/covariance-and-contravariance`.

- **Covariance** We can use a more derived type than originally specified.

- **Contravariance** We can use a more generic (less derived) type than originally specified.

- **Invariance** We are allowed to use only the type originally specified.

Covariance and contravariance are collectively known as *variance*.

Starting with the .NET Framework 4, in C# there are keywords to mark the generic type parameters of interfaces and delegates as *covariant* or *contravariant*. Covariant interfaces and delegates are marked with the *out* keyword (to indicate that values come out). Contravariant interfaces and delegates are associated with the *in* keyword (to indicate that values go in).

Let's go through our C# examples. Remember that IEnumerable<T> is covariant on T, and Action<T> is contravariant on T. Let us check the definition of the IEnumerable<T> interface in Visual Studio.

```
namespace System.Collections.Generic
{
    ...public interface IEnumerable<out T> : IEnumerable
    {
        ...IEnumerator<T> GetEnumerator();
    }
}
```

Author's Note: Notice that we can see that the word "out" is associated with the definition of IEnumerable. So, We can assign IEnumerable<DerivedType> to IEnumerable<BaseType>.This is why, we can assign IEnumerable<string> to IEnumerable<object>.

Now check the definition of the Action<T> delegate in Visual Studio. We will see this:

```
namespace System
{
    ...public delegate void Action<in T>(T obj);
}
```

Alternatively, check the definition IComparer<T> interface in Visual Studio. We will see this:

```
//      The type of objects to compare.
public interface IComparer<in T>
{
    ...int Compare(T x, T y);
}
}
```

Note   Notice that we can see that the word *in* is associated with the definition of Acion<T>. So, we can assign Action<BaseType> to Action<DeriveType>.

The bottom line: Since IEnumerable<T> is covariant on T, we can convert from IEnumerable<string> to IEnumerable<object>. Values come out from these cases (covariance).

On the other hand, since Action<T> is contravariant on T, we can also convert Action<object> to Action<string>. Values go into these objects (contravariance).

To test both of these flavors, we will discuss covariance with generic interfaces and contravariance with generic delegates. I suggest that you try to implement the remaining two cases: covariance with generic delegates and contravariance with generic interfaces.

Demonstration 9: Covariance with Generic Interfaces

```
using System;
using System.Collections.Generic;

namespace CovarianceWithGenericInterfaceEx
{
    class Parent
    {
        public virtual void ShowMe()
        {
            Console.WriteLine(" I am from Parent, my hash code is :" +
            GetHashCode());
        }
    }
    class Child : Parent
    {
        public override void ShowMe()
        {
            Console.WriteLine(" I am from Child, my hash code is:" +
            GetHashCode());
        }
    }
```

```
class Program
{
    static void Main(string[] args)
    {

        //Covariance Example

        Console.WriteLine("***Covariance with Generic Interface
        Example***\n");
        Console.WriteLine("***IEnumerable<T> is covariant");
        //Some Parent objects
        Parent pob1 = new Parent();
        Parent pob2 = new Parent();
        //Some Child objects
        Child cob1 = new Child();
        Child cob2 = new Child();
        //Creating a child List
        List<Child> childList = new List<Child>();
        childList.Add(cob1);
        childList.Add(cob2);
        IEnumerable<Child> childEnumerable = childList;
            /* An object which was instantiated with a more derived type
            argument (Child) is assigned to an object instantiated with a
            less derived type argument(Parent). Assignment compatibility
            is preserved here. */
        IEnumerable<Parent> parentEnumerable = childEnumerable;
        foreach (Parent p in parentEnumerable)
        {
            p.ShowMe();
        }
    Console.ReadKey();
    }
}
}
```

Output

```
***Covariance with Generic Interface Example***

***IEnumerable<T> is covariant
I am from Child, my hash code is:21083178
I am from Child, my hash code is:55530882
```

Analysis

Go through the comments included in the program for a better understanding.

Demonstration 10: Contravariance with Generic Delegates

```csharp
using System;

namespace ContravarianceWithGenericDelegatesEx
{
    //A generic delegate
    delegate void aDelegateMethod<in T>(T t);
    class Vehicle
    {
        public virtual void ShowMe()
        {
            Console.WriteLine(" Vehicle.ShowMe()");
        }
    }
    class Bus: Vehicle
    {
        public override void ShowMe()
        {
            Console.WriteLine(" Bus.ShowMe()");
        }
    }
```

```csharp
class Program
{
    static void Main(string[] args)
    {
        Console.WriteLine("***Contra-variance with Generic Delegates
        example ***");
        Vehicle obVehicle = new Vehicle();
        Bus obBus = new Bus();
        aDelegateMethod<Vehicle> delVehicle = ShowVehicleType;
        delVehicle(obVehicle);
        //Contravariance with Delegate
        //Using less derived type to more derived type
        aDelegateMethod<Bus> delChild = ShowVehicleType;
        delChild(obBus);
        Console.ReadKey();
    }

    private static void ShowVehicleType(Vehicle p)
    {
        p.ShowMe();
    }
}

}
```

Output

```
***Contra-variance with Generic Delegates example ***
Vehicle.ShowMe()
Bus.ShowMe()
```

Analysis

Like in the previous case, go through the comments in this program to get a better understanding.

Students ask:

In the preceding program, you used a static method (ShowVehicleType (…)) with generic delegates. Can you use the same concept with non-static methods?

Teacher says: Obviously, you can.

Summary

This chapter discussed the following:

- ✓ Generics in C#

- ✓ Why generics are important

- ✓ The advantages of generic programming over non-generic programming

- ✓ The keyword *default* in the context of generics

- ✓ How to impose constraints in generic programming

- ✓ Covariance with generic interfaces

- ✓ Contravariance with generic delegates

CHAPTER 13

Exception Handling

Discussions on Exception Handling

Teacher starts the discussion: In general, when we write code for an application, we have the expectation that it will always execute without any problem. But sometimes, we encounter sudden surprises when we execute those programs. These surprises may occur in various ways and through some careless mistakes (e.g., trying to implement the wrong logic, or ignoring some loopholes in the code paths of the program, etc.) However, it is also true that many of the failures are beyond the control of a programmer. We often call these unwanted situations *exceptions*. Handling these exceptions are essential when we write an application.

Definition

We can define an exception as an event, which breaks the normal execution/instruction flow.

When exceptional situations arise, an exception object is created and thrown into the method that created the exception. That method may or may not handle the exception. If it cannot handle the exception, it will pass the responsibility to another method. (Similar to our daily life, when a situation goes beyond our control, we seek advice from others). If there is no method to take the responsibility of handling a particular exception, an error dialog box appears (indicating an unhandled exception) and the execution of the program stops.

© Vaskaran Sarcar 2018
V. Sarcar, *Interactive C#*, https://doi.org/10.1007/978-1-4842-3339-9_13

POINTS TO REMEMBER

An exception handling mechanism deals with runtime errors in .NET, and if not handled
properly, an application will die prematurely. Therefore, we should try to write applications that
can detect and handle surprises in a graceful manner and prevent the premature death of the
application.

Let's begin with a simple example. The following program will compile successfully
but it will raise an exception during runtime because we have overlooked the fact that
the divisor (b) is 0 (i.e., we are going to divide 100 by 0).

Demonstration 1

```
using System;

namespace ExceptionEx1
{
    class Program
    {
        static void Main(string[] args)
        {
            Console.WriteLine("***Exploring Exceptions.***");
            int a=100, b=0;
            int c = a / b;
            Console.WriteLine(" So, the result of a/b is :{0}", c);
            Console.ReadKey();
        }
    }
}
```

Output

System.DivideByZeroException: 'Attempted to divide by zero.'

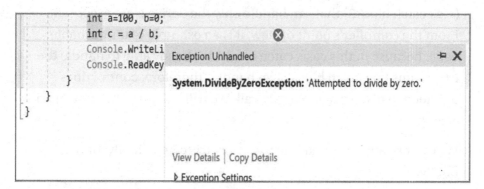

Teacher continues: Before going forward, I'll highlight some key points about the exception handling mechanism. You must go through these points repeatedly.

- All exceptions in .NET are objects.

- System.Exception is the base class for the exceptions.

- Any method in an application can raise surprises during the application's runtime. If such a situation occurs, in programming terminology, we say that the method has thrown an exception.

- We use the following keywords to deal with C# exceptions: try, catch, throw, finally

- We try to guard an exception with try/catch block. The code that may throw an exception is placed inside a try block and this exceptional situation is handled inside a catch block.

- We can associate multiple catch blocks with a try block. When a particular catch block handles the sudden surprises, we say that the catch block has caught the exception.

- The code in the finally block must execute. A finally block is generally placed after a try block or a try/catch block.

- When an exception is raised inside a try block, the control jumps to the respective catch or finally block. The remaining part of the try block will not be executed.

- Exceptions follow the inheritance hierarchy. Sometimes we may encounter compile-time errors if we place a catch block (e.g., catch block1) that can handle a parent class exception before a catch block (e.g., catch block2) that can handle only the derive class exception. From the compiler's point of view, it is an example of unreachable code, because in this case, catch block1 is already able to handle the exceptions that catch block2 can handle. Therefore, control does not need to reach catch block2 at all. We will examine this case in an example.

- We can use any combination: try/catch, try/catch/finally, or try/ finally.

- The code in finally block must execute.

- If we do not handle exceptions, the CLR will catch it on our behalf and our program may die prematurely.

  There is a key difference with Java: here all exceptions are implicitly unchecked. Therefore, there is no concept of the *throws* keyword in C#. This is a hot topic of debate.

Teacher continues: Now let's see how to handle the exception that we encountered in the previous example.

Demonstration 2

```csharp
using System;

namespace ExceptionEx1Modified
{
    class Program
    {
        static void Main(string[] args)
        {
            Console.WriteLine("***Exploring Exceptions***");
            int a = 100, b = 0;
            try
            {
```

```
        int c = a / b;
        Console.WriteLine(" So, the result of a/b is :{0}", c);
    }
    catch (Exception ex)
    {
        Console.WriteLine("Encountered an exception :{0}",
        ex.Message);
    }
    finally
    {
        Console.WriteLine("I am in finally.You cannot skip me!");
    }
    Console.ReadKey();
        }
    }
}
```

Output

```
***Exploring Exceptions***
Encountered an exception :Attempted to divide by zero.
I am in finally.You cannot skip me!
```

Analysis

We can confirm the following points from the output of the program:

- When an exception is raised inside a try block, the control jumped to the respective catch block. The remaining part of the try block did not execute.

- The code in the finally block executed even though we encountered an exception.

- We used a common property called Message. In System.Exception, there are some well-known properties. You can easily see them in Visual Studio.

```
namespace System
{
    public class Exception : ISerializable, _Exception
    {
        public Exception();
        public Exception(string message);
        public Exception(string message, Exception innerException);
        protected Exception(SerializationInfo info, StreamingContext context);

        public virtual string Source { get; set; }
        public virtual string HelpLink { get; set; }
        public virtual string StackTrace { get; }
        public MethodBase TargetSite { get; }
        public Exception InnerException { get; }
        public virtual string Message { get; }
        public int HResult { get; protected set; }
        public virtual IDictionary Data { get; }

        protected event EventHandler<SafeSerializationEventArgs> SerializeObjectState;

        public virtual Exception GetBaseException();
        public virtual void GetObjectData(SerializationInfo info, StreamingContext context);
        public Type GetType();
        public override string ToString();
    }
}
```

As indicated by the arrow, in most cases, you may need these three properties: Message, StackTrace, and InnerException. This chapter uses the Message and StackTrace Properties in various examples. From the screenshot, you can easily see that these are read-only properties (they have only the get property). For your immediate reference, I have expanded these three properties to show their descriptions.

- *StackTrace property:* With this property, we can get the hierarchy of the method calls that caused the exception. It gives us a string representation of the immediate frames on the call stack.

```
//
// Summary:
//     Gets a string representation of the immediate frames on the call stack.
//
// Returns:
//     A string that describes the immediate frames of the call stack.
public virtual string StackTrace { get; }
```

- *Message property:* Describes the current exception.

```
//
// Summary:
//     Gets a message that describes the current exception.
//
// Returns:
//     The error message that explains the reason for the exception, or an empty string
//     ("").
public virtual string Message { get; }
```

- *InnerException property:* Gets the System.Exception instance that caused the current exception.

```
//
// Summary:
//     Gets the System.Exception instance that caused the current exception.
//
// Returns:
//     An object that describes the error that caused the current exception. The System.Exception.InnerException
//     property returns the same value as was passed into the System.Exception.#ctor(System.String,System.Exception)
//     constructor, or null if the inner exception value was not supplied to the constructor.
//     This property is read-only.
public Exception InnerException { get; }
```

Students ask:

Sir, we could easily put an if block like if(b==0) before the division operation to avoid a 0 divisor, and in that case, we can easily exclude the use of the try/catch block.

Teacher clarifies: "You are considering only this simple example, which is why it appears to you this way. Yes, in this case, your divisor is fixed and you can guard your code in that way. However, think of a case where the value of *b* is also computed at runtime, and you cannot predict the value earlier. Also, if you need to put guards like this in all probable cases, your code may look clumsy and clearly unreadable."

Teacher continues: For your ready reference, the following are some exception classes that are defined in the language specification.

System.ArithmeticException	A base class for exceptions that occur during arithmetic operations, such as System.DivideByZeroException and System.OverflowException.
System.ArrayTypeMismatchException	This is thrown when a store into an array fails because the actual type of the stored element is incompatible with the actual type of array.
System.DivideByZeroException	This is thrown when an attempt to divide an integral value by zero occurs.
System.IndexOutOfRangeException	This is thrown when an attempt to index an array via an index that is less than zero or outside the bounds of the array.
System.InvalidCastException	This is thrown when an explicit conversion from a base type or interface to a derived type fails at run time.
System.NullReferenceException	This is thrown when a null reference is used in a way that causes the referenced object to be required.
System.OutOfMemoryException	This is thrown when an attempt to allocate memory (via new) fails.
System.StackOverflowException	This is thrown when the execution stack is exhausted by having too many pending method calls; typically indicative of very deep or unbounded recursion.
System.TypeInitializationException	This is thrown when a static constructor throws an exception, and no catch clauses exist to catch it.
System.OverflowException	This is thrown when an arithmetic operation in a checked context overflows.

For a more detailed list of exceptions, you can press Ctrl+Alt+E in Visual Studio and expand the Common Language Runtime Exceptions option, as shown in the following screenshot.

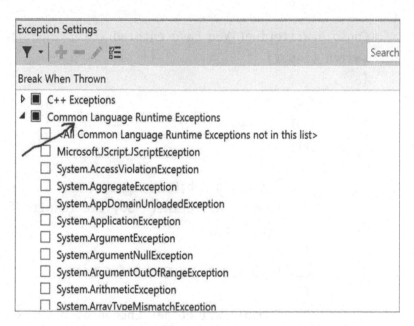

Now consider the following example to examine how to handle multiple exceptions with multiple catch blocks in our program.

Demonstration 3

```
using System;

namespace HandlingMultipleEx
{
    class Program
    {
        static void Main(string[] args)
        {
            Console.WriteLine("***Handling multiple Exceptions***");
            string b1;
            int input;
            Console.WriteLine("Enter your choice( 0 or 1)");
```

```
            b1 = Console.ReadLine();
            //Checking whether we can parse the string as an integer
            if (int.TryParse(b1, out input))
            {
                Console.WriteLine("You have entered {0}", input);
                switch (input)
                {
                    case 0:
                        int a = 100, b = 0;
                        try
                        {
                            int c = a / b;
                            Console.WriteLine(" So, the result of a/b is
                            :{0}", c);
                        }
                        catch (DivideByZeroException ex)
                        {
                            Console.WriteLine("Encountered an exception
                            with integers:{0}", ex.Message);
                            Console.WriteLine("Encountered an exception
                            with integers:{0}", ex.StackTrace);
                        }
                        catch (Exception ex)
                        {
                            Console.WriteLine("In Choice0.Exception
                            block ..{0}",ex.Message);
                        }
                        break;
                    case 1:
                        int[] myArray = { 1, 2, 3 };
                        try
                        {
                            Console.WriteLine(" myArray[0] :{0}",
                            myArray[0]);
```

```csharp
                Console.WriteLine(" myArray[1] :{0}",
                myArray[1]);
                Console.WriteLine(" myArray[2] :{0}",
                myArray[2]);
                Console.WriteLine(" myArray[3] :{0}",
                myArray[3]);
            }
            catch (IndexOutOfRangeException ex)
            {
                Console.WriteLine("Encountered an exception
                with array elements :{0}", ex.Message);
                Console.WriteLine("Encountered an exception
                with array elements :{0}", ex.StackTrace);
            }
            catch (Exception ex)
            {
                Console.WriteLine("In Choice1.Exception
                block ..{0}", ex.Message);
            }

            break;
        default:
            Console.WriteLine("You must enter either 0 or 1");
            break;
        }
    }
    else
    {
        Console.WriteLine("You have not entered an integer!");
    }
    Console.ReadKey();
    }
  }
}
```

Output

Case 1: User entered 0.

```
***Handling multiple Exceptions***
Enter your choice( 0 or 1)
0
You have entered 0
Encountered an exception with integers:Attempted to divide by zero.
Encountered an exception with integers:   at HandlingMultipleEx.Program.
Main(String[] args) in C:\Feluda_June12,2017Onwards\MyPrograms\CSharpPro
gs\CSharpBasicsProgs\InteractiveCSharpSolution\HandlingMultipleEx\Progra
m.cs:line 24
```

Case 2: User entered 1.

```
***Handling multiple Exceptions***
Enter your choice( 0 or 1)
1
You have entered 1
 myArray[0] :1
 myArray[1] :2
 myArray[2] :3
Encountered an exception with array elements :Index was outside the bounds of the array.
Encountered an exception with array elements :   at HandlingMultipleEx.Program.Main(Strin
g[] args) in C:\Feluda_June12,2017Onwards\MyPrograms\CSharpProgs\CSharpBasicsProgs\Intera
ctiveCSharpSolution\HandlingMultipleEx\Program.cs:line 44
```

Case 3: User entered a string.

```
***Handling multiple Exceptions***
Enter your choice( 0 or 1)
hjk
You have not entered an integer!
```

Analysis

We can confirm the following points from the output of the program:

- When an exception is raised, only one catch clause is executed. For example, if the block- catch (DivideByZeroException ex){..} can handle the exception, the block- catch (Exception ex){..} does not need to come into the picture.

- In the preceding program, all types of exceptions (except DivideByZeroException and IndexOutOfRangeException) are caught inside the block- catch (Exception ex) and *this block must be placed as the last catch block because System.Exception class is base class for all exceptions.*

Quiz

Can you predict the output?

Demonstration 4

```
using System;
namespace Quiz1Exception
{
    class Program
    {
        static void Main(string[] args)
        {
            Console.WriteLine("***Exploring Exceptions***");
            int a = 100, b = 0;
            try
            {
                int c = a / b;
                Console.WriteLine(" So, the result of a/b is :{0}", c);
            }
            catch (ArithmeticException ex)
            {
```

```
            Console.WriteLine("Encountered an exception :{0}",
            ex.Message);
        }
        //Error:Exceptions follows the inheritance hierarchy.
        //So, we need to place catch blocks properly.
        catch (DivideByZeroException ex)
        {
            Console.WriteLine("Encountered an DivideByZeoException
            :{0}", ex.Message);
        }
        Console.ReadKey();
    }
  }
}
```

Output

Compiler error.

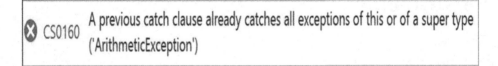

CS0160   A previous catch clause already catches all exceptions of this or of a super type
('ArithmeticException')

Analysis

Exceptions follow the inheritance hierarchy. Therefore, we need to place catch blocks properly. In this case, DivideByZeroException is a subclass of ArithmeticException (which in turn is a subclass of Exception). You can check this easily in Visual Studio.

```
namespace System
{
    ...public class DivideByZeroException : ArithmeticException
    {
        ...public DivideByZeroException();
```

POINTS TO REMEMBER

So, when you deal with multiple catch blocks, you need to place more specific exception clause first.

Other Variations of the catch Clause

Teacher continues: So far, we have seen different catch blocks. We will take note that instead of catch(<Exceptionname> <exceptionReference>), you can simply use catch(<Exceptionname>) or catch{}. So, the following block of code will not raise any compilation error. It is one variation of the catch clause.

```
catch (Exception)
{
    Console.WriteLine("Encountered an Exception");
}
```

This block is also OK. Here is another variation of the catch clause.

```
catch ()
  {
      Console.WriteLine("Encountered an Exception");
  }
```

However, it is strongly recommended that you try to avoid both of these variations of catch blocks.

Quiz

Will the code compile?

```
//some code before
catch (Exception)
{
 Console.WriteLine("Encountered an Exception");
}
catch { }
//some code after
```

Answer

Yes. However, in Visual Studio 2017, you will see this warning message:

 CS1058 A previous catch clause already catches all exceptions. All non-exceptions thrown will be wrapped in a System.Runtime.CompilerServices.RuntimeWrappedException.

Quiz

Will the code compile?

```
//some code before
catch { }
catch (Exception)
{
  Console.WriteLine("Encountered an Exception");
}
//some code after
```

Answer

No. In Visual Studio 2017, you see this error message:

❌ CS1017   Catch clauses cannot follow the general catch clause of a try statement

Explanation

As per language specification, a catch clause that does not name an exception class can handle any exception. Also, there are some exceptions that do not derive from System. Exception. These are called *non-CLS exceptions*. Some .NET languages, including C++/ CLI, support these exceptions. In Visual C#, we cannot throw non-CLS exceptions but we can catch them. By default, a Visual C# assembly catches non-CLS exceptions as wrapped exceptions (see the warning message in the output of the previous Quiz). Therefore, we can also get them in the block-catch (Exception ex){..}.

Experts suggests that you use catch{} when you know that you need to perform some specific task (e.g., write a log entry) in response to non-CLS exceptions but you do not need to access the exception information. For more information on this topic, you can go to `https://docs.microsoft.com/en-us/dotnet/csharp/programming-guide/exceptions/how-to-catch-a-non-cls-exception`.

Teacher continues: We have another variation of a catch block, which was introduced in C# 6.0.

The following is a third variation of the catch clause.

```
catch (WebException ex) when (ex.Status == WebExceptionStatus.Timeout)
 {
//some code
 }
```

In this scenario, *when* clause acts like a filter. So, in this case, if a WebException is thrown but the Boolean condition (which is followed by when) is not true, this catch block will not handle that exception. Therefore, with this kind of filter, we can catch the same exception again but handle it in a different catch block, as follows:

```
catch (WebException ex) when (ex.Status == WebExceptionStatus.Pending)
 {
   //some code
 }
```

Or,

```
catch (WebException ex) when (ex.Status == WebExceptionStatus.
ProtocolError)
 {
//some code
 }
```

Teacher continues: Now let's look at how a method can throw an exception. A method can throw an exception with the *throw* keyword. In the following example, we have thrown a DivideByZeroException from the Divide method when the divisor is 0, and then we handled it inside a catch block.

Demonstration 5

```csharp
using System;

namespace ThrowingExceptionEx
{
    class Program
    {
        static int a = 100, b = 0, c;
        static void Divide(int a, int b)
        {
            if (b != 0)
            {
                int c = a / b;
            }
            else
            {
                throw new DivideByZeroException("b comes as Zero");
            }
        }
        static void Main(string[] args)
        {
            Console.WriteLine("***Exploring Exceptions:Throwing an
            Exception Example***");
            try
            {
                Divide(a, b);
                Console.WriteLine("Division operation completed");
            }
            catch (DivideByZeroException ex)
            {
                Console.WriteLine("Encountered an exception :{0}", ex.Message);
            }
            Console.ReadKey();
        }
    }
}
```

Output

```
***Exploring Exceptions:Throwing an Exception Example***
Encountered an exception :b comes as Zero
```

Students ask:

Sir, what are the different ways to raise an exception?

Teacher says: In general, there are two different ways that exceptions can be raised.

Method 1: We have just seen that any method can raise an exception by using the throw keyword. This statement immediately raises the exception and control never comes to the statement that immediately follows the throw statement.

Method 2: When we process C# statements and exceptions, we can encounter exceptions due to wrong logic, loopholes, and so forth.

Teacher continues: Sometimes we need to repeatedly throw (called *rethrow*) an exception. It is necessary in some situations; for example, when we want to write a log entry or when we want to send a new higher-level exception.

The following is the format to rethrow an exception:

```
try
{
  //some code
 }
catch(Exception ex)
{
 //some code e.g. log it now
 //Now rethrow it
 throw;
 }
```

Note   If you use `throw` `ex` instead of `throw;` the program will not have any compilation issues, but if you examine the StackTrace property, you see that it is different from the original one. Therefore, it is strictly recommended that you use `throw;` only when you truly want to rethrow the original exception. See the Demonstration 6 output to confirm this.

Demonstration 6

```
using System;

namespace RethrowingExceptionEx
{
    class Program
    {
        static int a = 100, b = 1, c;
        static void Divide(int a, int b)
        {
            try
            {
                b--;
                c = a / b;
                //some code
            }
            catch(Exception ex)
            {
                //some code e.g. log it now
                Console.WriteLine("a={0} b={1}", a,b);
                Console.WriteLine("Message: {0}", ex.Message);
                Console.WriteLine("StackTrace: {0}", ex.StackTrace);
```

```
            //Now rethrow it
            throw; //will throw the current exception
            //throw  new ArithmeticException();//throwing the parent
            class exception
        }
    }
    static void Main(string[] args)
    {
        Console.WriteLine("***Exploring Rethrowing an Exception
        Example***");
        try
        {
            Divide(a, b);
            Console.WriteLine(" Main.Divide() is completed");
        }
        catch (DivideByZeroException ex)
        {
            Console.WriteLine("\na={0} b={1}", a, b);
            Console.WriteLine("Message: {0}", ex.Message);
            Console.WriteLine("StackTrace: {0}", ex.StackTrace);
        }
        catch (Exception ex)
        {
            Console.WriteLine("\nIn catch(Exception ex)");
            Console.WriteLine("a={0} b={1}", a, b);
            Console.WriteLine("Message: {0}", ex.Message);
            Console.WriteLine("StackTrace: {0}", ex.StackTrace);
        }
        Console.ReadKey();
    }
  }
}
```

Output

```
***Exploring Rethrowing an Exception Example***
a=100 b=0
Message: Attempted to divide by zero.
StackTrace:    at RethrowingExceptionEx.Program.Divide(Int32 a, Int32 b) in C:\Feluda_June12,20170
nwards\MyPrograms\CSharpProgs\CSharpBasicsProgs\InteractiveCSharpSolution\RethrowingExceptionEx\Pr
ogram.cs:line 13

a=100 b=1
Message: Attempted to divide by zero.
StackTrace:    at RethrowingExceptionEx.Program.Divide(Int32 a, Int32 b) in C:\Feluda_June12,20170
nwards\MyPrograms\CSharpProgs\CSharpBasicsProgs\InteractiveCSharpSolution\RethrowingExceptionEx\Pr
ogram.cs:line 23
    at RethrowingExceptionEx.Program.Main(String[] args) in C:\Feluda_June12,2017Onwards\MyPrograms
\CSharpProgs\CSharpBasicsProgs\InteractiveCSharpSolution\RethrowingExceptionEx\Program.cs:line 32
```

Analysis

Now you can see why the logging in the first case was important. As soon as we encountered the exception, we logged it and then we see that the divisor (b) became 0 in the Divide() method. If you did not log it, then when you see the final log statements, you may wonder why you got this exception when b is 1.

Uncomment the `throw new ArithmeticException();` line in the preceding program, as follows:

```
//Now rethrow it
//throw; //will throw the current exception
throw  new ArithmeticException();//throwing the parent class exception
}
```

You will receive the following output:

```
StackTrace:     at RethrowingExceptionEx.Program.Divide(Int32 a, Int32 b) in C:\Feluda_June12,2
017Onwards\MyPrograms\CSharpProgs\CSharpBasicsProgs\InteractiveCSharpSolution\RethrowingExcept
ionEx\Program.cs:line 13

In catch(Exception ex)
a=100 b=1
Message: Overflow or underflow in the arithmetic operation.
StackTrace:     at RethrowingExceptionEx.Program.Divide(Int32 a, Int32 b) in C:\Feluda_June12,2
017Onwards\MyPrograms\CSharpProgs\CSharpBasicsProgs\InteractiveCSharpSolution\RethrowingExcept
ionEx\Program.cs:line 24
   at RethrowingExceptionEx.Program.Main(String[] args) in C:\Feluda_June12,2017Onwards\MyProg
rams\CSharpProgs\CSharpBasicsProgs\InteractiveCSharpSolution\RethrowingExceptionEx\Program.cs:
line 32
```

Students ask:

Sir, it appears that we can rethrow any exception in a situation like this. Is this correct?

Teacher says: Yes but obviously, that is not recommended. However, when you learn to create your own exception, you may combine this original exception with your custom exception message and then rethrow it for better readability.

Creating a Custom Exception

Teacher continues: Sometimes we want to define our own exception to get messages that are more meaningful. Before we proceed further, we must remember these points:

- In an exception hierarchy, we notice two major types of exception classes: *SystemException* and *ApplicationException.* A SystemException is thrown by a runtime (CLR), and an ApplicationException is thrown by user programs (so far, we have used System Exception's). Initially, it was suggested that user-defined exceptions should derive from ApplicationException class. However, later MSDN suggested this: "You should derive custom exceptions from the Exception class rather than the ApplicationException class. You should not throw an ApplicationException exception in your code, and you should not catch an ApplicationException exception unless you intend to rethrow the original exception." (See https://msdn.microsoft.com/en-us/library/system. applicationexception.aspx.)

- When we create our own exception, the class name should end with the word Exception. (See https://docs.microsoft.com/en-us/ dotnet/standard/exceptions/how-to-create-user- defined-exceptions.)

- Supply the three overloaded versions of constructors (as described in Demonstration 7).

We will try to follow all of these suggestions when we create our own exceptions.

Demonstration 7

```
using System;

namespace CustomExceptionEx1
{
    class ZeroDivisorException : Exception
    {
        public ZeroDivisorException() : base("Divisor is zero"){ }
        public ZeroDivisorException(string msg) : base(msg){ }
        public ZeroDivisorException(string msg, Exception inner) :
        base(msg, inner)
        { }
    }
    class TestCustomeException
    {
        int c;
        public int Divide(int a, int b)
        {
            if (b == 0)
            {
```

```
            //Ex.Message= "Divisor should not be Zero"
            throw new ZeroDivisorException("Divisor should not be Zero");
            //Ex.Message= "Divisor is Zero"
            //throw new ZeroDivisorException();
        }
        c = a / b;
        Console.WriteLine("Division completed");
        return c;
    }
}
class Program
{
    static void Main(string[] args)
    {
        Console.WriteLine("***A Custom Exception Example***");
        int a = 10, b = 1, result;
        try
        {
            b--;
            TestCustomeException testOb = new TestCustomeException();
            result = testOb.Divide(a, b);
        }
        catch (ZeroDivisorException ex)
        {
            Console.WriteLine("Caught the custom exception: {0}",
            ex.Message);
        }
        finally
        {
            Console.WriteLine("\nExample completed");
            Console.ReadKey();
        }
    }
}
```

Output

```
***A Custom Exception Example***
Caught the custom exception: Divisor should not be Zero

Example completed
```

Analysis

We have used the second overloaded version of the constructor. If you want to use the default constructor (which was commented earlier), there is a different message.

```
***A Custom Exception Example***
Caught the custom exception: Divisor is zero

Example completed
```

Summary

This chapter answered the following questions.

- ✓ What is an exception?
- ✓ How can we handle errors in our program?
- ✓ What are the common keywords used when we deal with exceptions in C#?
- ✓ How should we place try, catch, and block in our program and for what purpose?
- ✓ What are the different variations of the catch clause?
- ✓ How can we use exception filters in our program?
- ✓ How can we classify exceptions?
- ✓ How do we make a custom exception?

CHAPTER 14

Memory Cleanup

Teacher starts the discussion: Managing memory is an important concern for programmers. But .NET tried to make their lives easier by taking the responsibility of clearing those objects that have no use after a particular point. In programming, we call them *dirty objects* or *unreferenced objects.*

The garbage collector program runs in background as a low-priority thread and keeps track of dirty objects. .NET runtime on regular intervals can invoke this program to remove unreferenced or dirty objects from memory.

However, there is a catch. Some objects require special teardown codes to release resources. A very common example is when we open one or more files and then perform some operation (e.g., reading, writing, etc.) but forget to close the file(s). A similar kind of attention may be needed in other situations, such as when we deal with unmanaged objects, locking mechanisms, or operating system handles in our programs, and so forth. Programmers explicitly need to release those kinds of resources.

In general, when programmers put their efforts to clean up (or release) memory, we say that they try to dispose of the objects, but when CLR automatically handles releasing the resources, we say that garbage collector is performing its job or that garbage collections are taking place.

POINTS TO REMEMBER

Programmers can release resources by explicitly disposing the objects, or CLR automatically releases resources through a garbage collection mechanism.

© Vaskaran Sarcar 2018
V. Sarcar, *Interactive C#*, https://doi.org/10.1007/978-1-4842-3339-9_14

How the Garbage Collector Works

Teacher continues: A generational garbage collector is used to collect short-lived objects more frequently than longer-lived objects. We have three generations here: 0, 1, and 2. Short-lived objects are stored in generation 0. The longer-lived objects are pushed into the higher generations—either 1 or 2. The garbage collector works more frequently in the lower generations than in the higher ones.

Once we create an object, it resides in generation 0. When generation 0 is filled up, the garbage collector is invoked. The objects that survive garbage collection in the first generation are promoted to the next higher generation—generation 1. The objects that survive garbage collection in generation 1 enter the highest generation—generation 2.

Note   You can remember the 3-3 rule: Garbage collection works in three different phases, and in general, a garbage collector is invoked in three different cases.

Three Phases of Garbage Collection

The following are the three different phases of garbage collection:

- Phase 1 is the *marking phase,* in which the live objects are marked or identified.

- Phase 2 is the r*elocating phase*, in which it updates the references of the objects that will be compacted in phase 3.

- Phase 3 is the c*ompacting phase*, which reclaims memory from dead (or unreferenced) objects, and the compaction operation is performed on the live objects. It moves the live objects (that survived until this point) to the older end of the segment.

Three Cases to invoke the Garbage Collector

The following are three common cases of invoking garbage collector:

- In case 1, we have low memory.

- In case 2, our allocated objects (in a managed heap) surpass a defined threshold limit.

- In case 3, the System.GC() method is invoked.

I said earlier that the GC.Collect() method can be used to force the garbage collection mechanism. There are many overloaded versions of this method. In the following example, we use GC.Collect(Int32), which forces an immediate garbage collection from generation 0 through the specified generation.

To understand the concepts, let's examine the following program and output. We are bringing garbage collector into action by invoking System.GC() (case 3).

Demonstration 1

```
using System;

namespace GarbageCollectionEx4
{
    class MyClass
    {
        private int myInt;
        //private int myInt2;
        private double myDouble;

        public MyClass()
        {
            myInt = 25;
            //myInt2 = 100;
            myDouble = 100.5;
        }
        public void ShowMe()
        {
```

```
        Console.WriteLine("MyClass.ShowMe()");
    }
    public void Dispose()
    {
        GC.SuppressFinalize(this);
        Console.WriteLine("Dispose() is called");
        Console.WriteLine("Total Memory:" + GC.GetTotalMemory(false));
    }
    ~MyClass()
    {
        Console.WriteLine("Destructor is Called..");
        Console.WriteLine(" After this destruction total Memory:" +
        GC.GetTotalMemory(false));
        //To catch the output at end, we are putting some sleep
        System.Threading.Thread.Sleep(60000);
    }
}

class Program
{
    public static void Main(string[] args)
    {
        Console.WriteLine("*** Exploring Garbage Collections.***");
        try
        {
            Console.WriteLine("Maximum Generations of GC:" +
            GC.MaxGeneration);
            Console.WriteLine("Total Memory:" +
            GC.GetTotalMemory(false));
            MyClass myOb = new MyClass();
            Console.WriteLine("myOb is in Generation : {0}",
            GC.GetGeneration(myOb));
            Console.WriteLine("Now Total Memory is:{0}",
            GC.GetTotalMemory(false));
            Console.WriteLine("Collection occured in 0th
            Generation:{0}", GC.CollectionCount(0));
```

```
Console.WriteLine("Collection occured in 1th
Generation:{0}", GC.CollectionCount(1));
Console.WriteLine("Collection occured in 2th
Generation:{0}", GC.CollectionCount(2));

//myOb.Dispose();

GC.Collect(0);//will call generation 0
Console.WriteLine("\n After GC.Collect(0)");

Console.WriteLine("Collection occured in 0th
Generation:{0}", GC.CollectionCount(0));//1
Console.WriteLine("Collection occured in 1th
Generation:{0}", GC.CollectionCount(1));//0
Console.WriteLine("Collection occured in 2th
Generation:{0}", GC.CollectionCount(2));//0
Console.WriteLine("myOb is in Generation : {0}",
GC.GetGeneration(myOb));
Console.WriteLine("Total Memory:" +
GC.GetTotalMemory(false));

GC.Collect(1);//will call generation 1 with 0
Console.WriteLine("\n After GC.Collect(1)");

Console.WriteLine("Collection occured in 0th
Generation:{0}", GC.CollectionCount(0));//2
Console.WriteLine("Collection occured in 1th
Generation:{0}", GC.CollectionCount(1));//1
Console.WriteLine("Collection ccured in 2th
Generation:{0}", GC.CollectionCount(2));//0
Console.WriteLine("myOb is in Generation : {0}",
GC.GetGeneration(myOb));
Console.WriteLine("Total Memory:" +
GC.GetTotalMemory(false));

GC.Collect(2);//will call generation 2 with 1 and 0
Console.WriteLine("\n After GC.Collect(2)");
```

```
            Console.WriteLine("Collection occured in 0th
            Generation:{0}", GC.CollectionCount(0));//3
            Console.WriteLine("Collection occured in 1th
            Generation:{0}", GC.CollectionCount(1));//2
            Console.WriteLine("Collection ccured in 2th
            Generation:{0}", GC.CollectionCount(2));//1
            Console.WriteLine("myOb is in Generation : {0}",
            GC.GetGeneration(myOb));
            Console.WriteLine("Total Memory:" +
            GC.GetTotalMemory(false));

        }
        catch (Exception ex)
        {
            Console.WriteLine("Error:" + ex.Message);
        }

        Console.ReadKey();
    }
  }
}
```

Output

```
Total Memory:38060
myOb is in Generation : 0
Now Total Memory is:38060
Collection occured in 0th Generation:0
Collection occured in 1th Generation:0
Collection occured in 2th Generation:0

 After GC.Collect(0)
Collection occured in 0th Generation:1
Collection occured in 1th Generation:0
Collection occured in 2th Generation:0
myOb is in Generation : 1
Total Memory:40416

 After GC.Collect(1)
Collection occured in 0th Generation:2
Collection occured in 1th Generation:1
Collection ccured in 2th Generation:0
myOb is in Generation : 2
Total Memory:40520

 After GC.Collect(2)
Collection occured in 0th Generation:3
Collection occured in 1th Generation:2
Collection ccured in 2th Generation:1
myOb is in Generation : 2
Total Memory:40572
Destructor is Called..
 After this destruction total Memory:48764
```

Analysis

Go through the theory again to understand the output. Then try to understand how garbage collection happened. We can see that whenever we call generation 2, the other generations are also called.

You can also see that the object that we have created was originally placed in generation 0.

Students ask:
Sir, how can we call destructors?

Teacher says: You cannot call the destructor. The garbage collector takes care of that responsibility.

Students ask:
What is a managed heap?

Teacher says: When CLR initializes the garbage collector, it allocates a segment of memory to store and manage the objects. This memory is known as the *managed heap*.

Teacher continues: In general, Finalize() (or the destructor of the object) is invoked to clean up the memory. Hence, we can provide the destructor to free up some unreferenced resources held by our objects, in that case, we need to override the Object class's Finalize() method.

Students ask:
When does the garbage collector call the Finalize() method?

Teacher says: We never know. It may call instantly when an object is found with no references, or later when the CLR needs to reclaim some memory. But we can force the garbage collector to run at a given point by calling System.GC.Collect(), which has many overloaded versions. (We already saw one such usage by invoking GC.Collect(Int32)).

Students ask:
Why is compaction necessary?

Teacher continues: When the GC removes all the intended objects (i.e., those objects with no reference) from the heap, the heap contains scattered objects. For simplicity, you can assume this as our heap.After the garbage collector's cleanup operation, it may look like the following (white blocks are represented as free/available blocks):

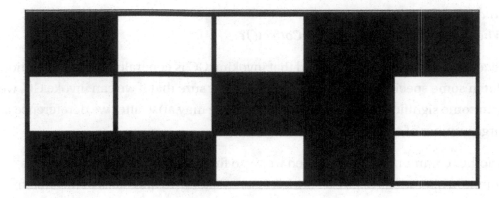

You can see that if we need to allocate five contiguous memory blocks in our heap now, we cannot allocate them, although collectively we have enough spaces to hold them. To deal with this kind of a situation, the garbage collector needs to apply the compaction technique, which moves all remaining objects (live objects) to one end to form one continuous block of memory. So, after compaction, it may look like this:

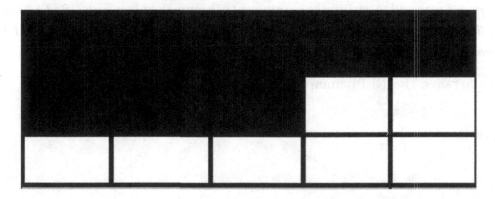

Now we can easily allocate five contiguous blocks of memory in the heap.

In this way, a managed heap is different from an old unmanaged heap. (Here we do not need to iterate through a linked list of addresses to find spaces for a new data. We can simply use the heap pointer; so, instantiating an object under .NET is faster). After the compaction, objects generally stay at the same area, so accessing them also becomes easier and faster (because page swapping is less). This is why Microsoft also believes that although the compaction operation is costly, the overall gain due to that effect is greater.

Students ask:

When should we invoke the GC.Collect()?

Teacher says: I already mentioned that invoking GC is generally a costly operation. But in some special scenarios, we are absolutely sure that if we can invoke GC, we'll gain some significant benefits. Such an example may arise after we dereference a large number of objects in our code.

Another common example is when we try to find memory leaks through some common operations (e.g., executing a test repeatedly to find leaks in the system). After each of these operations, we may try to gather different counters to analyze memory growth and to get the correct counters. We may need to call GC.Collect() at the beginning of each operation.

We will discuss memory leak analysis shortly.

Students ask:

Suppose we need to reclaim some amount of memory at some specified period of time when our application is running. How should we proceed to fulfill the demand?

Teacher says: The .NET framework provides a special interface, IDisposable.

```
using System.Runtime.InteropServices;

namespace System
{
    //
    // Summary:
    //     Provides a mechanism for releasing unmanaged resources.
    [ComVisible(true)]
    public interface IDisposable
    {
        //
        // Summary:
        //     Performs application-defined tasks associated with freeing, releasing, or resetting
        //     unmanaged resources.
        void Dispose();
    }
}
```

We need to implement this IDisposable interface, and as an obvious action, we need to override its Dispose() method. When a developer wants to free up the resources, it is the best practice. Another key advantage with this kind of approach is that we are aware when our programs are going to free up unreferenced resources.

POINTS TO REMEMBER

When we are implementing the IDisposable interface, we assume that the programmer will call the Dispose() method correctly. Some experts still suggest that as a precautionary measure, we should implement a destructor also. This approach may become useful if Dispose() is not called. I agree that this kind of dual implementation can make more sense in real-world programming.

C# provides a special support in this context. You can use the "using statement" to reduce your code size and make it more readable. It is used as a syntactic shortcut for the try/finally block.

Memory Leak Analysis

In general, when a computer program runs over a long period of time but fails to release memory resources that are no longer needed, we can feel the impact of memory leak (s) (e.g., machines become slow over time or in the worst case, the machines can crash). With this information, it is apparent that "how fast it comes to our attention" depends on the *leaking rate* of our application.

Consider a very simple example. Suppose that we have an online application where users need to fill in some data and then they click a Submit button. Now assume that the developers of the application mistakenly forgot to deallocate some memory that is no longer needed once a user presses the Submit button, and due to this misjudgement, the application is leaking 512 bytes per click. We probably won't notice any performance degradation in some initial clicks. But what happens if thousands of online users are using the application simultaneously? If one lakh(1,00,000) users press the Submit button, we will eventually lose 48.8 MB of memory, one crore(100,000,00) clicks leads to the loss of 4.76 GB, and so on.

In short, even if our application or program is leaking a very small amount of data per execution, it is quite obvious that we will see some kind of malfunctioning over a period of time; for example, we may notice that our device is crashing with a System. OutOfMemoryException, or operations in the device becomes so slow that we need to restart our application often.

In an unmanaged language like C++, we need to deallocate the memory when the intended job is done; otherwise, over a period of time, the impact of memory leaks will be huge. In managed code, CLR's garbage collector rescues us from most of these cases. Still, there are cases that we need to handle with care; otherwise, we may notice the impact of memory leaks.

If garbage collector is working properly, we can say that at a given point of time, if an object has no reference, the garbage collector will find that object, it will assume that the object is no longer needed and so, it can reclaim the memory occupied by that object.

So, how can we detect leaks? The windbg.exe is a common tool to find memory leaks in a large application. Apart from this, we can use other graphical tools, like Microsoft's CLR Profiler, SciTech's Memory Profiler, Red Gate's ANTS Memory Profiler, and so forth to find the leaks in our system. Many organizations have their own memory leak tool to detect and analyze leaks.

In the latest editions of Visual Studio, there is a diagnostic tool to detect and analyze memory leaks. It is very user-friendly, easy to use, and you can take different memory snapshots in different period of time. Markers in the tool indicate garbage collector activities. The real power of this tool is that you can analyze data in real time while the debugging session is active. The spikes in the graph can draw the programmer's attention immediately. Demonstration 2 includes a sample snapshot after executing the following program.

Demonstration 2

```
using System;
using System.Collections.Generic;

namespace AnalyzingLeaksWithSimpleEventEx1
{
    public delegate string MyDelegate(string str);

    class SimpleEventClass
    {
        public int ID { get; set; }

        public event MyDelegate SimpleEvent;
```

```
public SimpleEventClass()
{
    SimpleEvent += new MyDelegate(PrintText);
}
public string PrintText(string text)
{
    return text;
}

static void Main(string[] args)
{
    IDictionary<int, SimpleEventClass> col = new Dictionary<int,
    SimpleEventClass>();
    for (int objectNo = 0; objectNo < 500000; objectNo++)
    {
        col[objectNo] = new SimpleEventClass { ID = objectNo };
        string result = col[objectNo].SimpleEvent("Raising an event ");
        Console.WriteLine(objectNo);
    }
    Console.ReadKey();
}
}
}
```

Snapshots from Diagnostic Tool

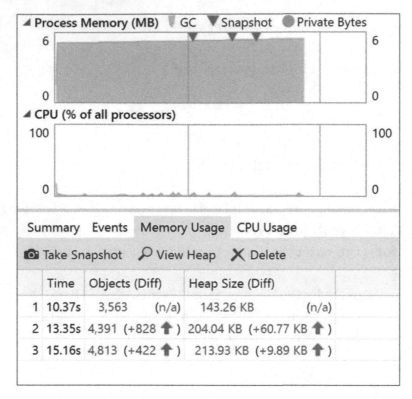

This is a screenshot of the Diagnostic Tool window; it includes three different snapshots to analyze memory usage at a given point of time.

We can see how the heap size is growing over time. If you notice carefully, you'll see that we are registering an event in our code

```
SimpleEvent += new MyDelegate(PrintText);
```

but never unregistered it.

I have also presented a case study with Microsoft's CLR Profiler to analyze the memory leak associated with a program. This tool is free and very easy to use (though presently it has lost the popularity to other tools). You can download the CLR Profiler (for .NET Framework 4) from `https://www.microsoft.com/en-in/download/confirmation.aspx?id=16273` *(Note: the link works fine at the time of this writing but it can be changed/ removed in future).*

Let us analyse the leaks associated with a different program but in this case, we will use CLR profiler.

Consider the following program (I took the snapshots once the program finished its execution):

Demonstration 3

```
using System;
using System.IO;//For FileStream

//Analysis of memory leak with an example of file handling

/* Special note: To use the CLR profiler:
   use the command: csc /t:exe /out:AnalyzingLeaksWithFileHandlingEx1.exe
   Program.cs to compile
   General Rule: csc /out:My.exe File.cs  <- compiles Files.cs and
   creates My.exe
   (you may need to set the PATH environment variable in your system)*/
namespace AnalyzingLeaksWithFileHandlingEx1
{
  class Program
      {
          class FileOps
          {
              public void readWrite()
              {

                  for (int i = 0; i < 1000; i++)
                  {
                      String fileName = "Myfile" + i + ".txt";
                      String path = @"c:\MyFile\" + fileName;
                      {
                          FileStream fileStreamName;
                          try
                          {
                              fileStreamName = new FileStream(path,
                              FileMode.OpenOrCreate, FileAccess.
                              ReadWrite);
```

```csharp
                        //using (fileStreamName = new
                        //FileStream(path, FileMode.OpenOrCreate,
                        FileAccess.ReadWrite))
                        {
                            Console.WriteLine("Created file no :
                            {0}", i);
                            //Forcefully throwing an exception , so
                            that we cannot close //the file
                            if (i < 1000)
                            {
                                throw new Exception("Forceful
                                Exception");
                            }
                        }
                        // FileStream not closed
                        // fileStreamName.Close();
                    }
                    catch (Exception e)
                    {
                        Console.WriteLine("Caught exception" + e);

                    }
                }
            }
        }
    }
    static void Main(string[] args)
    {
        FileOps filePtr = new FileOps();
        {
            filePtr.readWrite();
            Console.ReadKey();
        }
    }
}
}
```

Snapshots from CLR Profiler

A sample report from CLR Profiler may look like this:

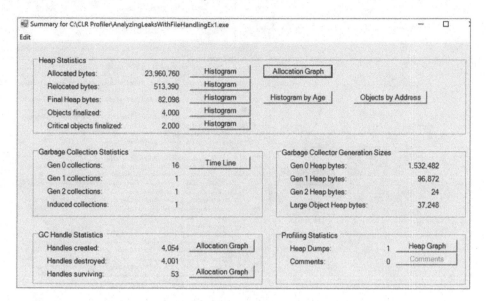

Analysis

From this screenshot, you can see the number of times the garbage collector needed to clean up different generations. Also, if you open the corresponding histograms, you can see the issues with the exceptions are related to file handling. For your reference, I am opening the final heap bytes histograms, objects finalized histograms, and relocated objects histograms after the execution of the program.

This is the final heap bytes histogram:

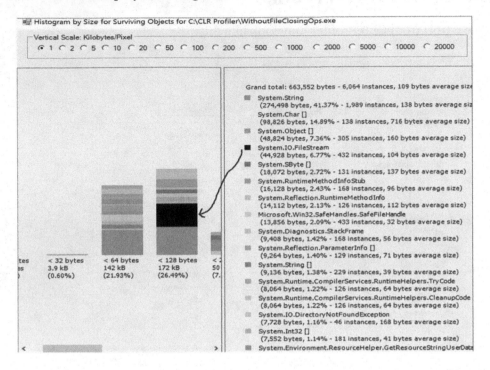

This is the finalized objects histogram:

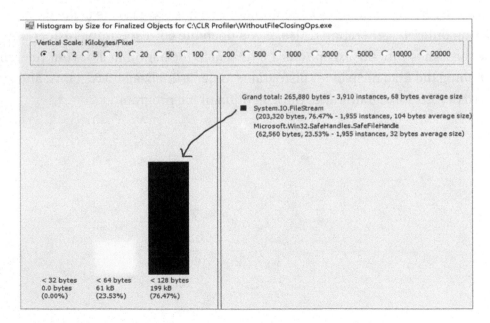

This is the relocated objects histogram:

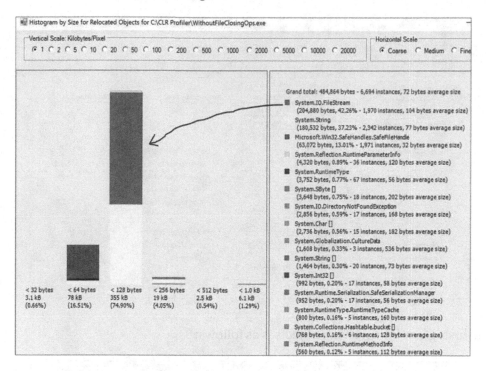

Let us modify the program

Now we are enabling the `using` statement in the preceding program, like this:

```
try
{
    //fileStreamName = new FileStream(path, FileMode.OpenOrCreate, FileAccess.ReadWrite);
    using (fileStreamName = new FileStream(path, FileMode.OpenOrCreate, FileAccess.ReadWrite))
    {
```

Now we have this report:

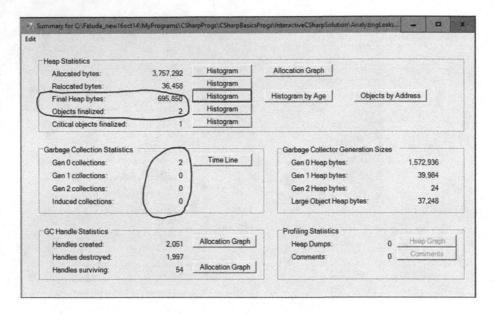

The histogram for surviving objects is as follows:

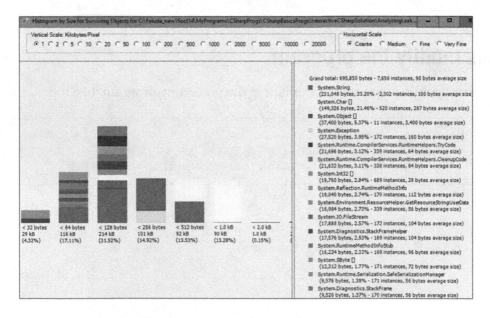

The histogram for relocated objects is as follows:

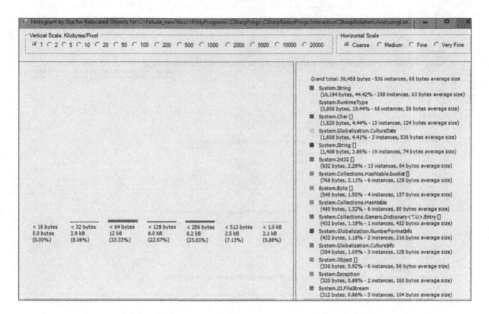

Analysis

Now we can see the difference: System.IO.FileStream instances are not a concern anymore. Also note that the garbage collector needed to perform much less than in the previous case.

Apart from this, you must note another important characteristic: if we analyze the IL code, we will see a try/finally block.

In this case, the compiler has created try/finally blocks for us since we are experimenting with the `using` statement. I already mentioned that `using` statements act as a syntactic shortcut for the try/finally block.

POINTS TO REMEMBER

According to Microsoft, the `using` statement ensures that the Dispose() method is called even if an exception occurs while you are calling methods on the object. You can achieve the same result by putting the object inside a try block and then calling the Dispose() method in a finally block; in fact, this is how the `using` statement is translated by the compiler.

So, the line of code:

```
using (FileStream fileStreamName = new FileStream(path, FileMode.
OpenOrCreate, FileAccess.ReadWrite))
{
  //lines of codes
}
```

converts into this:

```
FileStream fileStreamName = new FileStream(path, FileMode.OpenOrCreate,
FileAccess.ReadWrite);
try
{
  //lines of codes
}
finally
{
if (fileStreamName != null) ((IDisposable) fileStreamName).Dispose();
}
```

Teacher continues: Let's move on to another discussion. We must remember one key point in this context: If we pass the current object in the GC.SuppressFinalize() method, the Finalize() method (or destructor) of the current object won't be called.

Consider the following three programs and their output to understand how we can reclaim memory in C#.

Demonstration 4

```
using System;

namespace GarbageCollectionEx1
{
    class MyClass : IDisposable
    {
        public int Sum(int a, int b)
        {
            return a + b;
        }
        public void Dispose()
        {
            GC.SuppressFinalize(this);
            Console.WriteLine("Dispose() is called");
        }
```

```csharp
        ~MyClass()
        {
            Console.WriteLine("Destructor is Called..");
            System.Threading.Thread.Sleep(5000);
        }
    }
    class Program
    {
        static void Main(string[] args)
        {
            Console.WriteLine("*** Exploring Garbage Collections.
            Example-1***");
            MyClass myOb = new MyClass();
            int sumOfIntegers = myOb.Sum(10,20);
            Console.WriteLine("Sum of 10 and 20 is: " + sumOfIntegers);
            myOb.Dispose();
            Console.ReadKey();
        }
    }
}
```

Output

Note that the Dispose() method is called and the destructor of the object is not called.

```
*** Exploring Garbage Collections.Example-1***
Sum of 10 and 20 is: 30
Dispose() is called
```

Demonstration 5

Now we have commented out the line //GC.SuppressFinalize(this); and we did not call the Dispose() method; that is, both lines are commented out.

```csharp
using System;

namespace GarbageCollectionEx2
{
    class MyClass : IDisposable
    {
        public int Sum(int a, int b)
        {
            return a + b;
        }
        public void Dispose()
        {
            //GC.SuppressFinalize(this);
            Console.WriteLine("Dispose() is called");
        }
        ~MyClass()
        {
            Console.WriteLine("Destructor is Called..");
            //To catch the output at end, we are putting some sleep
            System.Threading.Thread.Sleep(15000);
        }
    }
    class Program
    {
        static void Main(string[] args)
        {
            Console.WriteLine("*** Exploring Garbage Collections.
            Example-2***");
            MyClass myOb = new MyClass();
            int sumOfIntegers = myOb.Sum(10, 20);
            Console.WriteLine("Sum of 10 and 20 is: " + sumOfIntegers);
```

```
        //myOb.Dispose();
        Console.ReadKey();
    }
  }
}
```

Output

The destructor method was called in this case.

```
*** Exploring Garbage Collections.Example-2***
Sum of 10 and 20 is: 30
Destructor is Called..
```

Demonstration 6

Now we are commenting out the line //GC.SuppressFinalize(this); in the preceding program but invoking the Dispose().

```
using System;

namespace GarbageCollectionEx3
{
    class MyClass : IDisposable
    {
        public int Sum(int a, int b)
        {
            return a + b;
        }
        public void Dispose()
        {
            //GC.SuppressFinalize(this);
            Console.WriteLine("Dispose() is called");
        }
        ~MyClass()
        {
```

```
            Console.WriteLine("Destructor is Called..");
            //To catch the output at end,we are putting some sleep
            System.Threading.Thread.Sleep(30000);
        }
    }
    class Program
    {
        static void Main(string[] args)
        {
            Console.WriteLine("*** Exploring Garbage Collections.
            Example-3***");
            MyClass myOb = new MyClass();
            int sumOfIntegers = myOb.Sum(10, 20);
            Console.WriteLine("Sum of 10 and 20 is: " + sumOfIntegers);
            myOb.Dispose();
            Console.ReadKey();
        }
    }
}
```

Output

Both the Dispose() method and the destructor are called now.

```
*** Exploring Garbage Collections.Example-3***
Sum of 10 and 20 is: 30
Dispose() is called
Destructor is Called..
```

Quiz

If you understand the programs we discussed so far, predict the output here.

Note that our program structure is similar to GarbageCollectionEx1; the only difference is that one class is containing another class.

```
using System;

namespace GarbageCollectionEx1._1
{
    class MyClassA : IDisposable
    {
        MyClassB classBObject;
        class MyClassB : IDisposable
        {
            public int Diff(int a, int b)
            {
                return a - b;
            }
            public void Dispose()
            {
                GC.SuppressFinalize(this);
                Console.WriteLine("MyClass B:Dispose() is called");
            }
            ~MyClassB()
            {
                Console.WriteLine("MyClassB:Destructor is Called..");
                System.Threading.Thread.Sleep(5000);
            }
        }

        public int Sum(int  a, int b)
        {
            return a + b;
        }
        public int Diff(int a, int b)
        {
```

```
        classBObject = new MyClassB();
        return classBObject.Diff(a, b);
    }
    public void Dispose()
    {
        GC.SuppressFinalize(this);
        Console.WriteLine("MyClassA:Dispose() is called");
        classBObject.Dispose();
    }
    ~MyClassA()
    {
        Console.WriteLine("MyClassA:Destructor is Called..");
        System.Threading.Thread.Sleep(5000);
    }
}

class Program
{
    static void Main(string[] args)
    {
        Console.WriteLine("*** Quiz:Exploring Garbage
        Collections.***");
        MyClassA obA = new MyClassA();
        int sumOfIntegers = obA.Sum(100, 20);
        int diffOfIntegers = obA.Diff(100, 20);
        Console.WriteLine("Sum of 10 and 20 is:{0}",sumOfIntegers);
        Console.WriteLine("Difference of 10 and 20 is:{0}",
        diffOfIntegers);
        obA.Dispose();
        Console.ReadKey();
    }
}
}
```

Output

```
*** Quiz:Exploring Garbage Collections.***
Sum of 100 and 20 is:120
Difference of 100 and 20 is:80
MyClassA:Dispose() is called
MyClass B:Dispose() is called
```

Quiz

Now let us comment out the code in the previous program as follows:

```
public void Dispose()
{
    GC.SuppressFinalize(this);
    Console.WriteLine("MyClassA:Dispose() is called");
//classBObject.Dispose();
}
```

What will be output?

Answer

```
*** Quiz:Exploring Garbage Collections.***
Sum of 100 and 20 is:120
Difference of 100 and 20 is:80
MyClassA:Dispose() is called
MyClassB:Destructor is Called..
```

Analysis

Notice that this time the Dispose () of MyClassA and destructor of MyClassB is invoked.

Summary

This chapter answered the following questions:

- ✓ What is garbage collection (GC)? How does it work in C#?

- ✓ What are the different GC generations?

- ✓ What are the different ways to invoke the garbage collector?

- ✓ How can we force GC?

- ✓ What is a memory leak?

- ✓ What are the probable causes of memory leaks?

- ✓ How can we use the Dispose() method effectively to collect memory?

- ✓ How do we use memory leak analysis with Visual Studio's diagnostic tool and Microsoft's CLR Profiler?

PART III

Become a Hero in the Real World

This section's highlights:

- An overview of the most fascinating design pattern concepts in programming

- Three important design patterns, including real-world examples and computer-world examples

CHAPTER 15

An Introduction to Design Patterns

Introduction

Teacher starts the discussion: Over a period of time, software engineers were facing a common problem during software development. There were no standards to instruct them on how to design and proceed. The issue became significant when a new member (experienced or inexperienced does not matter) joined the team, and he/she was assigned to do something from scratch or to modify something in the existing architecture. Since there were no standards, understanding the system architecture required huge efforts. *Design patterns* address the issue and make a common platform for all developers. Note *that these patterns are to be applied and reused in object-oriented designs.*

Around 1995, four authors—Erich Gamma, Richard Helm, Ralph Johnson, and John Vlissides presented their book, *Design Patterns: Elements of Reusable Object-Oriented Software* (Addison-Wesley, 1995)), in which they initiated the concept of *design patterns in software development.* These authors became known as the Gang of Four (GoF). They introduced 23 design patterns that were developed based on the experiences of software developers over a long period of time. Now, if any new member joins in a development team and he knows that the new system is following some specific design patterns, immediately he can get some idea with that design architecture. As a result, he can actively participate in the development process with the other team members within a very short period of time.

The first concept of real-life design pattern came from the building architect Christopher Alexander. He experienced some common problems repeatedly. So, he tried to address those issues with a related solution (for building design) in a well-uniformed manner. People believe that the software industry grasped the concept because software engineers can relate their products to building applications.

© Vaskaran Sarcar 2018
V. Sarcar, *Interactive C#*, https://doi.org/10.1007/978-1-4842-3339-9_15

Each pattern describes a problem that occurs over and over again in our environment, and then describes the core of the solution to that problem, in such a way that you can use this solution a million times over, without ever doing it the same way twice.

—Christopher Alexander

GoF ensures us that although the patterns were described for building and towns, the same concepts can be applied for the patterns in object-oriented design. We can substitute the original concepts of walls and doors with objects and interfaces. The common thing in both is that at the core, both types of patterns try to find some solutions in some specific context.

In 1995, the original concepts were discussed with C++. But C# came in 2000. In this book, we will try to examine three design patterns with C#. If you are familiar with any other popular programming languages, like Java, C++, and so forth, then you will understand the concepts very easily. I have chosen simple examples with easy-to-remember examples to help you to develop these concepts.

Key Points

- A design pattern is a general reusable solution for commonly occurring problems.

- Our aim is to make a template of how to solve a problem that can be used in many different situations.

- These are descriptions of communicating objects and classes that are customized to solve a general design problem in a particular context.

- Gang of Four discussed 23 design patterns that can be classified into three major categories.

- *Creational patterns:* These patterns abstract the instantiation process. We try to make a system that is independent from how the objects are composed, created, or represented. The following five patterns are in this category.

  - Singleton pattern

  - Prototype pattern

  - Factory Method pattern

  - Builder pattern

  - Abstract Factory pattern

- *Structural patterns:* Here we focus on how classes and objects can be composed to form relatively large structures. They generally use inheritance to compose interfaces or implementations. The following seven patterns fall into this category.

  - Proxy pattern

  - Flyweight pattern

  - Composite pattern

  - Bridge pattern

  - Facade pattern

  - Decorator pattern

  - Adapter pattern

- *Behavioral patterns:* Here our concentration is on algorithms and the assignment of responsibilities among objects. We also focus on the communication process among them. We need to give a sharp look on the way by which those objects can be interconnected. The following eleven patterns fall into this category.

  - Observer pattern

  - Strategy pattern

  - Template method pattern

  - Command pattern

  - Iterator pattern

  - Memento pattern

  - State pattern

  - Mediator pattern

  - Chain of responsibility pattern

  - Visitor pattern

  - Interpreter pattern

Here we are exploring only three design patterns: one from each category. I chose the simplest examples so that you can understand them easily. But you must think about each of them repeatedly, practice, try to connect them to other problems, and ultimately keep writing the code. This process will help you to master the subject.

Singleton Pattern

GoF Definition

Ensure a class only has one instance, and provide a global point of access to it.

Concept

A particular class should have only one instance. We will only use that instance when we are in need.

A Real-life Example

Suppose you are a member of a sports team. And your team is going to play against another team in a tournament. As per the rules of the game, the captains of the two sides must do a coin toss to decide which side will start the game in possession. So, if your team does not have a captain, you need to elect someone as a captain. And, your team must have only one captain.

A Computer-World Example

In a software system, sometimes we decide to use only one file system. Usually, we use it for centralized management of resources.

Illustration

In this example, we made the constructor private so that we cannot instantiate in a normal fashion. When we make an attempt to create an instance of the class, we are checking whether we already have an available copy or not. If we do not have any such copy, we'll create it; otherwise, we'll simply reuse the existing copy.

Class Diagram

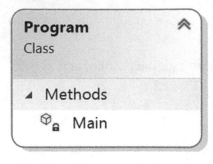

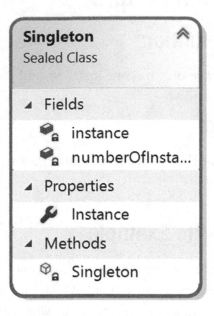

Solution Explorer View

The following shows a high-level structure of the parts of the program.

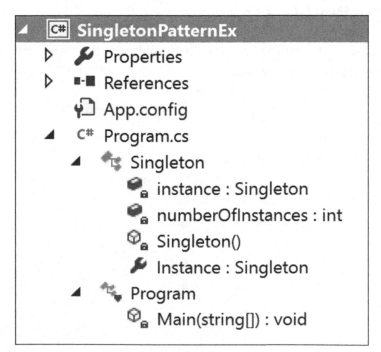

Discussion

We have implemented a very simple example to illustrate the concept of the singleton pattern. This approach is known as *static initialization*.

Initially, C++ specification had some ambiguity about the initialization order of static variables. But the .NET Framework resolved this.

The following are notable characteristics of this approach:

- The CLR (common language runtime) takes care of the variable initialization process.

- We will create an instance when any member of the class is referenced.

- The *public static* member ensures a global point of access. It confirms that the instantiation process will not start until we invoke the Instance property of the class (i.e., it supports lazy instantiation). The *sealed* keyword prevents further derivation of the class (so that its subclass cannot misuse it), *readonly* ensures that the assignment process will take place during the static initialization.

- Our constructor is private. We cannot instantiate the Singleton class outside. It helps us to refer the only instance that can exist in the system.

Implementation

```
using System;

namespace SingletonPatternEx
{
    public sealed class Singleton
    {
        private static readonly Singleton instance=new Singleton();
        private int numberOfInstances = 0;
        //Private constructor is used to prevent
        //creation of instances with 'new' keyword outside this class
        private Singleton()
        {
```

```
        Console.WriteLine("Instantiating inside the private
        constructor.");
        numberOfInstances++;
        Console.WriteLine("Number of instances ={0}", numberOfInstances);
    }
    public static Singleton Instance
    {
        get
        {
            Console.WriteLine("We already have an instance now.Use
            it.");
            return instance;
        }
    }
    //public static int MyInt = 25;
}
class Program
{
    static void Main(string[] args)
    {
        Console.WriteLine("***Singleton Pattern Demo***\n");
        //Console.WriteLine(Singleton.MyInt);
        // Private Constructor.So,we cannot use 'new' keyword.
        Console.WriteLine("Trying to create instance s1.");
        Singleton s1 = Singleton.Instance;
        Console.WriteLine("Trying to create instance s2.");
        Singleton s2 = Singleton.Instance;
        if (s1 == s2)
        {
            Console.WriteLine("Only one instance exists.");
        }
        else
        {
            Console.WriteLine("Different instances exist.");
        }
```

```
        Console.Read();
    }
  }

}
```

Output

```
***Singleton Pattern Demo***

Trying to create instance s1.
Instantiating inside the private constructor.
Number of instances =1
We already have an instance now.Use it.
Trying to create instance s2.
We already have an instance now.Use it.
Only one instance exists.
```

Challenges

Consider the following code. Suppose that we have added one more line of code in the Singleton class, as follows:

```csharp
public sealed class Singleton
{
    private static readonly Singleton instance=new Singleton();
    private int numberOfInstances = 0;
    //Private constructor is used to prevent
    //creation of instances with 'new' keyword outside this class
    private Singleton()
    {
    Console.WriteLine("Instantiating inside the private constructor.");
    numberOfInstances++;
    Console.WriteLine("Number of instances ={0}", numberOfInstances);
    }
    public static Singleton Instance
    {
        get
        {
            Console.WriteLine("We already have an instance now.Use it.");
            return instance;
        }
    }
    public static int MyInt = 25;   ←
}
```

And suppose our Main() method looks like this:

```
class Program
    {
        static void Main(string[] args)
        {
            Console.WriteLine("***Singleton Pattern Demo***\n");
            Console.WriteLine(Singleton.MyInt);
            Console.Read();
        }
    }
```

Now if you execute the program, you will see following output:

```
Instantiating inside the private constructor.
Number of instances =1
***Singleton Pattern Demo***

25
```

This is the downside of this approach. Inside Main(), you only tried to play with the MyInt static variable, but your application still made an instance of the Singleton class; that is, you have less control over the instantiation process. The instantiation process starts whenever you refer to any member of the class.

Still in most scenarios, this approach is mostly preferred in .NET.

Q&A Session

Question 1: **Why are we complicating things? We can simply write our Singleton class as follows:**

```
public class Singleton
    {
        private static Singleton instance;

        private Singleton() { }

        public static Singleton Instance
```

```
    {
        get
        {
            if (instance == null)
            {
                instance = new Singleton();
            }
            return instance;
        }
    }
 }
```

Answer: This approach can work in a single threaded environment. But consider a multithreaded environment. In a multithreaded environment, suppose two (or more) threads try to evaluate this:

```
if (instance == null)
```

And if they see that the instance is not created yet, each of them will try to create a new instance. As a result, we may end up with multiple instances of the class.

Question 2: Are there any alternative approaches to model a Singleton design pattern?

Answer: There are many approaches. Each of them has their own pros and cons. Let's discuss one of them called *Double Checked Locking*. MSDN outlined the approach as follows:

```
//Double checked locking
    using System;

    public sealed class Singleton
    {
        /*We are using volatile to ensure that
          assignment to the instance variable finishes before
          it's   access*/
        private static volatile Singleton instance;
        private static object lockObject = new Object();

        private Singleton() { }
```

```
public static Singleton Instance
{
    get
    {
        if (instance == null)
        {
            lock (lockObject)
            {
                if (instance == null)
                    instance = new Singleton();
            }
        }
        return instance;
    }
}
}
```

This approach can help us create the instances when they are really needed. But in general, a locking mechanism is expensive.

Question 3: Why are we marking the instance as volatile?

Answer: Let's look at what C# specification tells us: "The volatile keyword indicates that a field might be modified by multiple threads that are executing at the same time. Fields that are declared volatile are not subject to compiler optimizations that assume access by a single thread. This ensures that the most up-to-date value is present in the field at all times."

Simply put, the *volatile* keyword helps us to provide a serialize access mechanism; that is, all threads will observe the changes by any other thread as per their execution order. Remember that the *volatile* keyword is applicable to class (or struct) fields; we cannot apply them to local variables.

If you are interested to know more about different approaches of Singleton Patterns, you can go through Jon Skeets comments. He discussed various alternatives (with their pros and cons) to model a singleton pattern in his article at http://csharpindepth.com/Articles/General/Singleton.aspx.

Adapter Pattern

GoF Definition

Convert the interface of a class into another interface clients expect. Adapter lets classes work together that could not otherwise because of incompatible interfaces.

Concept

The core concept is best described by the examples given next.

A Real-Life Example

The most common example of this type is a power adapter. An AC power supply provides different types of sockets that adapt to the one needed. Consider another example. Very often, we need to charge our mobile phones using a charger through a switchboard. But if we discover that our mobile charger cannot be used (or plugged into) with a particular switchboard, we need to use an adapter. Even a translator who is translating languages can be considered following this pattern in real life.

So, you can imagine something like this: your application is plugged in into an adapter (which is x-shaped in this example) that enables you to use the intended interface. Without the adapter, you cannot join the application and the interface.

The following illustrates *before* using an adapter:

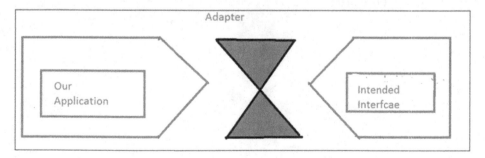

The following illustrates *after* using an adapter:

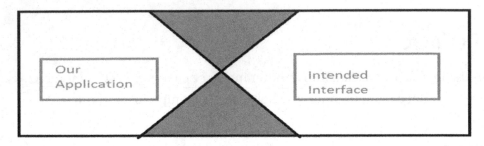

A Computer-World Example

The most common use of this pattern is best described by the following example.

Illustration

In this example, we can easily calculate the area of a rectangle. Note the Calculator class and its GetArea() method. We need to supply a rectangle in the GetArea() method to get the area of the rectangle. Now suppose that we want to calculate the area of a triangle, but our constraint is that we want to get the area of it through the GetArea() of the calculator. How can we do that?

To serve the requirement, we have made an adapter (CalculatorAdapter in the example) for the triangle and we are passing a triangle in its GetArea() method. The method will treat the triangle like a rectangle, and in turn, calls the GetArea() of the Calculator class to get the area.

Class Diagram

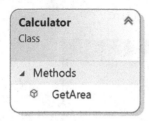

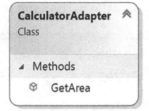

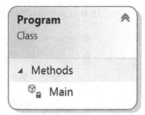

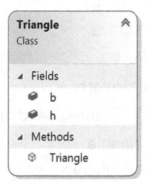

Directed Graph Document

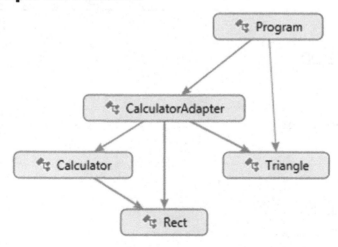

Solution Explorer View

The following is a high-level structure of the parts of the program:

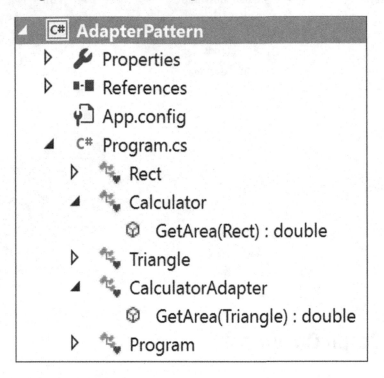

Implementation

```
using System;

namespace AdapterPattern
{
    class Rect
    {
        public double l;
        public double w;
    }
    class Calculator
    {
        public double GetArea(Rect r)
        {
```

```
        return r.l * r.w;
    }
}
//Calculate the area of triangle using Calculator and Rect type as
input.Whether we have Triangle.
class Triangle
{
    public double b;//base
    public double h;//height
    public Triangle(int b, int h)
    {
        this.b = b;
        this.h = h;
    }
}
class CalculatorAdapter
{

    public double GetArea(Triangle t)
    {
        Calculator c = new Calculator();
        Rect r = new Rect();
        //Area of Triangle=0.5*base*height
        r.l = t.b;
        r.w = 0.5*t.h;
        return c.getArea(r);
    }

}


class Program
{
    static void Main(string[] args)
    {
        Console.WriteLine("***Adapter Pattern Demo***\n");
        CalculatorAdapter cal=new CalculatorAdapter();
        Triangle t = new Triangle(20,10);
```

```
            Console.WriteLine("Area of Triangle is " + cal.GetArea(t)+"
            Square unit");
            Console.ReadKey();
        }
    }
}
```

Output

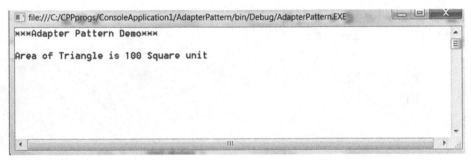

Let's modify the illustration.

We have already seen a very simple example of adapter design pattern. But if you want to follow object-oriented design principles, you may want to modify the example. One of the main reasons is that instead of using concrete classes, we need to use interfaces. So, keeping the previous goal in mind, let's modify our illustration.

The following are key characteristic of the new examples:

- Class Rect is implementing RectInterface and the CalculateAreaOfRectangle() method helps us calculate the area of a rectangle object.

- The Triangle class implements TriInterface and the CalculateAreaOfTriangle() method helps us calculate the area of a triangle object.

- Your constraint is that you need to calculate the area of the triangle by using RectInterface. To serve this purpose, we have made an adapter that can talk to RectInterface.

- Now notice the beauty of using this pattern: neither Rectangle nor Triangle code needs to change. We are using an adapter that helps us to talk to RectInterface and at high level, it appears that by using RectInterface method, we are computing the area of a triangle.

- Notice that the GetArea(RectInterface r) method does not know that through TriangleAdapter, it is getting a Triangle object instead of a Rectangle object.

- Note another important fact and usage. Suppose that you do not have many rectangle objects but your demand is greater. With this pattern, you can use some of the triangle objects that may behave like rectangle objects. How? Well, if you notice carefully, you will find that by using the adapter (though we are calling CalculateAreaOfRectangle()), it is actually invoking CalculateAreaOfTriangle(). So, we can modify the method body as per our need; for example, we could multiply the triangle area by 2.0 to get an area of 200 sq. units (just like a rectangle object with length of 20 units and breadth of 10 units). This could help in a scenario where you need to deal with objects that have an area of 200 square units.

- For better readability, we have not followed the C# standard naming conventions for interfaces in this example(i.e. we did not start with "I" for interfaces).

Solution Explorer View

The following is a high-level structure of the parts of the program:

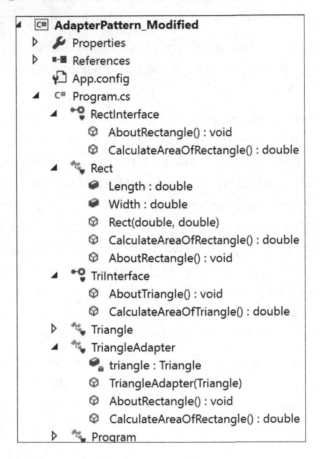

Implementation

```
using System;
namespace AdapterPattern_Modified
{
    interface RectInterface
    {
        void AboutRectangle();
        double CalculateAreaOfRectangle();
    }
    class Rect : RectInterface
```

```csharp
{
    public double Length;
    public double Width;
    public Rect(double l, double w)
    {
        this.Length = l;
        this.Width = w;
    }

 public double CalculateAreaOfRectangle()
 {
    return Length * Width;
 }

 public void AboutRectangle()
 {
  Console.WriteLine("Actually, I am a Rectangle");
 }
}

interface TriInterface
{
    void AboutTriangle();
    double CalculateAreaOfTriangle();
}
class Triangle : TriInterface
{
    public double BaseLength;//base
    public double Height;//height
    public Triangle(double b, double h)
    {
        this.BaseLength = b;
        this.Height = h;
    }

    public double CalculateAreaOfTriangle()
    {
```

```csharp
            return 0.5 * BaseLength * Height;
        }
        public void AboutTriangle()
        {
            Console.WriteLine(" Actually, I am a Triangle");
        }
    }

    /*TriangleAdapter is implementing RectInterface.
     So, it needs to implement all the methods defined
    in the target interface.*/
    class TriangleAdapter:RectInterface
    {
        Triangle triangle;
        public TriangleAdapter(Triangle t)
        {
            this.triangle = t;
        }

        public void AboutRectangle()
        {
            triangle.AboutTriangle();
        }

        public double CalculateAreaOfRectangle()
        {
            return triangle.CalculateAreaOfTriangle();
        }
    }

    class Program
    {
        static void Main(string[] args)
        {
            Console.WriteLine("***Adapter Pattern Modified Demo***\n");
            //CalculatorAdapter cal = new CalculatorAdapter();
            Rect r = new Rect(20, 10);
```

```
Console.WriteLine("Area of Rectangle is :{0} Square unit",
r.CalculateAreaOfRectangle());
Triangle t = new Triangle(20, 10);
Console.WriteLine("Area of Triangle is :{0} Square unit",
t.CalculateAreaOfTriangle());
RectInterface adapter = new TriangleAdapter(t);
//Passing a Triangle instead of a Rectangle
Console.WriteLine("Area of Triangle using the triangle adapter
is :{0} Square unit", GetArea(adapter));
Console.ReadKey();
}
/*GetArea(RectInterface r) method  does not know that through
TriangleAdapter,it is getting a Triangle instead of a Rectangle*/
static double GetArea(RectInterface r)
{
    r.AboutRectangle();
    return r.CalculateAreaOfRectangle();
}
}
}
```

Output

```
***Adapter Pattern Modified Demo***

Area of Rectangle is :200 Square unit
Area of Triangle is :100 Square unit
 Actually, I am a Triangle
Area of Triangle using the triangle adapter is :100 Square unit
```

Note

The GoF explained two types of adapters: class adapters and object adapters.

- Object adapters adapt through object compositions. The adapter that we discussed is an example of an object adapter. In many places, you will notice this typical class diagram for an object adapter.

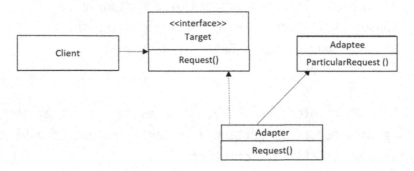

In our example, TriangleAdapter is the adapter that implements the RectInterface (Target interface) and Triangle is the Adaptee. You can see that the adapter holds the adaptee instance (i.e. object composition is implemented in this example).

- Class adapters adapts through subclassing. They are the supporters of multiple inheritance. But we know that in C#, multiple inheritance through classes is not supported. (We need interfaces to implement the concept of multiple inheritance).

Here is a typical class diagram for class adapters that support multiple inheritance:

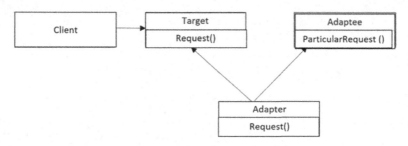

Q&A Session

Question: **How can we implement a class adapter design pattern in C#?**

Answer: We can subclass an existing class and implement the desired interface. Consider the following code block.

```
class ClassAdapter : Triangle, RectInterface
    {
        public ClassAdapter(double b, double h) : base(b, h)
        {
        }

        public void AboutRectangle()
        {
            Console.WriteLine(" Actually, I am an Adapter");
        }

        public double CalculateAreaOfRectangle()
        {
            return 2.0 * base.CalculateAreaOfTriangle();
        }
    }
```

But we must note that this approach may not be applicable in all scenarios; for example, when we need to adapt a method that is not specified in a C# interface. In those cases, object adapters are useful.

Visitor Pattern

GoF Definition

Represent an operation to be performed on the elements of an object structure. Visitor lets you define a new operation without changing the classes of the elements on which it operates.

Concept

In this pattern, we can separate an algorithm from the object structure on which it operates. Therefore, we can add new operations to existing object structures without modifying those structures. This way, we are following the open/close principle (an extension is allowed but modification is disallowed for entities like class, function, modules, etc.).

A Real-Life Example

We can think of a taxi-booking scenario. When the taxi arrives at our door and we enter the taxi, the "visiting" taxi takes control of the transportation.

A Computer-World Example

This pattern is very useful when we do plugging in public APIs. Clients can then perform operations on a class with a visiting class without modifying the source.

Illustration

Here we have presented a simple example to describe the visitor design pattern. You can see two class hierarchy here- left most one is representing the original class hierarchy. The rightmost one is created by us. Any modification/update operation in the IOriginalInterface hierarchy can be done through this new class hierarchy without disturbing the original code.

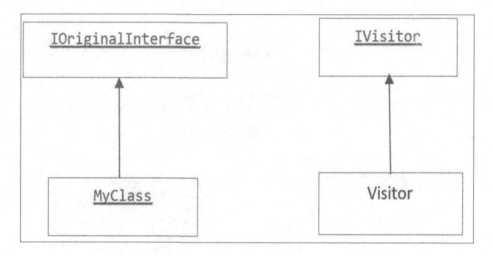

Consider a simple case. Suppose, in this example, we want to modify the initial integer value in MyClass but our constraint is that we cannot change the codes in the existing hierarchy.

To serve this requirement,in the following demonstration, we are separating the functionality implementations (i.e., algorithms) from the original class hierarchy and we put all our logic into the visitor class hierarchy.

Class Diagram

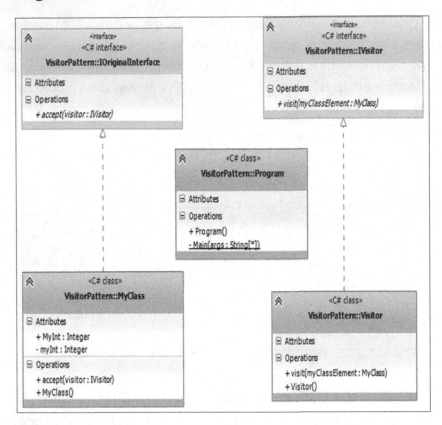

Solution Explorer View

The following is a high-level structure of the parts of the program:

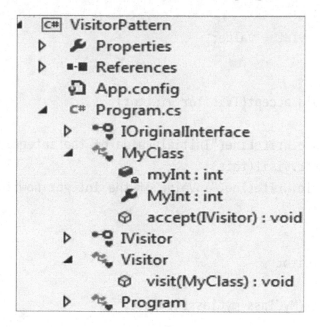

Implementation

```csharp
using System;

namespace VisitorPattern
{
    interface IOriginalInterface
    {
        void accept(IVisitor visitor);
    }
    class MyClass : IOriginalInterface
    {
        private int myInt = 5;//Initial or default value

        public int MyInt
        {
            get
            {
```

```
                return myInt;
            }
            set
            {
                myInt = value;
            }
     }
    public void accept(IVisitor visitor)
    {
        Console.WriteLine("Initial value of the integer:{0}", myInt);
        visitor.visit(this);
        Console.WriteLine("\nValue of the integer now:{0}", myInt);
    }
}

interface IVisitor
{
    void visit(MyClass myClassElement);
}
class Visitor : IVisitor
{
    public void visit(MyClass myClassElement)
    {
        Console.WriteLine("Visitor is trying to change the
        integer value");
        myClassElement.MyInt = 100;
        Console.WriteLine("Exiting from Visitor- visit");
    }
}
class Program
{
    static void Main(string[] args)
    {
        Console.WriteLine("***Visitor Pattern Demo***\n");
        IVisitor v = new Visitor();
        MyClass myClass = new MyClass();
```

```
        myClass.accept(v);
        Console.ReadLine();
    }
  }
}
```

Output

```
***Visitor Pattern Demo***

Initial value of the integer:5
Visitor is trying to change the integer value
Exiting from Visitor- visit

Value of the integer now:100
```

Q&A Session

***Question 1:* When should we consider implementing visitor design patterns?**

Answer: When we need to add capabilities without modifying the existing architecture. It is the primary aim of a visitor pattern. For this pattern, encapsulation is not the primary concern.

***Question 2:* Are there any drawbacks associated with this pattern?**

Answer: Encapsulation is not its key concern here. So, in many cases, we may break the encapsulation using visitors. If we frequently need to add new concrete classes to an existing architecture, the visitor hierarchy becomes difficult to maintain. For example, suppose we want to add another concrete class in the original hierarchy. Then in this case, we need to modify the visitor class hierarchy accordingly to serve the purpose.

Summary

This chapter introduced

- ✓ Design patterns
- ✓ Three Gang of Four design patterns: the singleton pattern, the adapter pattern, and the visitor pattern with C# implementations

CHAPTER 16

Winning Notes and the Road Ahead

Congratulations. You have reached the end of the journey. All of us can start a journey but only few among us can complete it with care. So, you are among the minority who have that extraordinary capability to cover the distance successfully. I believe that you have enjoyed your learning experience. The same experience can help you learn any new topic in this category. Earlier, I said that if you repeatedly think about the questions and answers discussed in the book, you will have more clarity about them, you will feel confident about them, and you will remake yourself in the programming world.

A complete coverage of the C# language and all of its features would need many more pages, which would make the size of the book too big to digest. So, what's next? You should not forget the basic principle: *learning is a continuous process*. This book was an attempt to encourage you to learn the core topics in depth, so that you can learn advanced topics and upcoming features smoothly.

Once you finish this book, you are ready to explore advanced features, such as collections, LINQ, concurrency, serialization, reflection, multithreading, parallel programming, asynchronous programming, design patterns, and more, in depth. With any of these, you will find that the concepts described in this book are very helpful to you.

Finally, I have a request of you: criticism is allowed but at the same time, please let me know what you liked in this book. In general, it is always easy to criticize but an artistic view and an open mind are required to discover the true efforts that are associated with any kind of work. Thank you and happy coding!

© Vaskaran Sarcar 2018
V. Sarcar, *Interactive C#*, https://doi.org/10.1007/978-1-4842-3339-9_16

APPENDIX A

Collect the Raw Materials

Fundamentals

C# is an object-oriented language. It has many similarities with Java, C++, and Visual Basic. Programmers often say that when the power and efficiency of C++ shook hands with the clean object-oriented design of Java and the simplification of Visual Basic, we got this powerful language. Let us quickly go through some fundamental questions and answers in this topic.

Theory

When we compile our .NET program using any .NET-obedient language like C#, initially our source code is converted into an intermediate code, which is known as MSIL (Microsoft Intermediate Language). IL code is interpreted by CLR. Upon program execution, IL code is converted into the binary executable code, or native code.

What is the purpose of IL code?

Answer:

It is operating system and hardware independent. This code is similar for each .NET language, so we can make cross-language relationships with it.

What is CLR?

Answer:

It is the most important concept in the .NET Framework. It is a framework layer that exists above operating systems and handles the execution of .NET applications. The programs must go through the CLR so that there is no direct communication with the OS.

© Vaskaran Sarcar 2018
V. Sarcar, *Interactive C#*, https://doi.org/10.1007/978-1-4842-3339-9

How can we see the IL code for the following program?

Answer:

Consider this program.

```csharp
using System;
namespace ILCodeTest
{
    class Program
    {
        static void Main(string[] args)
        {
            Console.WriteLine("Check IL Code in C#");

            Console.WriteLine("Enter an integer");
            string a = Console.ReadLine();
            int myInt = int.Parse(a);
            Console.WriteLine("You have entered:" + a);

            double myDouble = 21.9;
            Console.WriteLine("your double value is : " + myDouble);

            float myFloat = 100.9F;
            Console.WriteLine("Your float value is : " + myFloat);

            Console.Read();
        }
    }
}
```

To see the IL code, do the following:

1. Open the Visual Studio command prompt.

2. Type **ildasm** and press Enter. The following window will pop up.

3. Drag the .exe to this window.

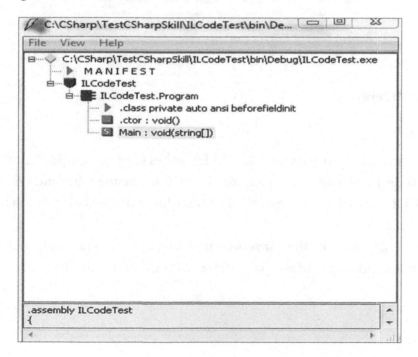

4.   Double-click Main:void(string[]).

What are JITers?

Answer:

It's full form is Just-in-time compilers. CLR invokes them to compile IL code to native executable code; for example, in .exe or .dll (which must be machine and OS specific). Afterward, CLR reuses the same compiled copy so that repeated compilation time can be saved/avoided.

When we call a function, the conversion of IL to native code takes place just in time, and the part that is not used in any particular run is never converted.

Which is faster, C# or C++?

Answer:

Actually, the competition was not the concern for Microsoft. But experts say that when a program runs over a very long period of time, we assume that all (or most) of the functions are already called and we have no (or minimum) just in time performance penalty. And in such cases, JITers can make the code faster than C++; otherwise, C++ is considered faster because C# has just-in-time performance penalty.

What is the difference between a project and a solution?

Answer:

A *project* contains executables and libraries (in general) to make an application or module. Their extension is .csproj in C# (e.g., Console Application, Class Library, Windows Form Application, etc.).

A *solution* is a placeholder that contains different logically related projects. The extension is .sln. (e.g., one of our solutions can contain a Console Application project and a Windows Form project).

C# does not allow two classes with the same name in a program. But in some cases, you may need the same name. How can you avoid the name conflicts?

Answer:

We can use a namespace in such a scenario.

What is the significance of the "using System"?

Answer:

We can access all classes defined in the System namespace (but not the classes in its child namespaces).

What is the significance of these lines?

```
class Program
    {
        static void Main(string[] args)
        {
        }
    }
```

413

Answer:

It is a standard signature of the Main() method of C#.

- Main: The entry point of our program.

- static: CLR can call the Main method without creating any object of the Program class.

- void: The method is returning nothing.

- string[] args: The list of parameters that can be passed to Main() while executing the program from the command line.

Can we have two or more Main() methods in a C# program? Will the program compile?

```csharp
using System;

namespace MultipleMainMethodTest
{
    class Program1
    {
        static void Main(string[] args)
        {
            Console.WriteLine("I am in Program -1");
        }
    }
    class Program2
    {
        static void Main(string[] args)
        {
            Console.WriteLine("I am in Program -2");
        }
    }
}
```

Answer:

We can have multiple Main() methods here but we need to specify the entry point; otherwise, we will get error like this:

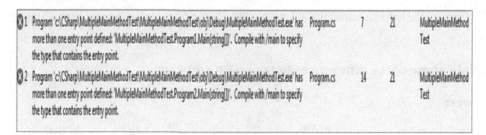

To run this program, go to project properties and set the startup object (I have chosen Program1 here):

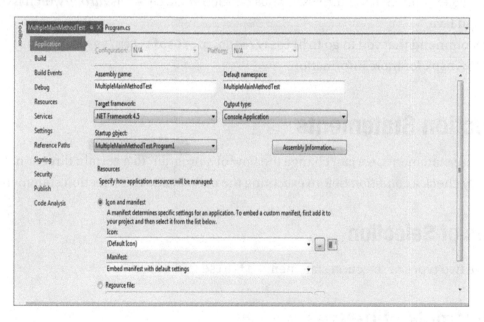

Now when you run the application, the output will look like this:

```
I am in Program -1
```

Explain some of the similarities between C# and Java.

Answer:

Both are object-oriented languages. Both have built-in garbage collection. C# does not allow multiple inheritance like Java. In managed code, it does not allow the use of pointers.

Explain some of the differences between C# and Java.

Answer:

C# supports the concepts of operator overloading, enumerations, preprocessor directives and pointers in unmanaged code, and delegates (like function pointers).

In Java, we have a special keyword, *throws*, in which any method can declare the unchecked exception that it throws. C# has no such syntax. C# has *throw*, which is also present in Java.

I recommend that you to go to `https://msdn.microsoft.com/en-us/library/ms836794.aspx` for more information.

Selection Statements

With these statements, we can change the flow of a program to a certain direction. We generally check a *condition* before executing the code inside the selection statements.

Types of Selection

We have two types of selection statements: `if-else` and `switch`.

An Example of if-else

```
using System;

namespace Example_if_else
{
    class Program
    {
```

```
static void Main(string[] args)
{
    Console.WriteLine("***Illustration -if-else***");
    string input;
    int number;
    Console.WriteLine("Enter a number");
    input = Console.ReadLine();
    //Checking whether we can parse the string as an integer
    if (int.TryParse(input, out number))
    {
        Console.WriteLine("You have entered {0}", input);
    }
    else
    {
        Console.WriteLine("Invalid input");
    }
    if (number % 2 == 0)
    {
        Console.WriteLine("{0} is an even number", number);
    }
    else
    {
        Console.WriteLine("{0} is an odd number", number);
    }
    Console.ReadKey();
}
}
}
```

Output 1: For Input 7

```
***Illustration -if-else***
Enter a number
7
You have entered 7
7 is an odd number
```

Output 2: For Input 24

```
***Illustration -if-else***
Enter a number
24
You have entered 24
24 is an even number
```

An Example of switch Statements

Unlike if-else, here we have a list of possible values for a variable. We pass the control to one of the case statements whose value matches with the variable in the switch statement.

```
using System;

namespace Example_switch
{
    class Program
    {
        static void Main(string[] args)
        {
            Console.WriteLine("***Illustration -switch statement***");
            Console.WriteLine("1-Below 40");
            Console.WriteLine("2-Between 41 and 60");
            Console.WriteLine("3-Between 60 and 79");
            Console.WriteLine("4-Above 80");
            Console.WriteLine("Enter your score");
            //Using Parse() instead of tryParse() just for a change.
            Though, it is suggested that //you use tryParse()
            int score = int.Parse(Console.ReadLine());
            switch (score)
            {
                case 1:
                    Console.WriteLine("Poor performance");
                    break;
```

```
        case 2:
            Console.WriteLine("Average performance");
            break;
        case 3:
            Console.WriteLine("Good performance");
            break;
        case 4:
            Console.WriteLine("Excellent performance");
            break;
        default:
            break;
    }
    Console.ReadKey();
    }
  }
}
```

Output

```
***Illustration -switch statement***
 1-Below 40
 2-Between 41 and 60
 3-Between 60 and 79
 4-Above 80
Enter your score
4
 Excellent performance
```

Can we place the default case between other case statements (i.e., not at the bottom)?

```
class Program
    {
        static int score;

        static void Main(string[] args)
        {
            switch (score)
            {
```

```
            case 1:
                Console.WriteLine("Poor performance");
                break;
            case 2:
                Console.WriteLine("Good performance");
                break;
            default:
                break;
            case 3:
                Console.WriteLine("Excellent performance");
                break;
        }
    }
}
```

Answer:

Yes, this is OK.

Quiz

Will the code compile?

```
using System;
namespace SelectionStmtsTests
{
    class Program
    {
        static int score;

        static void Main(string[] args)
        {
            switch (score)
            {
                case 1:
                    Console.WriteLine(" Poor performance");
                    break;
```

```
            case 2:
                Console.WriteLine(" Good performance");
                //break;
            default:
                break;
            case 3:
                Console.WriteLine(" Excellent performance");
                break;
        }

    }
  }
}
```

Answer:

No. In C#, we cannot fall through from one case label to another.

 CS0163   Control cannot fall through from one case label ('case 2:') to another

Quiz

What will the output be?

```
using System;

namespace SelectionStmtsTests2
{
    class Program
    {
        static int score;

        static void Main(string[] args)
        {
            int number = 5;
            if (number % 2 == 0)

                Console.WriteLine("{0} is an even number", number);
```

```
            Console.WriteLine("We have not used brackets for if
            statements");

        else
            Console.WriteLine("{0} is an odd  number", number);

    }
  }
}
```

Answer:

Compilation error. It is always a good practice to use brackets for your if-else blocks. You need to rewrite the section as follows:

```
int number = 5;
if (number % 2 == 0)
{
    Console.WriteLine("{0} is an even number", number);
    Console.WriteLine("We have not used brackets for if statements");
}
else
    Console.WriteLine("{0} is an odd  number", number);
```

Which one is faster-if-else or switch?

Answer:

Many of us believe that switch is faster. Actually, it depends on the situation. When we have a skewed distribution of inputs, the if-statement can perform better than switch. I suggest you to visit the online resource/discussion at www.dotnetperls.com/if-switch-performance.

Iteration Statements

Why do we need these statements?

Answer:

To create loops. Alternatively, simply to execute our code block/s up to some specified number of times.

Name the different types of iteration statements in C#.

Answer:

The while loop, the do...while loop, the for loop, and the foreach loop. The following is a typical example of the while loop:

```
Console.WriteLine("***Illustration: while loop***");
int i = 0;
while (i < 5)
 {
   Console.WriteLine("i is now {0}", i);
  i++;
}
```

How can you distinguish between while and do...while?

Answer:

With do...while, the condition is checked at the end of the loop. So, even if the condition is false, a do...while loop executes at least once.

Consider the following program and output. Note that we are checking whether the value of *j* is less than 10 in the *while* part, even if we're able to print the statement in do{..}.

Demonstration

```
using System;

namespace DoWhileEx
{
    class Program
    {
        static void Main(string[] args)
        {
            Console.WriteLine("***Illustration:do...while***");
            int j = 5;
            do
            {
                Console.WriteLine("Inside loop:j is now {0}", j);
                j++;
            } while (j < 10);
            Console.WriteLine(" Outside loop: Final value in j is {0}", j);
            Console.ReadKey();
        }
    }
}
```

Output

```
***Illustration:do...while***
Inside loop:j is now 5
Inside loop:j is now 6
Inside loop:j is now 7
Inside loop:j is now 8
Inside loop:j is now 9
 Outside loop: Final value in j is 10
```

Theory

With a for loop, we can execute a block of statements repeatedly until the point where the specified expression is true. In other words, when the expression becomes false, control will come out. The for loop is also similar to while loop as per the functionality, but the key difference is that here we have an initializer, condition, and increment/decrement (loop expression). Every for loop has three sections: initializer, condition, and iterator, with a body like that shown here:

```
for(initialization section; condition section;iterator section)
{
// a block of statement/s
}
```

So, a typical example of for loop is shown in the following demonstration.

Demonstration

```
using System;

namespace ForLoopEx
{
    class Program
    {
        static void Main(string[] args)
        {
            Console.WriteLine("***Illustration: for loop***");
            for (int i = 0; i < 5; i++)
            {
                Console.WriteLine("i is now {0}", i);
            }
            Console.ReadKey();
        }
    }
}
```

Output

```
***Illustration: for loop***
i is now 0
i is now 1
i is now 2
i is now 3
i is now 4
```

Write the corresponding code (shown in the preceding) using the while loop.

Answer:

```
int i = 0;
while (i < 5)
  {
    Console.WriteLine("i is now {0}", i);
    i++;
  }
```

Quiz

Will the code compile?

```
for (int i = 0;; i++)
{
 Console.WriteLine("i is now {0}", i);
}
```

Answer

Yes, but it will fall into an infinite loop.

Quiz

Will the code compile?

```
for (int i = 5; i<10; )
 {
  Console.WriteLine("i is now {0}", i);
 }
```

Answer

Yes, but it will also fall into an infinite loop.

Quiz

Will the code compile?

```
int i = 5;
while (i)
{
    Console.WriteLine("i is now {0}", i);
    i++;
  }
```

Answer

No. C# does not support this.

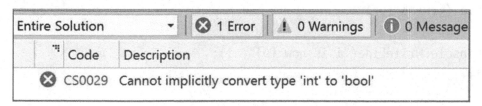

Quiz

Will the code compile?

```
int i = 5;
while ()
{
    Console.WriteLine("i is now {0}", i);
    i++;
}
```

Answer

No. C# does not support this.

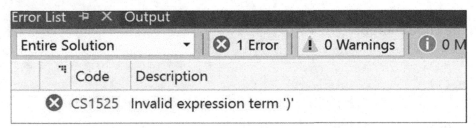

Quiz

Will the code compile?

```
int i = 5;
int j=0;
while (true&&true)
{
  Console.WriteLine("i is now {0}", i);
  i++;
}
```

Answer

Yes, but it will also fall into an infinite loop.

What is the difference between a for loop and a foreach loop?

Answer:

Experts often say that for is slightly faster. However, we will try to make it simpler:

- If we are dealing with collections and do not bother with the indexes, we normally use foreach. It is easier to write, we do not need to put any bounds for that operations.

- If we want to use/print/access every second or third item (or any such similar operation), the for loop is convenient.

- The for loop can work with other data and it is not restricted to collections.

According to MSDN: "The foreach statement is used to iterate through the collection to get the information that you want, but cannot be used to add or remove items from the source collection to avoid unpredictable side effects. If you need to add or remove items from the source collection, use a for loop."

Consider the following program and output. Here we use a foreach loop and its equivalent for loop.

```
using System;
using System.Collections.Generic;

namespace ForVsForEachDemo
{
    class Program
        {
            static void Main(string[] args)
            {
                List<int> list = new List<int>() { 1, 2, 3, 4, 5 };
                Console.WriteLine("Executing foreach loop");
                foreach (int i in list)
                {
                    Console.WriteLine("\t" + i);
                }
                Console.WriteLine("Executing for loop :");
                for (int i = 0; i < list.Count; i++)
```

429

```
            {
                int j = list[i];
                Console.WriteLine("\t" + j);
            }
            Console.ReadKey();
        }
    }
}
```

Output

```
Executing foreach loop
        1
        2
        3
        4
        5
Executing for loop :
        1
        2
        3
        4
        5
```

Note that we have done similar operations using for and foreach loops. Now notice that if you want to print the values, like 1,3,5 (or any particular order you like), writing code using the for loop is easier and we need to change only the increment part of the for loop, as follows (i.e., instead of i++, use i+=2):

```
for (int i = 0; i < list.Count; i+=2)
```

Note   Collections are advanced concepts. If you do not have any idea about collections, better to skip this question for now. You can learn about collections and then you can come back here.

Jump Statements

We use the following jump statements: break, continue, goto, return, and throw.

How can you differentiate break from continue?

Answer:

Consider the following program. In the first case, we use break, and in the second case, we use continue. Then let us analyze the output.

Demonstration

```
using System;

namespace BreakVsContinueStatements
{
    class Program
    {
        static void Main(string[] args)
        {
            Console.WriteLine("***Illustration -break vs continue***");
            int i = 5;
            while (i != 10)
            {
                i++;
                Console.WriteLine("i is now {0}", i);
                if (i == 8)
                {
                    Console.WriteLine(" Entered inside if loop");
                    break;
                    //continue;
                    //unreachable code
                    Console.WriteLine(" I am still in if  loop");
                }
            }
            Console.ReadKey();
```

```
        }
    }
}
```

Output

```
***Illustration -break vs continue***
i is now 6
i is now 7
i is now 8
 Entered inside if loop
```

Comment out the break statement and uncomment the continue statement in the preceding example, as follows:

```
...
 if (i == 8)
            {
                Console.WriteLine("Entered inside if loop");
                //break;
                continue;
              //Warning CS0162 :Unreachable code detected
                Console.WriteLine("I am still in if loop");
            }
.....
```

Output

```
***Illustration -break vs continue***
i is now 6
i is now 7
i is now 8
 Entered inside if loop
i is now 9 ←
i is now 10 ←
```

Analysis

Looking at the two sets of output, we can easily distinguish between break and continue. For break, we end the execution of the body of the loop but for continue, we skip the remaining portion of the loop and reach for an early start of the next iteration. We also notice that *I am still in if loop* never printed. The break statements work similarly inside switch statements also.

Theory

Now let us modify the program to show the goto statement. This statement transfers the control to a specified level in the statement block.

```csharp
using System;

namespace UseOfgoto
{
    class Program
    {
        static void Main(string[] args)
        {
            Console.WriteLine("***Illustration -goto statement***");
            int i = 5;
            //our label
            starttesting:
            while (i != 10)
            {
                i++;
                Console.WriteLine("i is now {0}", i);
                if (i == 8)
                {
                    Console.WriteLine("Entered inside if loop");
                    i++;//making i=9 now
                    goto starttesting;//transferring control
                    //Warning CS0162 :Unreachable code detected
                    Console.WriteLine("I am still in if loop");
                }
```

```
            }
         Console.ReadKey();
      }
   }
}
```

Output

```
***Illustration -goto statement***
i is now 6
i is now 7
i is now 8
 Entered inside if loop
i is now 10
```

Quiz

What will happen if we put the label before the statement int i=5, as follows?

```
//our label
   starttesting:
    int i = 5;
   while (i!=10)
     {
        i++;
      Console.WriteLine("i is now {0}", i);
      if (i == 8)
       {
          Console.WriteLine("Entered inside if loop");
          i++;//making i=9 now
          goto starttesting;//transferring control
          //unreachable code
          Console.WriteLine("I am still in if loop");
       }
     }
```

Answer:

We will fall into an infinite loop. Note that whenever i=8, we are incrementing it and then going to the specified label. The variable i is assigned to 5 again, so we fall inside this infinite loop.

Miscellaneous

What are the different uses of the using statement in C#?

Answer:

We use "using" to include namespace(s) in general, for example,

```
using System;
```

Another very common use is to ensure the correct use of IDisposable object. It helps call the Dispose method on the object in the correct way. Even we encounter an exception during the method call of the object, the Dispose() method will be called. So, in simple terminology, we can avoid use of try and finally blocks. Remember that in the using block, we cannot modify the object (it is readonly there).

Suppose that we have written the following program:

```
using System;
using System.IO;

namespace AnalysisOfUsingStatement
{
    class Program
    {
        static void Main(string[] args)
        {
            using (FileStream s = new FileStream(@"c:\MyFile.txt",
            FileMode.OpenOrCreate))
            {
                // our code
                BinaryWriter bw = new BinaryWriter(s);
                bw.Write("Hello World!");
            }
```

```
            Console.ReadKey();
        }
    }
}
```

Now open the IL code. We'll see this:

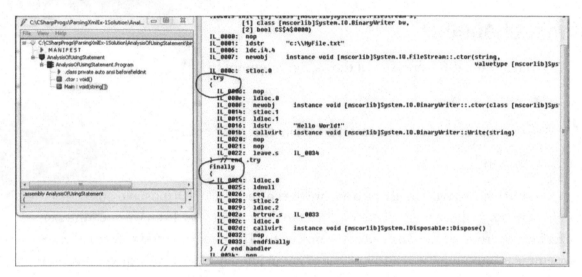

CLR is converting the using statement into a try{} and finally{} block. We discussed this in the chapter on memory clean-up. We'll learn about these concepts in detail in the discussions of Exception Handling(Chapter 13) and Memory Cleanup (Chapter 14).

Strings

In C#, we can use the string keyword to represent strings. We can also use the System.String alias here. We represent them inside double quotes like this:

```
string title = "Welcome to C# Basics";
```

Strings are represented with the keyword *string* (or System.String). These are an *immutable* sequence of Unicode characters. C# provides different methods associated with strings. We will test some of them.

To concatenate, we can use the + operator. Here is an example.

```
string helloMrX= "Hello" + " Mr. X";
```

We can also use the *string.Concat(string s1, string s2)* method. Here is an example.

```
string.Concat("hello", "world!");
```

To print characters in a string, in uppercase (or lowercase), we can use the : ToUpper() or ToLower() methods.

```
// To print characters in uppercase
string title = "Welcome to C# Basics";
Console.WriteLine(title.ToUpper());
// To print characters in lowercase
Console.WriteLine(title.ToLower());
```

Questions/Answers with code segments

How can we print double quotes in a line like "Welcome to 'Dream World'"?

Answer:

```
string doubleQuotesEx=@"Welcome to ""Dream World"" ";
Console.WriteLine(doubleQuotesEx);
```

How can we print URLS such as \\abcd\ef?

Answer:

```
string urlEx = @"\\abcd\ef";
Console.WriteLine(urlEx);
```

How can we remove whitespaces at the beginning of the string: "This line contains blank spaces at beginning.?

Answer:

```
string blankSpaceAtbeginning="This line contains blank spaces at beginning.";
Console.WriteLine(blankSpaceAtbeginning.Trim());
```

How we can remove the characters such as d, dot(.), blanks, and tab spaces at the end from the string: "This line contains blank and tab spaces at End."?

Answer:

```
char[] trimCharacters = { ' ', '\t','.' ,'d'};
string blankSpaceAtEnd = "This line contains blank and tab spaces at End.";
Console.WriteLine(blankSpaceAtEnd.TrimEnd(trimCharacters));
```

Output

```
This line contains blank and tab spaces at En
```

How can we traverse character by character in a String?

Answer:

Strings implement IEnumerable<char>. We can use the foreach loop in such a context:

```
string welcome = "Welcome, to C# Basics.";
 foreach (char c in welcome)
   {
     Console.Write(c);
   }
```

How we can distinguish between an empty string and a null string?

Answer:

If we want to calculate the length of an empty string, we'll get zero; but for a null string, we'll encounter a NullReferenceException.

You can test this with these lines of code:

```
string emptyString = String.Empty;
string nullString = null;
Console.WriteLine("Length of emptyString is {0}", emptyString.Length);//0
Console.WriteLine("Length of nullString is {0}", nullString.Length); //
Exception
```

Output

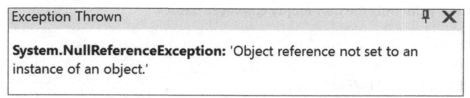

We can also distinguish them with the following lines of code:

```
Console.WriteLine(emptyString=="");//True
Console.WriteLine(nullString =="");//False
```

How can you test whether a string is null or empty?

Answer:

```
Console.WriteLine(string.IsNullOrEmpty(emptyString));//True
Console.WriteLine(string.IsNullOrEmpty(nullString));//True
```

Suppose you have the string: Welcome to C# programming. Then how can we print: ***Welcome to C# programming### ?

Answer:

```
string welcome = "Welcome to C# programming";
string welcome1=welcome.PadLeft(welcome.Length+3,'*');
string welcome2= welcome1.PadRight(welcome1.Length+3,'#');
Console.WriteLine(welcome2);
```

```
***Welcome to C# programming###
```

What will the output be?

```
string welcome = "Welcome to C# programming";
Console.WriteLine(welcome.PadRight(5,'*'));
```

Answer:

There is no change to the original string because the length of the string is already greater than 5.

Suppose we have read the following XML structure in a string. Write a program that can print only the non-empty employee names.

```
<EmpRecord>
<Employee1>
        <EmpName>Rohit</EmpName>
        <EmpId>1001</EmpId>
   </Employee1>
   <Employee2>
        <EmpName>Amit</EmpName>
        <EmpId>1002</EmpId>
   </Employee2>
   <Employee3>
        <EmpName></EmpName>
        <EmpId>1003</EmpId>
   </Employee3>
   <Employee4>
        <EmpName>Soham</EmpName>
        <EmpId>1004</EmpId>
   </Employee4>
</EmpRecord>";
```

Answer:

```
using System;
using System.Collections.Generic;

namespace ReadingXMLFormatEx
{
    class Program
```

```
{
    static void Main(string[] args)
    {
        string employee =
          @"<EmpRecord>
            <Employee1>
              <EmpName>Rohit</EmpName>
              <EmpId>1001</EmpId>
            </Employee1>
            <Employee2>
             <EmpName>Amit</EmpName>
             <EmpId>1002</EmpId>
            </Employee2>
            <Employee3>
             <EmpName></EmpName>
             <EmpId>1003</EmpId>
            </Employee3>
            <Employee4>
             <EmpName>Soham</EmpName>
             <EmpId>1004</EmpId>
            </Employee4>
           </EmpRecord>";
        string[] splt = { "<EmpName>", "</EmpName>" };
        List<string> empNamesList = new List<string>();
        string[] temp = employee.Split(splt, StringSplitOptions.
        RemoveEmptyEntries);
        for (int i = 0; i < temp.Length; i++)
        {
            if (!temp[i].Contains("<"))
            {
                empNamesList.Add(temp[i]);
            }
        }
        Console.WriteLine("Employee names are as below:\n");
        foreach (string s in empNamesList)
        {
```

```
            Console.WriteLine(s);
        }
        Console.ReadKey();
    }
  }
}
```

Output

```
Employee names are as below:

Rohit
Amit
Soham
```

Write a program to check whether a string is a palindrome or not.

Our Logic:

We will reverse the string and then check whether the original string and the reversed strings are same. If they are same, the string is a palindrome string.

```
Console.WriteLine("Enter the string:");
string s1 = Console.ReadLine();
//string s1 = "abccba";
char[] tempArray = s1.ToCharArray();
Array.Reverse(tempArray);
//change the reverse array to a string and compare
string reverseStr = new string(tempArray);
if (s1.Equals(reverseStr))
  {
   Console.WriteLine("String \" {0} \" is a palindrome string, reverse
   string of it is {1}", s1, reverseStr);
  }
  else
```

```
{
Console.WriteLine("String \"{0}\"is a Not palindrome string, reverse
string of it is {1}", s1, reverseStr);
}
```

Output 1: Positive Case

```
**Program to check palindrome strings***
Enter the string:
cam c mac
String " cam c mac " is a palindrome string, reverse string of it is :
 cam c mac
```

Output 2: Negative Case

```
**Program to check palindrome strings***
Enter the string:
hello world
String "hello world"is a Not palindrome string,reverse string of it is:
 dlrow olleh
```

How can you calculate the length of a string?

Answer:

```
Console.WriteLine("Enter a string");
string inputString = Console.ReadLine();
Console.WriteLine("Length of the string \"{0}\" is {1}", inputString,
inputString.Length);
```

Output

```
Enter a string
hello world
Length of the string "hello world" is 11
```

Write your own program segment to calculate the length of a string.

Answer:

```
Console.WriteLine("Enter a string");
string inputString = Console.ReadLine();
int len = 0;
foreach (char c in inputString)
{
 len++;
}
Console.WriteLine("Length of the string \"{0}\" is {1}", inputString, len);
```

Output

```
Enter a string :
Joe, how are you?
Length of the string "Joe, how are you?" is 17
```

Write your own program segment to reverse a string.

Answer:

Our Logic:

We will put string elements into a character array and then we traverse the array from the opposite direction.

```
Console.WriteLine("Enter a string");
string inputString = Console.ReadLine();
char[] tempArray=inputString.ToArray();
string outputString = String.Empty;
for (int i = tempArray.Length-1; i >= 0; i--)
{
 outputString = outputString + tempArray[i];
}
Console.WriteLine("Reversed string is {0}",outputString );
```

Output

```
Enter a string
hello abc!
Reversed string is !cba olleh
```

Write a program segment to check whether a string is a palindrome or not without reversing the string.

Answer:

Our Logic:

We will start with the middle position of the string and then proceed. Note that we can have a palindrome of even length (e.g., abccba), or we can have a palindrome string of odd length (e.g., abcdcba).So, we need to take care of both scenarios.

```
Console.WriteLine("Enter the string:");
string test = Console.ReadLine();
char[] testForPalindrome = test.ToCharArray();
int len = testForPalindrome.Length;
int mid = len / 2;
bool flag = true;
//odd palindrome
if (len % 2 != 0)
{
 int j = mid + 1;
 for (int i = mid - 1; i >= 0; i--)
 {
  if (testForPalindrome[i] != testForPalindrome[j])
  {
   flag = false;
  }
j++;
}
Console.WriteLine("The string {0} is palindrome? {1}", test, flag);
}
```

```
//even palindrome
else
{
 int j = mid;
 for (int i = mid - 1; i >= 0; i--)
 {
  if (testForPalindrome[i] != testForPalindrome[j])
   {
     flag = false;
    }
  j++;
 }
Console.WriteLine("The string {0} is palindrome? {1}", test, flag);
}
```

Output 1: Positive Case

```
Enter the string:
abc d cba
The string abc d cba is palindrome? True
```

Output 2: Negative Case

```
Enter the string:
hello jon!
The string hello jon! is palindrome? False
```

What is the difference between String and StringBuilder?

Answer:

Strings are immutable (not editable). This means that if we do some operations on a given string instance and if those operations cause some changes to the original string, then a new string instance with the updated value will be created (in a different location).

On the other hand, StringBuilder does not create a new instance for such an operation, which is why it is mutable. It updates the change in the existing instance.

Let's consider the following program and output. We will see that no new instance is created for StringBuilder. Remember the other basic differences, such as strings reside in the System namespace but StringBuilder resides in the System.Text namespace.

```
using System;
using System.Runtime.Serialization;//for ObjectIDGenerator
using System.Text;//for StringBuilder

namespace StringVsStringBuilderEx
{
    class Program
    {
        static void Main(string[] args)
        {
            Console.WriteLine("***String vs String builder***\n");
            ObjectIDGenerator idGenerator = new ObjectIDGenerator();
            bool firstTime = new bool();

            string myString = "Hello World";
            Console.WriteLine("{0} Instance Id now : {1}", myString,
            idGenerator.GetId(myString, out firstTime));
            //creates new instance ID
            myString = myString + ",programmer";
            Console.WriteLine("{0} Instance Id now : {1}", myString,
            idGenerator.GetId(myString, out firstTime));
```

```
StringBuilder myStringBuilder = new StringBuilder("Hello,
Mr StringBuilder");
Console.WriteLine("{0} Instance Id : {1}", myStringBuilder,
idGenerator.GetId(myStringBuilder, out firstTime));
//Do not create a new instance ID
myStringBuilder = myStringBuilder.Replace("Hello", "Welcome");
Console.WriteLine("{0} Instance Id : {1}", myStringBuilder,
idGenerator.GetId(myStringBuilder, out firstTime));
Console.ReadKey();
        }
    }
}
```

Output

```
***String vs String builder***

Hello World Instance Id now : 1
Hello World,programmer Instance Id now : 2
Hello , Mr  StringBuilder Instance Id : 3
Welcome , Mr  StringBuilder Instance Id : 3
```

Arrays

Arrays contain homogeneous data. Their length is fixed (System.Collection can provide dynamically sized arrays, however) and the elements in them are stored in a contiguous location. Arrays can be single dimensional or multidimensional.

Single Dimensional Arrays

Consider the following example. Here we have created and printed an array of integers. Note that this array is containing three integers.

Demonstration

```
using System;

namespace ArrayEx1
{
    class Program
    {
        static void Main(string[] args)
        {
            Console.WriteLine("** Demo: A simple array example ***");
            int[] myInts = new int[3];
            myInts[0] = 5;
            myInts[1] = 15;
            myInts[2] = 25;
            Console.WriteLine("Elements of myInts array are as follows:");
            for(int i=0;i<3;i++)
            {
                Console.WriteLine(myInts[i]);
            }
            Console.ReadKey();
        }
    }
}
```

Output

```
** Demo: A simple array example ***
Elements of myInts array are as follows:
5
15
25
```

Note

It is a simple demonstration and we know that there are only three elements in the array. But it is always better to use the Length property of the array (to traverse the array), as follows.

```
for (int i = 0; i < myInts.Length; i++)
{
  Console.WriteLine(myInts[i]);
}
```

We could have used either of these alternatives to create the array.

```
//Alternative approach-2
int[] myInts = new int[] { 5, 15,25 };
//Alternative approach-3
int[] myInts = { 5,15,25 };
```

Here we used integer arrays.You can create other types of arrays also.

Multidimensional Arrays

Multidimensional arrays come in two flavors: rectangular and jagged. In a rectangular array, each row has an equal number of columns. In a jagged array, each row can have a different number of columns. Individual dimensions at a given depth can have an unequal number of elements, regardless of other dimensions at the same depth. Each of these can contain other arrays, recursively.

Consider the following example. Here we are going to create a matrix with our preferred dimensions. Note that we have printed the output in a proper matrix form for better readability.

Demonstration

```csharp
using System;

namespace RectangularArrayEx
{
class Program
    {
        static void Main(string[] args)
        {
            Console.WriteLine("***Multidimensional array demo ***");
            Console.WriteLine("Enter how many rows you want?");
            String rowSize = Console.ReadLine();
            int row = int.Parse(rowSize);
            Console.WriteLine("Enter how many columns you want?");
            String columnSize = Console.ReadLine();
            int column = int.Parse(columnSize);
            int[,] myArray=new int[row,column];
            Console.WriteLine("Enter Data");
            for (int i = 0; i < row; i++)
            {
                for (int j = 0; j < column; j++)
                {
                    myArray[i,j] = int.Parse(Console.ReadLine());
                }
            }
            //Printing the matrix
            Console.WriteLine("Your matrix is as below:");
            for (int i = 0; i < row; i++)
            {
                for (int j = 0; j < column; j++)
                {
                 Console.Write(myArray[i, j]+"\t");
                }
```

```
                Console.WriteLine();
        }
      }
   }
}
```

Output

```
***A rectangular 2D array example ***
Enter how many rows you want?
3
Enter how many columns you want?
4
Enter all the 12 data from keyboard
1
2
3
4
5
6
7
8
9
10
11
12
Your matrix is as below:
1       2       3       4
5       6       7       8
9       10      11      12
```

In the preceding example, each row has an equal number of columns (three), so it is a rectangular two-dimensional (2D) array. Now let's create a jagged array.

If we want to create a jagged array in which the first row contains three elements, and the second row contains four elements, then the following diagram can represents our intention.

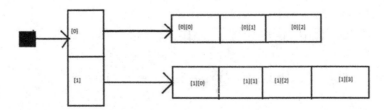

Similarly, in the following example, we have created a jagged array where we have three rows. The zeroth row contains three elements, the first row contains four elements, and the second row contains only two elements.

Demonstration

```
using System;

namespace JaggedArrayEx
{
    class Program
    {
        static void Main(string[] args)
        {
            Console.WriteLine("***Multidimensional jagged array
            demo***\n");
            int[][] myJaggedArray = new int[3][];
            myJaggedArray[0] = new int[3];
            myJaggedArray[1] = new int[4];
            myJaggedArray[2] = new int[2];
            //Entering data
            //1st row
            myJaggedArray[0][0] = 1;
            myJaggedArray[0][1] = 2;
            myJaggedArray[0][2] = 3;
            //2nd row
            myJaggedArray[1][0] = 4;
            myJaggedArray[1][1] = 5;
            myJaggedArray[1][2] = 6;
            myJaggedArray[1][3] = 7;
            //3rd row
            myJaggedArray[2][0] = 8;
            myJaggedArray[2][1] = 9;
```

```
            //Printing the elements
            foreach (int[] rows in myJaggedArray)
            {
                foreach (int i in rows)
                {
                    Console.Write(i + "\t");
                }
                Console.WriteLine();
            }
            Console.ReadKey();
        }
    }
}
```

Output

```
***Multidimensional jagged array demo***

1       2       3
4       5       6       7
8       9
```

What do you mean by the following line of code?

```
int[][] jaggedArray = new int[3][];
```

Answer:

jaggedArray refers to a 2D jagged array that contains *three(3)* 1D array. (D for dimensional.)

Quiz

What will the output be?

```
using System;

namespace QuizOnArray
{
    class Program
    {
        static void Main(string[] args)
        {
            Console.WriteLine("**Test on Array initialization***");
            int[] myIntArray = new int[4];
            for (int i = 0; i < myIntArray.Length; i++)
            {
                Console.WriteLine("myIntArray[" + i + "] is : {0}",
                myIntArray[i]);
            }
            Console.WriteLine();
            string[] myStringArray = new string[4];
            for (int i = 0; i < myStringArray.Length; i++)
            {
                bool value = string.IsNullOrEmpty(myStringArray[i]);
                if (value)
                {
                    Console.WriteLine("myStringArray[" + i + "] is null.");
                }
                else
                {
                    Console.WriteLine("myStringArray[" + i + "] is NOT  null.");
                }
            }
            Console.ReadKey();
        }
    }
}
```

Output

```
**Test on Array initialization***
myIntArray[0] is : 0
myIntArray[1] is : 0
myIntArray[2] is : 0
myIntArray[3] is : 0

myStringArray[0] is null.
myStringArray[1] is null.
myStringArray[2] is null.
myStringArray[3] is null.
```

Explanation

The elements of an array are initialized to their default values. int is a value type and its default value is 0. But a string is a reference type. The string array (myStringArray) is initialized with null references. We need to remember that for the reference type, we need to explicitly instantiate them; for example, we can instantiate the elements of the string array (myStringArray) like this:

```
myStringArray[0] = "abc";
```

and so on.

When do you prefer a jagged array over a rectangular array?

Answer:

Jagged arrays are basically an array of arrays. Each of the inner arrays can have different lengths. In many situations, a rectangular array may not need all the elements in a row. In such cases, jagged arrays are better because they support an unequal number of elements in a row. A typical example is a sparse matrix. (For a sparse matrix, most of the elements are zero; for a dense matrix, most of the elements are non-zero).

Quiz

What will the output be?

```
using System;
namespace QuizOnArray
{
  class Program
    {
        static void Main(string[] args)
        {
          Console.WriteLine("**Quiz on Arrays***");
          int[][] jaggedArray = new int[3][];
            jaggedArray[0] = new int[4] { 1, 2, 3, 4 };
            jaggedArray[1] = new int[6] { 5, 6, 7, 8, 9, 10 };
            jaggedArray[2] = new int[2] { 11,12 };
            Console.WriteLine(jaggedArray[0].GetUpperBound(0));//3
            Console.WriteLine(jaggedArray[1].GetUpperBound(0));//5
            Console.WriteLine(jaggedArray[2].GetUpperBound(0));//1
            Console.ReadKey();
        }
    }
}
```

Output

```
**Quiz on Arrays***
3
5
1
```

Quiz

Suppose the jagged array is the same as earlier. What is the output for the following line of code?

```
Console.WriteLine(jaggedArray[0].GetUpperBound(1));
```

Answer:

We will encounter IndexOutOfRangeException.

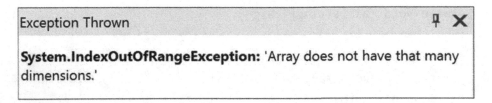

Quiz

Suppose the jagged array is same as earlier. What is the output for the following line of code?

```
Console.WriteLine(jaggedArray.GetUpperBound(0));//2
Console.WriteLine(jaggedArray.Length);//3
```

Answer:

2

3

Quiz

What is the output if we modify the jagged array like this?

```
int[][] jaggedArray=new int[4][];
jaggedArray[0]=new int[4]{1,2,3,4};
jaggedArray[1]=new int[6]{5,6,7,8,9,10};
jaggedArray[2]=new int[2] {10,20};
jaggedArray[3]=new int[3] {3,7,15};
Console.WriteLine(jaggedArray.Length);
```

Answer:

4

Quiz

What is the output for the rectangular array?

```
int[,] rectArray = new int[3,4];
Console.WriteLine(rectArray.Length);
```

Answer:

12 [Clue:3*4=12]

Enumerations

We create enumerations with the *enum* keyword. Enum is the base class for all enumerations in the .NET Framework. These are user-defined *value types*. We can assign a set of integral named constants through enumeration. The default integral type is System.Int32.

Here is a simple illustration of using enum.

Demonstration

```
using System;

namespace EnumEx1
{
    class Program
    {
        enum Values { val1, val2, val3,val4,val5 };
        static void Main(string[] args)
        {
            Console.WriteLine("** A simple use of enum ***");
            int x1 = (int)Values.val1;
            int x2 = (int)Values.val2;
            int x3 = (int)Values.val3;
            int x4 = (int)Values.val4;
            int x5 = (int)Values.val5;
            Console.WriteLine("x1={0}", x1);
            Console.WriteLine("x2={0}", x2);
            Console.WriteLine("x3={0}", x3);
            Console.WriteLine("x4={0}", x4);
            Console.WriteLine("x5={0}", x5);
            Console.ReadKey();
        }
    }
}
```

Output

```
** A simple use of enum ***
x1=0
x2=1
x3=2
x4=3
x5=4
```

Analysis

By default, each member is taking an integer value. In addition to that, the values for x1, x2, and x3 (which are basically constants) are automatically assigned. These assignments started from 0 and incremented automatically by 1 (e.g., x1 is containing 0, x2 is containing 1 and x3 is containing 2). And notice that this increment is happening according to their declaration order.

Is the declaration valid?

```
enum Values { val1 = 37, val2 = 69, val3 = 175 };
```

Answer:

Yes, it is perfect. We can assign explicitly to the members of the enumeration.

What will the output be?

```
using System;

namespace EnumQuizes
{
    class Program
    {
        enum Values { val1, val2 = 26, val3 = 12, val4, val5 };
        static void Main(string[] args)
        {
            Console.WriteLine("** Quiz on enum ***");
            int x1 = (int)Values.val1;//0
```

```
            int x5 = (int)Values.val5;//14
            Console.WriteLine(x1);
            Console.WriteLine(x5);
            Console.ReadKey();
        }
    }
}
```

Answer:

0

14

(Clue: val1 is initialized with 0 by default. But val3 is 12, so from there, values increased incrementally by 1.)

```
** Quiz on enum ***
0
14
```

What will the output be?

Demonstration

```
using System;

namespace EnumQuizes
{
    class Program
    {
        int a = 50;
        enum Values { val1, val2 = a, val3 = 12, val4, val5 };
        static void Main(string[] args)
        {
            Console.WriteLine("** Quiz on enum ***");
```

```
        int x1 = (int)Values.val1;//0
        int x5 = (int)Values.val5;//14
        Console.WriteLine(x1);
        Console.WriteLine(x5);
        Console.ReadKey();
    }
  }
}
```

Output

Compilation error.

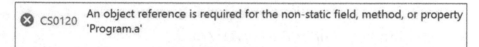

❌ CS0120 An object reference is required for the non-static field, method, or property 'Program.a'

So if we change int a =25 to static int a=25, will the preceding code compile?

Answer:

No.

❌ CS0133 The expression being assigned to 'Program.Values.val2' must be constant

Note

Therefore, the key point is to remember that we cannot use variables in this manner.

Quiz

Will the code compile?

```
using System;

namespace EnumQuizes
{
    class Program
    {
        const int MYCONST = 50;//ok
        enum Values { val1, val2 = MYCONST, val3, val4=21, val5 };
        static void Main(string[] args)
        {
            Console.WriteLine("** Quiz on enum ***");
            int x1 = (int)Values.val1;//0
            int x2 = (int)Values.val2;//50
            int x3 = (int)Values.val3;//50+1=51
            int x4 = (int)Values.val4;//21
            int x5 = (int)Values.val5;//21+1=22
            Console.WriteLine("x1={0}", x1);
            Console.WriteLine("x2={0}", x2);
            Console.WriteLine("x3={0}", x3);
            Console.WriteLine("x4={0}", x4);
            Console.WriteLine("x5={0}", x5);
            Console.ReadKey();
        }
    }
}
```

Answer:

Yes and we will get the following output. Note the commented lines to see how values are assigned (or incremented).

```
** Quiz on enum ***
x1=0
x2=50
x3=51
x4=21
x5=22
```

Can we replace the const keyword with a static readonly in the preceding code?

Answer:

No. We will encounter a compilation error.

> ❌ CS0133   The expression being assigned to 'Program.Values.val2' must be constant

Can we specify an alternative integral type to an enum like this?

```
enum Values :byte{ val1 , val2, val3 };
```

Answer:

Yes, it is perfect.

Will the code compile?

```
enum simpleColors : string
{
 red, green, yellow,black, blue,pink
};
```

Answer:

No. Only sbyte, short, ushort, int, uint, long, and ulong are allowed.

> ❌ CS1008   Type byte, sbyte, short, ushort, int, uint, long, or ulong expected

How can we check the default storage type of an enum?

Answer:

Consider the following example:

Demonstration

```
using System;

namespace EnumQuizesPart2
{
    class Program
    {
        enum Values { val1, val2 = 26, val3 = 12, val4, val5 };
        enum TrafficLight : byte
        {
            red, green = (int)Values.val3, yellow
        };
        static void Main(string[] args)
        {
            Console.WriteLine("** Quiz on enum ***");
            Console.WriteLine("Default  Storage type of Values is {0}",
            Enum.GetUnderlyingType(typeof(Values)));//System.Int32
            Console.WriteLine("Default  Storage type of TrafficLight is {0}",
            Enum.GetUnderlyingType(typeof(TrafficLight)));//System.Byte
            Console.ReadKey();
        }
    }
}
```

Output

```
** Quiz on enum ***
Default  Storage type of Values is System.Int32
Default  Storage type of TrafficLight is System.Byte
```

Quiz

What will the output be?

```csharp
using System;

namespace EnumQuizesPart3
{
    class Program
    {
        enum Values { val1, val2 = 100, val3 = 50, val4, val5 };
        static void Main(string[] args)
        {
            Console.WriteLine("** Quiz on enum ***");
            foreach (Values v in Enum.GetValues(typeof(Values)))
            {
                Console.WriteLine("{0} is storing {1}", v, (int)v);
            }
            Console.ReadKey();
        }
    }
}
```

Output

```
** Quiz on enum ***
val1 is storing 0
val3 is storing 50
val4 is storing 51
val5 is storing 52
val2 is storing 100
```

Notice that the output is displaying in the sorted order.

Quiz

What will the output be?

```
class Program
{
enum TrafficLight : byte
{
    red, green, yellow
};
enum Values { val1 = 12, val2 = (int)TrafficLight.green, val3, val4 = 200 };
 static void Main(string[] args)
  {
    Console.WriteLine("** A simple use of enum ***");
     foreach (Values v in Enum.GetValues(typeof(Values)))
        {
        Console.WriteLine("{0} is storing {1}", v, (int) v);
        }
   }
}
```

Output

```
** A simple use of enum ***
val2 is storing 1
val3 is storing 2
val1 is storing 12
val4 is storing 200
```

Note that the output is displaying in the sorted order.

Quiz

What will the output be?

```
class Program
{
enum TrafficLight : byte
{
    red, green=(int)Values.val3, yellow
};
enum Values { val1 = 12, val2 = (int)TrafficLight.green, val3, val4 = 200 };
 static void Main(string[] args)
  {
    Console.WriteLine("** A simple use of enum ***");
     foreach (Values v in Enum.GetValues(typeof(Values)))
        {
        Console.WriteLine("{0} is storing {1}", v, (int) v);
        }
  }
}
```

Output

Compilation error. We are actually supplying a circular definition. val2 is getting values from TrafficLight.green. val3 is dependent on that value (since it will be incremented by 1). But again, TrafficLight.green is dependent on val3.

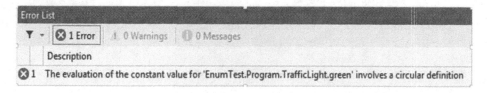

Quiz

What will the output be?

```
class Program
{
enum TrafficLight : byte
{
    red, green=(int)Values.val3, yellow
};
enum Values { val1 = 12, val2 = (int)TrafficLight.red, val3, val4 = 200 };
 static void Main(string[] args)
  {
    Console.WriteLine("** A simple use of enum ***");
     foreach (Values v in Enum.GetValues(typeof(Values)))
        {
        Console.WriteLine("{0} is storing {1}", v, (int) v);
        }
  }
}
```

Output

This time, the code can execute. We get the following output:

```
** A simple use of enum ***
val2 is storing 0
val3 is storing 1
val1 is storing 12
val4 is storing 200
```

Structures

In C#, structures are denoted by the keyword struct. They have many similarities with class but the fundamental difference is that they are value types (remember that a class is a reference type).

We can use structures in the following ways:

Demonstration

```
using System;

namespace StructsEx1
{
    struct MyStructure
        {
            public int i;
            public MyStructure(int i)
            {
                this.i = i;
            }
        }
    class Program
    {
        static void Main(string[] args)
        {
            Console.WriteLine("***Different ways of using structures in
            C# ***");
            MyStructure myS1 = new MyStructure();//OK
            myS1.i = 1;
            Console.WriteLine(" myS1.i={0}", myS1.i);

            //Another way of using structure
            MyStructure myS2 = new MyStructure(10);//OK
            Console.WriteLine(" myS2.i={0}", myS2.i);

            //Another way of using structure
            MyStructure myS3;
```

```
            myS3.i = 100;
            Console.WriteLine(" myS3.i={0}", myS3.i);
            Console.ReadKey();
        }
    }
}
```

Output

```
***Different ways of using structures in C# ***
myS1.i=1
myS2.i=10
myS3.i=100
```

Can a structure implement an interface?

Answer:

Yes. Consider the following program and output.

Demonstration

```
using System;
namespace StructureImplementsInterfaceEx
{
    interface IMyInterface
    {
        void ShowMe();
    }
    struct MyStructure : IMyInterface
    {
        public void ShowMe()
        {
            Console.WriteLine("MyStructure is implementing IMyInterface");
        }
    }
```

```
class Program
{
    static void Main(string[] args)
    {
        Console.WriteLine("***Demo:A Structure can implement an
        interface***");
        MyStructure myS = new MyStructure();
        myS.ShowMe();
        Console.ReadKey();
    }
}
}
```

Output

```
***Demo:A Structure can implement an interface***
MyStructure is implementing IMyInterface
```

Quiz

Will the code compile?

```
struct MyStructure1
 {
 }
struct MyStructure2 : MyStructure1
 {
 }
```

Answer

No, structures cannot be inherited.

> CS0527   Type 'MyStructure1' in interface list is not an interface

Quiz

Will the code compile?

```
class A
    {
    }
struct MyStructure2 : A
    {
    }
```

Answer

No, we cannot inherit structures from another class.

> ⊗ CS0527   Type 'A' in interface list is not an interface

Quiz

Will the code compile?

```
struct MyStructure1
 {
     int i = 25;
 }
```

Answer:

No, we cannot initialize here.

 'MyStructure': cannot have instance property or field initializers in structs

"Instances of structures can be created without a new keyword." Is this statement true?

Answer:

Yes. (See the first demonstration.)

Quiz

Will the code compile?

```
struct MyStructure3
    {
        MyStructure3()
        { }
    }
```

Answer

No. We cannot use the explicit parameterless constructor here.

 CS0568 Structs cannot contain explicit parameterless constructors

Can a structure contain properties?

Answer:

Yes. The following code will execute smoothly.

```
struct MyStructure3
    {
        private int myInt;
        public int MyInt
        {
            get
            {
                return myInt;
            }
            set
            {
                myInt = value;
            }
        }
    }
```

Give an example where structures are preferred than classes.

Answer

For lightweight objects, we prefer structures. If the size is small, the system can use structures more efficiently than classes. Most .NET Framework types are implemented as structs (e.g., System.Int32, System.Double, System.Byte, System. Boolean, etc.).

Quiz

Can we create a structure like this?

```
struct S
    {
        protected int i;
    }
```

Answer:

No. Microsoft clearly states that structs can implement an interface but they cannot inherit from another struct. For that reason, struct members cannot be declared as protected.

 CS0666   'MyStructure.i': new protected member declared in struct

Quiz

Will the code compile?

```
using System;

namespace QuizOnStructures
{
    #region Quizes-finishing parts
struct OuterStruct
{
    public void Show()
    {
        Console.WriteLine("OuterStruct.Show()");
    }
    internal struct InnerStruct
    {
        public void Show()
        {
            Console.WriteLine("InnerStruct.Show()");
        }
    }
}
#endregion
class Program
{
    static void Main(string[] args)
```

```
    {
        Console.WriteLine("***Quiz on structs***");
        OuterStruct.InnerStruct obS = new  OuterStruct.InnerStruct();
        //InnerStruct obS = new InnerStruct();//error
        obS.Show();
        Console.ReadKey();
    }
}
```

Answer

Yes. We will get following output:

```
***Quiz on structs***
InnerStruct.Show()
```

Quiz

Will the code compile?

```
using System;

namespace QuizOnStructures
{
  struct OuterStruct
    {
      public  void Show()
       {
           Console.WriteLine("I am in OuterStruct");
       }
    // internal struct InnerStruct
      protected  struct InnerStruct
      {
          public void Show()
          {
              Console.WriteLine("I am in InnerStruct");
```

```
            }
        }
    }
```

Answer

No. protected or protected internal is not allowed here.

 CS0666   'OuterStruct.InnerStruct': new protected member declared in struct

Highlight some of the key differences between structures and class in C#.

Answer:

Structures are value type, but classes are reference types.

Structures do not support inheritance but classes can support the concept (Do not consider multiple inheritance in this context).

We cannot have a default constructor (explicit parameterless constructor) for structure.

Fill in the blank: Structures are directly inherited from_____.

Answer:

System.ValueType
(Hint: Create a simple structure and check the IL code.)

APPENDIX B

FAQ

1. What is a class?

2. What is an object?

3. What is the difference between an object and a reference?

4. How can you differentiate a pointer from a reference?

5. How can you differentiate between a local variable and an instance variable?

6. What are the different types of constructors and why do we need them?

7. How can you differentiate between a user-defined parameterless constructor from a C#-provided default constructor?

8. What is the purpose of using the "this" keyword?

9. What are object initializers?

10. What are optional parameters?

11. What are the benefits of an object-oriented approach in real-world programming?

12. How can you implement the concept of inheritance in C#?

13. What are the different types of inheritance?

14. Does C# support multiple inheritance through class? If not, why?

15. Can you implement hybrid inheritance in C#? If not why?

16. What are the different uses of the "base" keyword in C#?

17. How does C#'s "base" keyword compare to Java's "super" keyword?

© Vaskaran Sarcar 2018
V. Sarcar, *Interactive C#*, https://doi.org/10.1007/978-1-4842-3339-9

18. How are constructors invoked in an inheritance hierarchy in C#?

19. How can you call a parent class method if its child class also contains a method with the same name?

20. How should you design an inheritance hierarchy?

21. What are the advantages of using inheritance?

22. How do you implement method overloading in C#?

23. How do you implement operator overloading in C#?

24. How do you implement method overriding in C#?

25. What is an abstract class? How do you use them in C#?

26. How do you achieve runtime polymorphism with abstract classes?

27. What is a method signature?

28. What is constructor overloading?

29. Can you overload the Main() method in C#?

30. Can you have multiple Main() methods in a C# program?

31. How do you achieve compile-time polymorphism?

32. How do you achieve runtime polymorphism?

33. Why is late binding necessary?

34. How do you use virtual, override, sealed, and abstract keywords in your program? Are there any restrictions?

35. What are the different techniques to prevent inheritance?

36. Which is preferable to use in an application: the "sealed" keyword or using a private constructor?

37. Differentiate between method overloading and method overriding.

38. Why can't constructors be abstract?

39. What is an interface?

40. How do you use an interface in your application?

41.   What are the basic characteristics of an interface?

42.   Can you implement multiple interfaces?

43.   How do you implement different interfaces that have a method with the same name?

44.   What are the different types of interfaces?

45.   How can you implement an interface explicitly?

46.   Why do we need explicit interface methods?

47.   What is a marker interface?

48.   What is the difference between an abstract class and an interface?

49.   When is using an abstract class preferable to using an interface?

50.   Are there any restrictions associated with an interface?

51.   How do you use properties in your C# application?

52.   What are the different types of properties?

53.   What is an automatic property?

54.   What are expression-bodied properties?

55.   What is a virtual property?

56.   What is an abstract property?

57.   Why should we use public properties instead of public fields?

58.   How are properties different from arrays?

59.   How can we impose some restrictions through properties?

60.   When should we use read-only properties and when do we avoid them?

61.   How are indexers used in a program?

62.   How are indexers different from properties?

63.   How do we use indexers with different types of interfaces? Are there any restrictions?

64.   How are interface indexers different from class indexers?

65.   What are static classes?

66.   What are static methods and static variables?

67.   Can you have static constructors? If so, when should we use them?

68.   How do you distinguish between implicit and explicit casting?

69.   How do you distinguish between boxing and unboxing?

70.   Name the ultimate base class in C#.

71.   Which one is implicit: boxing or unboxing?

72.   How do you distinguish between boxing and casting?

73.   How do you distinguish between upcasting and downcasting in C#?

74.   How are the "is" and "as" keywords used in an application? What are the significant differences between them?

75.   How do you distinguish between passing value types by value vs. passing value types by reference?

76.   How do you distinguish a "ref" parameter from an "out" parameter?

77.   Can you pass a reference type as a value (or vice versa)?

78.   Can a method return multiple values in C#?

79.   How do you distinguish value types from reference types?

80.   How do you check if a class or a structure is a value type in C#?

81.   When should you prefer value types to reference types and vice versa?

82.   What are pointer types in C#?

83.   How do you distinguish "const" from "readonly"?

84.   How do you implement the OOP principles in C#?

85.   How do you differentiate abstraction from encapsulation?

86.   How do you implement composition and aggregation in a C# application?

87. What are the challenges and drawbacks associated with OOP?

88. What is a delegate? Why do we need it?

89. How do you use delegates in a program?

90. Why is a delegate often called a *type-safe function pointer*?

91. What is a multicast delegate?

92. How do you achieve covariance and contravariance using delegates?

93. What are events? How do you use them?

94. How do you pass data with event arguments?

95. What are event accessors? How do you use them?

96. What are anonymous methods? How do you use them?

97. What is a lambda expression? How is it different from an anonymous method?

98. What are the basic differences between func, action, and predicate delegates?

99. What is an exception? How do you handle it in your program?

100. What are the common keywords used with exceptions in C#?

101. How can you classify exceptions?

102. How should you place try, catch, and blocks in a program? What are their purposes?

103. What are the different variations of a catch clause?

104. How are exception filters used?

105. How do you write your own exceptions?

106. What are generics in C#?

107. Why are generics important?

108. How is the keyword "default" used in generics?

109. How do you impose constraints in generic programming?

110. How are covariance and contravariance used in generic programming?

111. What is garbage collection (GC)? How does it work in C#?

112. What are the GC generations?

113. What are the ways to invoke the garbage collector?

114. How do you force GC?

115. What is a memory leak?

116. What are the probable causes of memory leaks?

117. What are the effects of memory leaks?

118. How do you use the Dispose() method to effectively collect memory?

119. How do destructors work in C#?

120. Can you call destructors?

121. Name some of the common tools to detect memory leaks.

122. When do you prefer to use an interface to an abstract class?

APPENDIX C

References

Joseph Albahari and Ben Albahari, *C# 6.0 in a Nutshell*, 4th Edition (O'Reilly, 2015).
Christian Nagel, Bill Evjen, Jay Glynn, Karli Watson, and Morgan Skinner.
Professional C# 4.0 and .NET 4 (Wrox, 2010).
Vaskaran Sarcar, *Design Patterns in C#* (2015).

Useful Online Resources/Web Sites

- www.codeproject.com

- www.c-sharpcorner.com

- www.csharp-station.com

- www.dotnetperls.com

- www.programmersheaven.com

- www.sanfoundry.com

- www.tutorialsteacher.com/csharp/csharp-tutorials

- https://docs.microsoft.com/en-us/dotnet/csharp/programming-guide/index

- https://en.wikipedia.org/

- https://msdn.microsoft.com

V. Sarcar, *Interactive C#*, https://doi.org/10.1007/978-1-4842-3339-9

Index

A

Abstract class, 157, 482–483
    access modifier, 114
    child class, 111, 116
    compilation error, 119
    compiler error, 119–120
    defined, 110
    fields, 114
    interface, 137, 139
    protected access, 121
    runtime polymorphism, 114
    subclasses, 110–111
Abstraction, 6, 232, 242, 484
Abstract property, 157
Access modifier, 114
Accessors, 145
Action delegate, 281
Adapter pattern
    class, 389
    class adapters, 398–399
    definition, 387
    execution, 392–393
    GetArea(), 388
    implementation, 390–391, 394, 396, 398
    MyClass, 401
    object adapters, 398
    Solution Explorer, 390, 394
Aggregation, 233, 238, 240

Anonymous functions, 278
Anonymous method, 275–278
Arrays, 212–213, 296, 304, 320, 323
    as keyword, 203
    multidimensional, 450–452, 454, 456, 458–459
    single dimensional, 449–450
Association, 233–234
Asynchronous programming, 407

B

base keyword, 52–54, 56, 60, 481
Behavioral patterns, 378
Binary operator, 76, 79
Boxing, 291–292, 484
    defined, 188
    generic programming, 193
    heap, 189
    performance analysis, 191, 193
    typecasting operations, 190
Built-in data types, 5

C

Casting, 188, 484
catch clause, 325, 327–329, 339, 485
Child class method, 59–60
Class, 11
Collections, 407

© Vaskaran Sarcar 2018
V. Sarcar, *Interactive C#*, https://doi.org/10.1007/978-1-4842-3339-9

Get the eBook for only $5!

Why limit yourself?

With most of our titles available in both PDF and ePUB format, you can access your content wherever and however you wish—on your PC, phone, tablet, or reader.

Since you've purchased this print book, we are happy to offer you the eBook for just $5.

To learn more, go to http://www.apress.com/companion or contact support@apress.com.

Apress®